ULENDO

ULENDO

—

Walking Where Vultures Fly

IAIN MACDONALD

Published by Iain Macdonald

© Iain Macdonald, 2021

iainmacd@mango.zw

All rights reserved.
No part of this publication may be reproduced,
stored in a retrieval system
or transmitted in any form by any means
– electronic, mechanical, photocopying,
recording, or otherwise –
without the express written permission
of the publisher.

ISBN: 978-1-77920-889-7 (paperback)
ISBN: 978-1-77920-890-3 (ebook)

This book was designed by Iain Macdonald
and set by TextPertise, Harare

Cover design by Juliet Kind, Harare.
Photo by Hu Chen on Unsplash

*This book is dedicated to those people
who step outside the confines
of their safe environment
to experience the world
where it counts most:
on foot,
surrounded by nature,
in the African bush.*

Contents

Foreword, by Brian Jackman	ix
Preface	xi
Acknowledgements	xiv

Part One: Growing Up

My first safari	2
My forebears	11
Childhood memories	21
Primary school years	29
Childhood in Lusaka	59
Moving South	75
Secondary school years	86
College years	93
National service	96
Film school and teaching	100
Call-ups	106

Part Two: Life as a Safari Guide

The Luangwa Valley	111
Walking-camp construction	131
Lukusuzi National Park	153
Interesting events from my diaries	159
Meeting lion and leopard on walks	203
North Luangwa National Park	214
The Selous Game Reserve, Tanzania	245

Part Three: What a Walking Guide Should Know

What makes a good safari guide?	262
Walking safaris	277
Guns and gun handling for safari work	310
Tracking	314
Finding your way back	329
Droppings	339
The Kill	344
Conservation	353

Foreword

by Brian Jackman

Born in Lusaka in 1946, Iain Macdonald worked for a time as a teacher in Malawi, but *ulendo* – the ChiChewa word for going on safari – had entered his blood at the age of four with his first safari to Senanga in Zambia's Western Province, and he never wavered from his ambition of becoming a walking guide.

His career in the bush began in 1975 at Chibembe Camp in Zambia's incomparable Luangwa Valley, where I went on several walking safaris with him. There he met Norman Carr, the legendary ex-warden and visionary conservationist, who trained him to be a walking guide. Coming from the man who famously reinvented the old-fashioned foot safari, it turned out to be the best possible apprenticeship in what is still regarded as Africa's finest walking country.

At that time, the Luangwa still had 100,000 elephants and a healthy population of black rhinos, whose presence added a certain frisson to every walk, especially when it involved tiptoeing through tall stands of kasensi grass, or, as it is called in Zimbabwe, adrenaline grass. Those early days served him well, instilling the need for constant vigilance and imbuing him with a sixth sense that proved invaluable when walking in big-game territory.

During his years in the Valley he guided Judge Train, the head of WWF USA. He also met David Shepherd, the renowned elephant artist, and worked with Phil Berry, John Coppinger, Patrick Ansell,

Robin Pope and other Luangwa luminaries. Mark Carwardine, author and TV presenter, interviewed him for a radio programme.

After Chibembe, with the help of Mark and Delia Owens, he built his own bush camp in the North Luangwa National Park and ran it for three unforgettable years using porters for the first time.

In 2002, having always dreamed of exploring Tanzania's vast Selous Game Reserve, he joined the Selous Safari Camp as their Activities manager, where his tasks included accompanying honeymoon couples on fly-camping expeditions on which they sought their own 'Out of Africa' experience.

Packed with page after page of bush wisdom and nail-biting encounters with dangerous game, Iain Macdonald's story is even more compelling because it is true. It also brings out the admiration and respect he felt for his Zambian colleagues. As a writer, he has the rare knack of bringing the sights and sounds of Africa to life, and if you can't go on safari right now, this is the next best thing.

Brian Jackman

http://www.brian-jackman.co.uk

Preface

To explain the title: Ulendo is a Chichewa word for going on safari. It was a word used by District Governors who went out into the bush on government business. 'Where no vultures fly,' was the title of the first movie ever made about safaris in Africa. It came out in 1951.

In essence, this book is a celebration of walking safaris conducted from Chibembe Lodge in the South Luangwa Valley, Zambia, during what I consider to be their halcyon days. Photographic walking safaris, as opposed to hunting safaris on foot, evolved at Chibembe Lodge. They did not exist anywhere else in Africa at that moment.

Rhodesia, now Zimbabwe, from 1965 until 1980 was experiencing a vicious civil war where all its wild areas were out of bounds.

South Africa, where photographic safaris had been run successfully for many, many years, still adopted the traditional safari from a vehicle. Walking safaris came into being there much later, and mainly on private conservancies.

Botswana, prior to the discovery of diamonds was, a very poor country with very little infrastructure and no tourist industry to speak of.

Thanks to Hemingway and to Hollywood movies, Kenya had been the traditional safari destination of choice for many years. The purpose of a safari to Africa was to bag trophies, hang them on the wall of your den back home, and compete for pride of place on the Safari Club International trophy list. You did not go on safari to admire or learn about animals, by getting down to their level and putting yourself at risk. Without a professional hunter to blast the animal to bits if it charged, this was considered to be pure lunacy.

Tanzania, with the same safari opportunities that Kenya possessed, was going through rigorous agrarian reforms in which foreign tourists did not feature whatsoever.

Several critical factors made Chibembe Lodge an ideal place for the creation of walking safaris as a special entity. One was the presence of Norman Carr; another was its relationship with a large tract of unspoilt bush that was teeming with many varieties of game. Norman Carr had been a big-game hunter before the creation of national parks. When these came into being, he joined National Parks and worked his way to the top, becoming warden. At Independence in 1964, as many like him, he created his own safari company, using the skills he had developed as a hunter and his knowledge of local people and their customs. His walking safari prototype was a fusion of a typical hunting safari with that of a photographic safari, retaining the thrill of the hunt within a framework that was safe and more comfortable.

In his professional capacity as a surgeon, my father knew the Carr family. When he retired from surgery, he had gone on safari with Norman Carr's hunting company. His professional hunter on that safari was Peter Hankin, a close friend of Norman's. Therefore, it was a logical step that, when I was at an age to put my own passion for wild animals and adventure to the test, I would make contact with Norman and offer my services as a safari guide.

From that moment I never looked back. I later became safari manager at Chibembe and in the Selous Game Reserve, Tanzania.

Anybody who has been on a walking safari in the Luangwa Valley at any time will find that this book brings back happy memories. To those who have not had that pleasure, then it is time to take that step and allow yourself a treat that you will never forget.

This book describes how I grew up in Northern Rhodesia, was schooled in Southern Rhodesia, then took up guiding walking safaris at Chibembe Lodge when Norman Carr was manager. In the process I was lucky to meet many interesting characters. Phil Berry was Manager at Chibembe later on. He too had been in the Game Department. He did outstanding work in protecting Zambia's rhino population from extinction.

In addition, the book contains a few chapters from a Safari Guide Manual that I wrote that never saw the light of day.

Over the years, Chibembe attracted many influential people: Prince Bernard of the Netherlands, who was head of World Wide Fund for Nature at the time. Judge Train, head of WWF USA came on a walk with me and his wife. Prince Andrew, Aubrey Buxton, head of Anglia Television and instigator of the *Survival* series with his daughter Cindy. David Shepherd, the artist, and many more.

Iain Macdonald
June 2021

Acknowledgements

I would like to thank Wolf Jabs, who was a good friend of mine and provided me with the opportunity to set up my own walking safari business in the North Luangwa National Park.

I would also like to extend my good wishes to all the wonderful people I had the opportunity to work with during my safari days in the Luangwa Valley and the Selous Game Reserve.

Brian Jackman, who worked on the London *Times* colour supplement as wildlife correspondent, became my friend and has kindly written a Foreword to this book.

Roger Stringer of TextPertise did a wonderful job in realising my objectives with the book and enabling it to use some of the design elements that I found so fascinating in the 1907 edition of Sir Percy Fitzpatrick's *Jock of the Bushveld* (London: Longman) that was illustrated by E. Caldwell

Unless otherwise indicated, all the photographs in the book were taken by me.

All the margin illustrations were drawn or painted by me, as were the sketches for the maps. Juliet Kind assisted in digitising them all, and designed the cover.

Iain Macdonald

Part One

Growing Up

My first safari

In the early-morning sunlight, the white tents glinted between the trees on the rocky hillside above us. My mother lifted me onto the battered mudguard of the Chevrolet truck and pointed.

'Look, Iain! There it is! There's the camp we couldn't find last night. It's been there all the time!'

In the distance we could hear a muffled roar. Fish Eagles called from somewhere high up in the dazzling blue sky. An imposing baobab tree squatted on the horizon. The distant thunder was the Zambezi river. I was four years old, and this was my very first safari.

We had come a long, long way on terrible roads to this remote district in what was then Barotseland, a semi-autonomous province that had its own Paramount Chief, the Litunga, in the west of Northern Rhodesia, because Father wanted to hunt big game. Few people came there. We had finally reached Senanga.

In 1902, Lewanika, the Paramount Chief of the Barotse people, was invited to London to meet King Edward VII. When asked what he would say to the King, he was quoted as saying: 'When we kings meet, we always have plenty to talk about.' Queen Victoria had bestowed on him special rights, which were not honoured by President Kaunda on Zambia's independence in 1964. He was presented with a full British admiral's uniform, which is still worn on big occasions to this day. Each year when the Zambezi floods, the Paramount Chief moves his palace to a drier site in a ceremony known as the Kuomboka. The royal barge, the Nalikwanda, is propelled by more than forty paddlers wearing bright scarlet hats.

The Zambezi, which flows sedately for most of its course between reed-studded banks over a sandy floor, has its might suddenly challenged: a belt of very hard black basalt rock intrudes into the riverbed to form a barrier on which millions of years of battering appears to have had little effect. Much the same happens further downstream, but on a much larger scale, at the Victoria Falls. The might of water is broken up into numerous smaller channels that cascade through narrow gaps in the black shiny rocks, forming their own little waterfalls.

As the shadows lengthened, and having reached what Father considered to be the end of the road, we spent a very dismal night huddled around the vehicles. We had a Ford pick-up truck, driven by Father, with Mother and me on the front seat, and Yotam, our garden-boy from Lusaka, sitting on the luggage behind, and a ten-ton Chevrolet lorry borrowed for the occasion, with a driver, from Stanley Puffet, a farmer friend of Father's. In the vehicles were enough supplies for a week's hunting trip. Our cook and house-boy rode in the lorry, the driver's spanner-boy sitting behind, guarding the luggage.

We had been travelling for two punishing days on frightful dirt roads. Our first night had been spent at Sesheke on the banks of the Zambezi at a small private rest house. I remember a prowling leopard with a very long twitchy tail and glinting eyes that looked at me from a metal cage with evil intentions.

We expected to find the camp ready for our occupation. It had been set up by the local District Commissioner because Father was a high-ranking surgeon in the Northern Rhodesia civil service at the time. However, with no camp in sight and the light

A baobab more than a thousand years old.

A sable bull antelope
with long lyre-shaped horns.

A Fish Eagle
calls to its mate flying above.

dying fast, Father decided to stop and make camp using whatever we could scrounge from the lorry – not easy when you have no idea where anything is and you can't see! It was all very depressing. To add to our woes, the countryside had recently been burnt. Everything you touched put a black smear on your skin, and we were soon all covered in black soot. After much hauling and heaving, Mother managed to find a camping box with the tinned food. My nose started bleeding. The box with the Coleman lamps was found, but the methylated spirit needed to light them was in another box. At least Father, who smoked a pipe, had matches in his pocket.

We ate baked beans with spoons off tin plates, sitting on camping boxes by torchlight. My face became smeared with tomato sauce and black ash. My bleeding nose added extra colour. As a reminder that we were in the wilds of Africa, a hyena called nearby. Father went off to find his rifle. This was 1950.

Father would be off before light with his tracker and Yotam in the Ford pick-up while our cook prepared lunch. Mother and I would go for short walks in the vicinity of the camp. We collected large shiny red-and-black seeds from the pod mahogany tree. Close to the camp, Father shot an impressive sable antelope with very long lyre-shaped horns; he picked us up so that we could see it. I was fascinated by the glistening droppings that spilled onto the hard, dry ground like pawpaw pips.

The Zambezi teems with tiger fish – ferocious game fish with red fins, large silver scales and long, sharp teeth like a piranha's. They favour fast-flowing water. Father was a keen fisherman; however, his knowledge was limited to fishing for salmon and

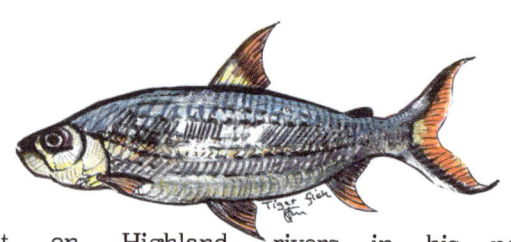

trout on Highland rivers in his native Scotland. This was different. This was coarse fishing at its most abrasive: the line was thick, green cord; the spoons were bronze with a hook as long as your finger. The spoon was attached to a short length of wire trace because tiger fish can bite through an ordinary fishing line.

On the first attempt, Father cast far out into the turbulent water. The line became snagged around the reel, and while he was trying to untangle it, an enormous tiger fish seized the spoon; with a ferocious tug that took Father entirely by surprise, it nearly had him in the river. That was about it. Father never fished again. The rod and reel remained in the linen cupboard outside the toilet back home, along with all the other sporting equipment, never to be used again.

I fished for tilapia in a small tributary of the main river with a line weighted with lead taken from .22 bullets – the same Brno .22 that I would use to good effect for most of my school years.

Camping in those days had been developed into a fine art. The District Commissioner of the day would 'go on Ulendo', taking with him all the paraphernalia and equipment needed for life away from civilisation. Ulendo was the local word for going on safari. It is a word that I always associated with going out into the bush on an adventure.

In colonial days, these safaris enabled the DC to visit remote regions under his jurisdiction, where the influence of the colonial system barely reached. His job was to settle disputes that could not be dealt with by the traditional courts, overseen by the chiefs.

Northern Rhodesia, now Zambia, covers a vast area: it is three times the area of England, Scotland and Wales put together. Even today, to reach some of these areas requires a powerful 4×4 and a considerable amount of determination.

Our camp had been set up on white sand under shade provided by leafy mahogany trees. The tents were white, with a flysheet that extended beyond the sleeping section and gave an extra layer of protection from the sun: you could sit on canvas folding chairs in the shade on this veranda portion. Outside each tent was a canvas hand-basin on a folding wooden tripod with a special pocket for the soap and a string for the hand-towel.

The bathroom was enclosed within a circular thatched wall, open to the sky. It contained a huge galvanised-iron bath tub that sat on a soft bed of grass. There was no door: the wall curved round itself like the entrance to a maze because there was no other form of privacy. The bath tub was filled in the evening with water that smelled of mud, heated on a fire and brought in by Yotam. Having a bath by paraffin lamp each evening was a special treat. The lamp attracted large moths, which cast flickering shadows on the grass walls that smelt of dry earth. You had to try hard not to drop the soap on the sand or to lose it in the murky water.

Mother was a keen photographer. For this occasion, she had invested in one of the first cine cameras; I don't think she had the faintest idea how to use it.

Galvanised iron bath tub

A fisherman using traps to catch fish at the Sioma Falls on the Zambezi river, close to where we had our camp on my first safari.

Mongu, the administrative centre for the western province of Zambia.
A young girl paddles her father up the Zambezi one evening.

On the return journey, to break up the tedium of bumping along on bad dirt roads, we spent a day aboard one of the regular barges that went up and down the Zambezi ferrying people and goods. These motor barges had steel hulls. They were about fifteen metres long with a big inboard engine that made a lot of noise and poured out a steady cloud of exhaust fumes. At the end of the day, they moored at one of several government rest camps along the river. We spent one night in one of these and made contact with the Ford and Chevrolet trucks for the last leg to Livingstone. I have a vague recollection of Father firing at basking crocodiles as we chugged downriver – and bringing one aboard which came alive later.

Our last night was spent with Gene and Marie Schultz in Livingstone. To our dismay, the suitcase containing Mother's camera had fallen off the back of the truck. It had also contained all my clothes. The spanner-boy had not noticed it going. Sadly, I have no photographic record of this very special safari.

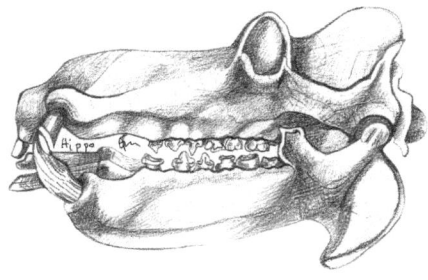

My paternal grandparents pose outside the gamekeeper's lodge on Darnaway estate, seat of the Earl of Moray.
In 1592, the Earl of Moray was murdered by the Earl of Huntly.
My father stands on his father's left.

My maternal grandfather and grandmother.
My grandmother holds my uncle Charles.
The lady on the right may well be
my Great-Aunt Dora who lived in Bath.

Darnaway castle, built in 1810,
home of the Earl of Moray.

The Findhorn river flows through the Darnaway estate
and is an excellent salmon river.

My forebears

My great-great-grandfather, Edward St John Daniel, distinguished himself as a midshipman in the Crimean War, when, at the age of seventeen, he won the Victoria Cross, one of the youngest ever to receive such an award. He went on to fight in the Indian Mutiny, the Second Burma Campaign, and a Maori uprising in New Zealand.

He was seventeen years old, a midshipman in the Royal Navy (Naval Brigade) during the Crimean War, when the following deeds took place for which he was awarded the VC.

On 17 October 1854 at Sebastopol, he was one of the volunteers from HMS *Diamond* who brought in powder to the battery from a wagon under very heavy fire, a shot having disabled the horses. On 5 November, at the Battle of Inkerman, as aide-de-camp to the captain, William Peel, he remained at his side throughout a long and dangerous day. On 18 June 1855 he was again with his captain in the first scaling party at the assault on the Redan, binding up his superior officer's severely wounded arm and taking him back to a place of safety.

In the Indian Mutiny his commanding officer, William Peel, suffered a wound to his thigh and, rather than take a train to the ship that would take him home for recuperation as befitted an officer, he chose to travel by cart. The cart had earlier been used to ferry a smallpox victim; he caught smallpox and died shortly after. Peel's father, Sir Robert Peel was the British Prime Minister and founder of the Conservative Party.

During this period of 'derring-do', Midshipman Daniel, now Lieutenant, found time to marry Barbara

The *London Gazette* announced the acts of bravery that earned my great-great grandfather, Edward St John Daniel, his Victoria Cross.

Edward St John Daniel's Victoria Cross

Lord Ashcroft VC Collection

Photo: Michael Daniels

Numb. 21971.   649

SUPPLEMENT TO
The London Gazette
Of TUESDAY the 24th of FEBRUARY.

Published by Authority.

TUESDAY, FEBRUARY 24, 1857.

War Office, 24th February, 1857.

THE Queen has been graciously pleased to signify Her intention to confer the Decoration of the Victoria Cross on the undermentioned Officers and Men of Her Majesty's Navy and Marines, and Officers, Non-commissioned Officers, and Men of Her Majesty's Army, who have been recommended to Her Majesty for that Decoration, —in accordance with the rules laid down in Her Majesty's Warrant of the 29th of January, 1856— on account of acts of bravery performed by them before the Enemy during the late War, as recorded against their several names, viz.:—

ROYAL NAVY (INCLUDING THE NAVAL BRIGADE EMPLOYED ON SHORE) AND ROYAL MARINES.

652 SUPPLEMENT TO THE LONDON GAZETTE, FEBRUARY 24, 1857.

Name and Rank.	Act of Bravery for which recommended.
Edward St. John Daniels, Midshipman............	2nd. On the 5th November, 1854, at the Battle of Inkerman, for joining the Officers of the Grenadier Guards, and assisting in defending the colours of that Regiment, when hard pressed at the Sandbag Battery. (Sir S. Lushington is authorized to make this statement by the Lieutenant-General Commanding the Division, His Royal Highness the Duke of Cambridge, who is ready to bear testimony to the fact.) 3rd. On the 18th June, 1855, for volunteering to lead the Ladder Party at the assault on the Redan, and carrying the first ladder until wounded. Sir Stephen Lushington recommends this Officer:—1st. For answering a call for volunteers to bring in powder to the Battery, from a waggon in a very exposed position under a destructive fire, a shot having disabled the horses. (This was reported by Captain Peel, commanding the Battery at the time.) 2nd. For accompanying Captain Peel at the Battle of Inkermann as Aide-de-camp. 3rd. For devotion to his leader, Captain Peel, on the 18th June, 1855, in tying a tourniquet on his arm on the glacis of the Redan, whilst exposed to a very heavy fire. (Despatch from Sir S. Lushington inclosed in letter from Admiral Lord Lyons, 10th May, 1856.)
Wm. Nathan Wright Hewett.	

Bedford, who bore him a daughter, Barbara Anne Trefusis Daniel, my great-grandmother. This period is covered by the adventures of Harry Flashman in the very entertaining historical novels by George Macdonald Fraser. Flashman – the fictional character from Thomas Hughes's semi-autobiographical *Tom Brown's School Days* who went to Rugby school – was a cad, a bully and a coward.

However, Daniel's story doesn't end there. With the death of William Peel, Lieutenant Daniel seems to have gone to pieces. The conditions at the time must have been ghastly: no anaesthetics, no antibiotics, appalling hygiene; Florence Nightingale bore witness to that in her heroic work with the wounded. In those days, post-traumatic stress disorder had not been recognised. You just had to grin, bear it, and carry on regardless – without the assistance of counselling. In an incident when he was goaded by a fellow officer, a fight ensued in which the officer died. He jumped ship to avoid a court martial and his VC was forfeited by Queen Victoria.

He died at the age of just thirty-one and was buried in Hokitika Cemetery in New Zealand. However, his story doesn't end there. According to one researcher, he may not have died in 1868, and may not be the man buried at Hokitika; the author Jack London has also described meeting an elderly man in 1902 whose story had 'uncanny parallels' with that of Edward St John Daniel (see http://www.danielvc.com/esjd/Summary).

In 1981, the family attempted to have his VC restored, but it was 'considered inappropriate to reverse the decision made in 1861 by Queen Victoria'. His Victoria Cross is in Lord Ashcroft's collection at the Imperial War Museum, London.

My father grew up in Dyke, a small village on the west coast of Scotland. His father was gamekeeper to the Earl of Moray on his Darnaway estate, which bordered the Findhorn river. His duties were to protect the birds, fish and other game that lived on the estate so that the Earl and his invited guests could enjoy themselves with rod and gun; it would also have entailed protecting and breeding pheasants for shooting. As the estate included highland, moorland grouse would also have been his concern, along with deer. The Findhorn river is a salmon river and also contains brown and sea trout.

My father, along with his brothers and sisters, walked across the estate to school in all weather to the nearby village of Dyke. Father did well at his school work and was sponsored by a rich uncle to study surgery at Edinburgh University, where he qualified. His first experience as a surgeon was on the meat boats going to and from Argentina. After that he accepted a posting to Northern Rhodesia in 1930. He was then thirty years' old. By that stage in his life Father knew all there was to know about guns and fishing rods.

As a gamekeeper's son, he grew up having strong opinions about cats: he detested them. His father would shoot any cat on sight, as they killed the pheasant chicks. My mother was very fond of cats and it was she who introduced the first cat into our lives. He was called Moosie, after Mersa Matruh, the site of a battle in North Africa during the Second World War. Father became very fond of Moosie and cats became part of our lives ever after.

Father also became a very good golfer and was

the Northern Rhodesia golf champion in the year I was born. He had a scratch handicap. His name appears to this day on the board in the Ndola Golf Club, and he designed the Chainama Hills Golf Course outside Lusaka, built in 1955.

My mother was born in Grahamstown, a small university town in the Eastern Cape of South Africa. Her father came from a well-established 1820 settler family who had come out to South Africa on the ship the Stentor from Cardiganshire in Wales. My great-grandfather was the Rector of Queenstown. He took the whole family back to England, where he became the Rector of St Thomas à Becket Church in Pensford. There my grandfather, Arthur Griffith-Green, a mining engineer, met and fell in love with Adela, the daughter of Henry Theodore Perfect, the Rector of the Church of St Mary in the neighbouring parish of Stanton Drew.

His gold-mining aspirations took him back to Africa, and in particular to Rhodesia, where he became involved in the first Chimurenga or Umvukela in 1896 – the uprising against the white settlers that Cecil Rhodes had brought in to develop the country. Matabeleland is home to the Ndebele people who, in turn, are related to the Zulus. They had arrived in the country in 1840 and spread their influence over all the local people in the region.

The European prospectors working in remote areas were made to join a troop for their own protection. Grandfather was involved in a skirmish: a Matabele warrior threw an assegai at him but it was deflected by the bandolier he

A studio photograph of my maternal grandfather on his return from the Klondike.

St Thomas à Becket Church, Pensford, Somerset, where my great-grandfather was Rector. My grandfather met my grandmother, the daughter of the vicar of Stanton Drew, an adjacent parish.

Photo (cropped) by Robert Cutts, <https://commons.wikimedia.org/wiki/File:St_Thomas_%C3%A0_Becket_Church,_Pensford,_Somerset_(4418378418).jpg>, under Creative Commons licence 2.0.

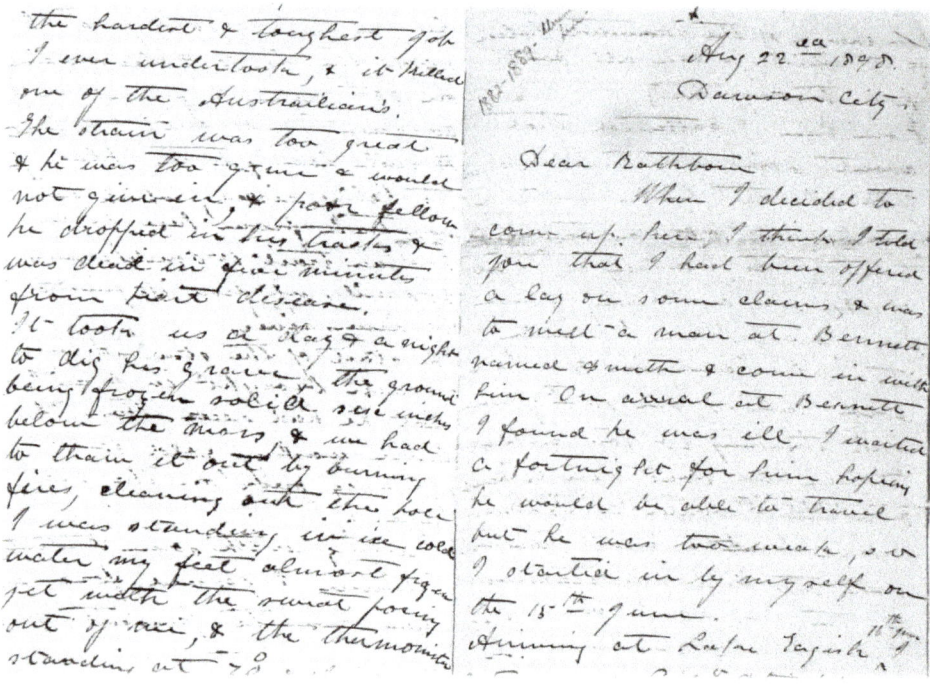

The letter sent to a friend by my Grandfather from Dawson City on 22 August 1898 while he was looking for gold during the Klondike gold rush in the Yukon.

wore across his chest. Convinced that his assegai had hit home, the warrior came at him in a rush, his short stabbing spear poised for the final thrust. Grandfather had to act quickly: he drew his revolver and fired, bringing the incident to a swift close.

Having had enough of the dust and heat of Rhodesia, he caught a ship to America to join the Klondike Gold Rush in the frozen wastes of the Yukon. He would have taken a ship to the east coast of America from Cape Town, then a train across the prairies on the new railroad to the Pacific coast, then another ship up the coast to Skagway, and then travelled by mule or on foot to Dawson City. It was 1898, the start of winter and already bitterly cold. I have a letter written by him from Dawson City on 22 August:

Meeting with some Australians, I joined forces with them. Well it was the hardest and longest job I ever undertook and it killed one of the Australians. The strain was too great and he was too game and would not give in. Poor fellow, he dropped in his tracks and was dead in five minutes from heart disease.

It took us a day and a night to dig his grave, the ground being frozen solid ... inches below the moss and we had to thaw it out by burning fires, clearing out the hole. I was standing in ice-cold water, my feet almost frozen ... clouds of mosquitoes ... we had to carry everything on our backs, blankets, grub, pick, dish, shovel and cooking things.

He never did make his fortune. Having survived the Klondike and the Matabele Rebellion, Grandfather returned to Grahamstown and decided to settle

The Japanese invade Tientsin during the 'Tientsin incident' in June 1939.

The Tientsin incident was an international incident created by a blockade by the Imperial Japanese Army's Japanese Northern China Area Army of the British settlements in the north China treaty port of Tientsin (modern day Tianjin) in June 1939. Originating as a minor administrative dispute, it escalated into a major diplomatic incident.

https://en.wikipedia.org/wiki/Tientsin_incident

Mother bravely asked the Japanese soldiers for their photograph.

down. He married Adela Perfect, and their children were my uncle Charles and my mother. Three years later, during the Boer War, Grandfather accepted a post as an engineer on a dam project in a remote area of the country. While there he developed appendicitis and died soon after, leaving my Grandmother with very little money.

My Grandmother had lived a very protected life in England and was not equipped to bring up two young children in a foreign land. Her family implored her to return to England, but she decided to stick it out and do the best she could. My mother grew up very poor. The clothes she wore were hand-me-downs. Her mother would eke out an existence by taking in boarders from St Andrew's College close by.

Mother went to the nearby Diocesan School for Girls. Her early childhood made her very strong. She never complained. Like my father, she suffered from tuberculosis: she had a severe form of the disease and the treatment at the time was to collapse one lung. To do this, several ribs were removed, but she nevertheless lived a very active life, playing golf and smoking, and lived to the age of ninety. She knew the value of money and was very thrifty without being mean. She even bought shares on the stock market and made a profit.

Mother took up nursing at the Johannesburg General Hospital and from there got a posting to Tientsin in China. In 1937, when the Japanese invaded China, she was captured but later managed to escape with an American doctor. Those who were not so lucky had to spend the rest of the Second World War in a detention camp where conditions were very harsh. Few survived. I have several photo albums of her time spent in China. (The movie, *On*

Devil's Coachman

Wings of Eagles, also known as *The Last Race*, about Eric Liddell, gold medallist at the 1924 Paris Olympics, takes place in a similar situation.) She was very courageous and even went down the Yangtse river by barge and as far as Korea by herself.

Mother returned to Africa and was posted to Northern Rhodesia, where she met my father, who was now divorced. His wife had taken their two children – a boy, David, my half-brother, and Jean, my half-sister – back to England. My mother was forty-five when she married my father, and I was born a year later by caesarian section in Lusaka Central (European) Hospital, Northern Rhodesia.

Childhood memories

My early schooling was in Lusaka. First a kindergarten, then a government junior school, which is still there to this day. I had many friends. My school reports were good. What little I remember of my kindergarten days was Mother making ginger biscuits for my morning tea.

My interest in nature manifested itself at this time when I became fascinated by the red velvet mites that appeared in the sand pit in the school vegetable garden. These are tiny red fluffy arachnids that come out during the rains and feed on termites, among other things. Their genus name is *Dinothrombium*; they are about as big as a sugar bean.

When I was little I had a large head so I was called *Bwana Chimsolo* in the Bemba language, which meant the master with the big head. I was highly strung and classified as a 'late developer'. I suffered acute migraine headaches if I became too excited, which often happened at birthday parties. By the time we sat down to the table to eat the birthday cake and jellies, I was feeling sick. This problem persisted right though my early school years and I learned to anticipate the onset of an attack only much later on.

Every three years Father had to take long leave, which necessitated a trip back to Scotland for six months on a mail boat from Cape Town. From Lusaka we caught the train to Cape Town, a distance of 2,300 kilometres, and spent a few nights with my Uncle Charles who was a Canon of the Church of England and living in Gordon's Bay.

With my parents in Edinburgh.

Auchnacloich, the farmhouse we stayed in.

My mother disbudding dahlias in front of our house in Lusaka. I am holding Sally.

Inverue, the old farmhouse at Nega Nega. I am holding my father's rifle.

My father and the Ford Zephyr in Nairn.

Showing off my new Diana pellet gun.

The train was pulled by huge steam engines that consumed large quantities of coal and in the process belched out clouds of white smoke. It was all very exciting for a young boy – the rhythmic clatter of the wheels over the points, the wail of the whistle as the engine approached a siding.

The railway line passed through Bechuanaland, where the local people made wooden toys that they sold to passengers through the coach windows at the stations along the way. The toy trains had windows burned into the wood with hot metal, but more important to me were the model aeroplanes with propellers that spun in the wind. However, if you leaned too far out of the window you ran the risk of getting a smut in your eye from the engine, which was very painful.

Those train journeys were magical. My mother took along my favourite books, written and illustrated by Jean de Brunhoff, about the adventures of Babar the elephant, his wife, Celeste, and Cornelius, the wisest elephant at court – characters that I remember vividly to this very day. We would have a coupé to ourselves and I insisted on sleeping on the top bunk. I would lower a piece of string down to Mother, sitting below me, and she would hook small items on to it that I would haul up. The cranes in Cape Town harbour fascinated me.

When I was much older, I shared a compartment with a man who had a glass eye that he would remove and put in a glass of water on the basin before he went to sleep. All through the night it clinked when the train went over the points.

Before meals, a waiter in a starched white uniform would walk along the

corridors, summoning passengers to the dining car by rapping on a three-note xylophone. While we were at dinner, the bedroom attendant would make up the beds with stiff white sheets. The seats and bolsters had shiny green covers and there was a small aluminium wash-hand basin between the windows. On the walls were photographs of the scenic wonders of South Africa, wild game and sandy beaches stretching to infinity.

The dining car was very posh – a term supposedly used to identify which side of the ship your cabin was situated on the long sea passage from England to India: Port Out, Starboard Home. This was to avoid the sun, but only the very grand passengers were able to secure a cabin on the cool side of the ship.

We were all were allocated sittings. The cutlery, cruets and coffee pots were all silver, stamped with the logo of South African Railways, and the napkins starched white. The greatest thrill of all was my seeing for the first time the sea, the mountains, some with snow on them, and the vineyards snaking across the well-tended hillsides.

From Cape Town it was all aboard a Union Castle liner that took us to Southampton. I have always been drawn to harbours to this very day. When I was working in Livorno, Italy, much later as a language teacher, I would go down to the harbour and sketch the tugs. I still have a sea trunk with a tin lining, complete with stickers, dating from those days.

I was fascinated by the flying fish that would appear suddenly from the sea and fly across the waves before disappearing into the water. Deck quoits were played on the wooden decks, and each day

Father would bet on how far the ship had travelled. When crossing the equator, Neptune appeared from the depths and officiated at a ceremony in which the crew, dressed in wigs and fancy dress, initiated anybody who had not crossed the equator before. I dared not show my face.

On my second trip – which was still not many years after the end of the Second World War and most of London was still in ruins – I was put into a children's home while my parents went shopping. It was somewhere between Southampton and London. I was not expecting this and was devastated. I would walk to the gate each day and look up the road, expecting to see them returning to pick me up, but they didn't. I was grief-stricken. After several days my mother couldn't bear it and they came and collected me. I wouldn't talk to them for days after that.

In London, Father hired a car and we drove up to Scotland. Before we left, Mother shut her right hand in the car door and later discovered that one of the diamonds from her engagement ring had fallen out. Just before the car was returned to the hire company six weeks later, she spotted her diamond, wedged in the rubber of the running-board.

In Bath we went to a Lyons Corner House tea-shop with my great aunt Dora, a very dignified lady. I chose a Swiss roll, which I managed to unravel and, by holding one end, I could eat from the bottom upwards. This behaviour, in the presence of Aunt Dora, was most embarrassing for my mother, who was very much in awe of her. I was scolded.

In Nairn we met up with my Scottish auntie, Frances. We stayed in an old farm house called Auchnacloich across the fields from my aunt's house. The barn smelled strongly of cow-dung and hay, a smell that I grew very fond of. Walking across the fields to my aunt's house, Murnachy, there were rabbits bouncing about, and we had to contend with Geordie, an Aberdeen Angus bull with a very bad attitude. I remember the smell of gorse and the exhilaration of seeing heather for the first time and the brilliantly coloured cock pheasants strutting about in the fields. Once, we went to the Braemar gathering and I saw highland dancing and throwing the caber. I was introduced to shortbread and floury baps and high teas in front of the fire, which were bigger than the teas I was used to, yet it was far too early for supper.

It was my birthday and my aunt went to a great deal of trouble to put on a birthday party for me, inviting several little children from the neighbourhood. There were multicoloured jellies in little paper cups. I disgraced myself by punching my young cousin Lesley on the nose. My older cousin, Sandra, wore her thick brown hair in plaits. She was good on the swing in their garden. They had Cairn Terriers.

We had a picnic on the Findhorn river and lit a fire to cook sausages. My aunt got her feet wet, so she took off her stockings and put them next to the fire to dry, whereupon they burst into flames. I thought this was very funny.

I caught a tiny trout in the Brodie Burn and took it home to the Marine Hotel, where I put it in the basin in the hope that it would revive. It was a brown trout with pink and black spots along its sides and a golden belly. It died, sadly. I also remember the swings in the children's playground and the merry-go-round.

I would go out with Father and shoot woodpigeons on a neighbour's farm. We would stack several stooks of wheat to form a blind. I shot a rook one evening as we were coming home with the shotgun. They were circling around a copse of trees, cawing loudly. My first time with the shotgun.

On one occasion we were walking through a paddock that contained a herd of Highland cattle. A hare got up, which Father fired at, whereupon the cows vaulted the fence and disappeared.

We met up with an old farmer friend who took us out with a ferret to shoot rabbits. The ferret was sent down one rabbit hole and the rabbits burst out of another. The myxomatosis virus came along later and spoilt all that.

We would go out to lochs in the vicinity and fish for trout from a boat rowed by my uncle Walter. Lochen Tutachad had a surfeit of tiny trout. Trolling the fly behind the boat was considered fair game.

Mother and I would walk along the beach at Nairn and accompany Father when he played golf. I can remember the wonderful smell of the clubhouse. You could look across the Cromarty Firth to the Black Isle. On one of the fairways were the ice houses for salmon. Father bought me a bag of miniature clubs and wanted me to take up golf – and take it up seriously. I had lessons from the club professional and continued playing until I went to university but then gave it up and sold my clubs. I had an eighteen handicap at the time.

In Nairn I would fish in the harbour using a small hand-line and worms that I dug up in my aunt's garden. On one occasion I caught a flounder but usually it was eels, which are slimy and wind themselves around the line and become impossible to remove. Once a wizened pensioner came up to me as I was struggling to get an eel off my hook and he removed it for me. He paid me a couple of apples for it. No activities were permitted on Sundays.

On a previous trip to Nairn, when I was just one year old, Mother was wheeling me down the high street and put her purse in my pram. Unknown to her I had chucked it out; she never found it again.

We visited my Uncle Peter, who lived in Edinburgh in a big house on Hermitage Drive near the Braid Hills. My Uncle always had Springer Spaniels. One of these had nipped the tip of aunty Renee's nose when it was asleep under the seat on a train journey. She bent down to talk to it and it got a fright and snapped at her.

We stayed at the Braid Hills Hotel, which was up the hill from the house. Father played golf on the Braid Hills Golf Course. I loved the smell of the garden with its damp leaves and the apple trees with real apples on them and the garden shed with the lawn-mower and tools hanging on hooks on the walls. At the bottom of the garden was a stone wall and beyond that was the river. Red squirrels scampered about in the trees.

Primary school years

At the age of six years and ten months, I became a boarder at a newly established boarding school called Springvale situated on an old tobacco farm an hour's drive outside Salisbury, the capital of Southern Rhodesia. Today it takes the better part of a day to get to Harare from Lusaka by road. In those days, the road was a narrow tarmac strip-road and, although there were no border formalities, you had to spend a night on the road. As an only child, I think my parents were worried that I would become too spoilt and pampered. I needed to be toughened up. Mother spent hours and hours sewing on name tags. The uniform was to be bought in Salisbury at Barbours store.

Before I started at Springvale, we went down to South Africa for a seaside holiday in East London. We started out in an enormous modern hotel with many floors. I kept getting lost in the maze of rooms and corridors. We moved to a cheaper one out of town close to the beach, which suited us all much better. We ate ice creams in a beach-side cafe that had a jukebox. My birthday was coming up, so Father took me into town and asked me what I wanted. I walked into a hardware shop and pointed to a hammer. That was what I wanted most of all.

At the start of my first term we stayed in the old Meikles Hotel right in the heart of Salisbury. It had a wide veranda along the pavement and a dining room with a moulded tin roof. Outside on the pavement, alongside Cecil Square with its fountain, were the flower-sellers. The square was renamed Africa Unity Square in 1983, although its design remains modelled on the Union Jack.

In the basement of Barbours was the toy department. A visit there after the tedious business of buying uniforms was a delight.

Our daily uniform was a tomato-coloured airtex shirt with short sleeves that buttoned half-way down, khaki shorts with an elastic waistband, and short socks, which most of us wore with sandals. Our smart outfit was a scarlet-coloured poplin shirt with a grey tie, grey shorts with a belt that had a coiled-snake buckle, and a grey jacket with the school badge on the pocket in red. This was the Jerusalem cross. Because the school was built on red-oxide soil, the red in the uniform was cleverly designed to take this into account. On our heads we wore cotton floppy hats, and it was one of the golden rules that you never went outdoors without a hat. If you played in the cricket first-team, however, you could wear a grey cap with the red school badge on the front.

When it came time to say goodbye, I jumped into my father's arms and clung around his neck in a vice-like grip and refused to let go. The beginning of term was always a hard time for us little guys. I was desperately homesick.

In the entrance hall to the school was a stout wooden bench that I would sit on when feeling miserable. Above it was a wooden propeller, made in Britain for flying boats after the Second World War. The bench and propeller are still there to this day.

Living so far away, it was difficult for my parents to visit and take me out on Sundays. They tried to come up at least once a term for a Sunday, which was all the time that the school allowed. Saying goodbye was the hardest part. As the afternoon wore on,

I became more and more depressed. We had to be back at school in time for showers and roll-call at 4.30. After that it was chapel in our smart uniform: grey shorts, grey jacket, grey tie.

The school estate was an exciting playground for us. As we grew older, we were given more access to it so that we could appreciate just what it held in store. It was criss-crossed by numerous vleis, valley bottoms through which water seeps forming marshy areas with reeds and ferns. Usually a narrow stream flows down the middle, but not always; sometimes the water goes underground.

Along the margins of these vleis are granite outcrops consisting of enormous boulders of differing sizes heaped on top of one another, some balancing in the most spectacular fashion as though put there by a gigantic hand. All this was embedded in brachystegia woodland, which turns many shades of red in September. It was there that I developed a fascination for birds and wildlife in general.

In days gone by, the Shona people used the caves hidden under these boulders as burial places, their belief being that the anger of the deceased is cooled by the presence of water. The corpses were walled in with stones and the walls covered with clay. In the caves were pots that would have contained beer and food for the afterlife.

Before the Shona were the Bushmen – the San (or Khoe-San/Khoisan). They were the original inhabitants of southern Africa for many thousands of years:

> The largest genomic study ever conducted among Khoe and San groups reveals that these

'Boxing glove' – one of the impressive granite kopjes on the Springvale estate that we visited on Sunday walks with our teachers.

This kopje had the best paintings. These were fascinating images painted by San artists depicting people and rituals of a bygone age!

This kopje, called 'Everest', was one that was used during a wide game that I organised when I was a teacher at the school during a Rhodes and Founders weekend.

A painting depicting San hunting with bows and arrows.

groups from southern Africa are descendants of the earliest diversification event in the history of all humans -- some 100,000 years ago, well before the 'out-of-Africa' migration of modern humans. (https://www.sciencedaily.com/releases/2012/09/120920141139.htm)

They must have come into conflict with the Shona, who arrived from East Africa with their cattle and goats. The San believed that all beasts belonged to them and they would have shot them with their tiny poisoned arrows and received brutal retribution in return.

They used the same caves as dwelling places and painted their exquisite renderings of wildlife in ochre and oxide on their smooth walls. We used to find beads and shards of pottery in the earth of these caves – and sometimes large venomous snakes. Hyraxes (also called dassies) dwell in the kopjes and they are the favoured prey of black mambas, whose venom is second to none in terms of toxicity. We would clamber all over these kopjes, which all had names that were well known to all of us: Blakes, Everest, Boxing Glove, Apple Slice, Cigarette. It was a miracle that no one broke any bones, was bitten by snakes or got trapped in the tunnels.

I started as a boarder in the last term of 1952 because my birthday was on 22 September. I was out of step with the other boys, who had been there for a term already. Miss Hill taught us arithmetic. She had come to the school with the headmaster and was of a similar age. She was a stern disciplinarian, had her hair tied in a bun and wore spectacles.

One exercise involved using cardboard money.

Springvale School
Marandellas, Rhodesia.
9 July 1955
Sunday Evening

Dear Margaret Macdonald

I'm so keen that Iain should sing a solo in next term's carol service but he hates it so. I've tried him alone, hidden away singing unaccompanied. The result was angelic, the only word for it. I think he has the most beautiful voice of any child I have taught – always perfectly in tune.

I think if he isn't seen, he won't mind too much. I do not want it to be a misery for him in any way, but it's such a waste of a lovely voice if it isn't heard.

Jean Preston (Grade One teacher, Music)

Springvale School
Marandellas, Rhodesia
26 November 1955

My Dear Margaret

I'm longing to see you on the 3rd and here is a warning! Bring a large hankie! (Both of you!) It'll help to mop up the tears when you hear Iain sing his little solo!

He did it yesterday in the chapel, just for me – Jean played the piano. I sat there with pricking eyes and swallowing hard whilst Mackie, his face the same colour as his shirt, hands held rigidly at his sides with the fingers all working madly, took a very deep breath and sang the first verse of Once in Royal David's City.

I suppose its just that straight clearness of little boys' voices that gets one – it was very touching, just Iain and me in the chapel – his voice is stronger than last year I'm sure.

Lou Godwin

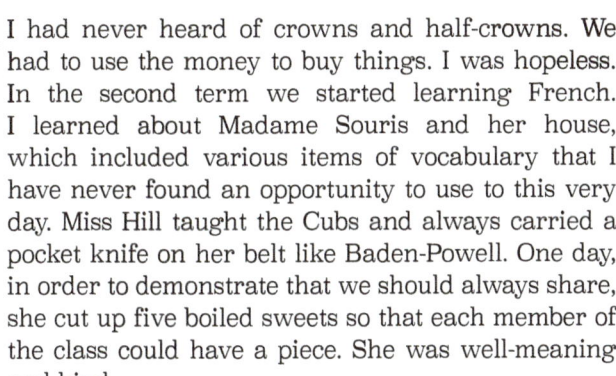

I had never heard of crowns and half-crowns. We had to use the money to buy things. I was hopeless. In the second term we started learning French. I learned about Madame Souris and her house, which included various items of vocabulary that I have never found an opportunity to use to this very day. Miss Hill taught the Cubs and always carried a pocket knife on her belt like Baden-Powell. One day, in order to demonstrate that we should always share, she cut up five boiled sweets so that each member of the class could have a piece. She was well-meaning and kind.

Lou Godwin was the nurse in the sanatorium. She used to take the first-year boys on a walk up to the railway-line so that we could put pennies on the line. The pennies had holes through the middle. The engines were diesel–electric and when they approached our crossing they would hoot their horns; we could hear the hooting during the night as they approached the siding. The next day, filled with high expectations, we would go and look to see if the pennies had been squashed flat.

Our first-year form teacher was Jean Preston. She was from England, dark-haired and beautiful. I adored her. She discovered that I had a clear singing voice and wanted me to sing a solo. She wrote to my mother about this. Lou Godwin warned her to bring a handkerchief to hear me sing. I had just turned seven. It was the end of term. I dreaded the thought of standing up in front of all the school and invited parents. I started well, then lost confidence and stopped. Miss Preston started playing the melody from the beginning and I started again and finished the piece. I remember telling one of the senior boys that I had run out of petrol.

In my second term I went up to school from Lusaka with a friend of mine, Tim Jones, and his sister Lis in his father's shiny green Land-Rover station wagon. Lis was starting as a boarder at Chisipite Junior School. Tim's father, Glyn Jones, was high up in the provincial government and later became the last Governor General of Nyasaland before independence.

Tim and I sat facing each other on upholstered bench seats with our school trunks stacked beside us. I was fascinated by the small windows set into the roof and decided that they must be for photographing giraffe. We stopped for the night at the Blue Jay Inn at Banket. My mother had given me a red Shuko Ferrari racing car with rubber wheels. I made it scoot down the corridors outside our room on the smooth concrete, which was ideal for these purposes. As we approached the school we saw a pall of smoke on the horizon. 'Let's hope it's the school burning down.' Sadly, it wasn't.

Our form-room was large with big windows and it was tucked away from the rest of the school. It looked out on to granite rocks and beyond those to enormous *Brachystegia* trees and the first-eleven cricket field. The drive skirted the field. We had it all to ourselves and played happily in the sand pit squeezed between the rocks. We had Dinky toys and made roads and raced them up and down and around and around. It was our own safe haven where we could play without interference from the older boys. There was a flower bed in which we planted our own flowers. I was overwhelmed by my first sighting of Love-in-a-Mist (*Nigella*).

With Christmas approaching at the end of my first term, we made Christmas cards in art lessons and paper chains from coloured paper to decorate

the windows of our classroom. It rained. When the fields were flooded we couldn't play cricket, so we ran steeplechase on the farm roads, splashing through puddles in our brown Tomy Takkies and having lots of fun.

At Easter the chapel was decorated with enormous arrangements of flowers in vases attached to the stout, black, creosoted gum pillars down the aisle. A flower that I will always remember because it grew in abundance in the vleis on the estate was the Red Hot Poker. Yellow ground orchids also grew in the vleis. Gerald Coney, the groundsman and art teacher, would create an Easter pageant in the porch of the chapel. A large flat stone would be placed across the tomb. The remains of a fire and Roman helmets and spears borrowed from the theatre department would tell their story. On Easter Day, much to our amazement, the stone would be gone and the white cloth in which the body had been wrapped would be lying on the ground.

In my second term I got pneumonia. Looking back, I think it was due to homesickness. The sanatorium had not been built by then, so I lay in bed upstairs in what would become a dormitory. Lou Godwin, the sanatorium sister, was so worried about me that she fed me peeled grapes. It was half-term, and she brought a parent who was a doctor to my bedside. It was on his advice that I ended up in the local hospital. I had to endure penicillin injections for the first time.

After lunch every day of the week was rest period. Before rest began, the library opened and thus equipped with books we would spend an hour reading happily on our beds in silence. At the beginning of the rest period, the matron would

A production of Gilbert and Sullivan's *HMS Pinafore* at Springvale.
I am centre stage, in front of the mast, as the Captain's daughter, Josephine.

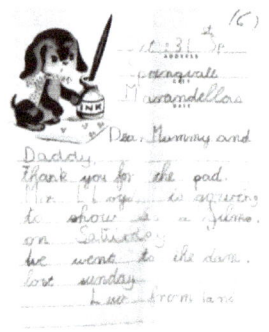

A letter home from boarding school.
My mother numbered each one.

Sunday outing on Springvale estate.
L to R: Me, Shepherd, Bromfield, Lis Jones, Slack, Tim Jones, Stephens.

Boxing with Christie at Springvale

The bench and propellor at Springvale.

unlock the tuck cupboard at one end of the dormitory and we were allowed to open our tuck boxes and take out four sweets. The matron knew exactly what constituted a sweet! The tuck shop opened during rest period. We had to put what we had bought into our tuck boxes, supervised by our eagle-eyed matrons. Heaven help the boy who tried to slip a few sweets into his pocket!

In the afternoon it was sport. After supper there was a movie. If I had played for a team in an away match that had involved a long journey in the school bus, I was feeling sick by the time the movie started. These were migraine headaches. The simple remedy was an aspirin. If I did not get an aspirin in good time, I would become nauseous, turn very pale and have to lie down. After my bout of pneumonia, Lou Godwin didn't want to take a chance, so she always admitted me to the sanatorium. This led the headmaster to suspect that I was malingering. It wasn't that at all: it was pure over-excitement. I learned with experience to predict the onset of the condition and took preventive measures in good time.

There was a sailing pool next to the chapel. In my first term I came equipped with a plastic replica of a Union Castle mailboat, the type we travelled on to England from Cape Town on long leave before the advent of the aeroplane. It developed a leak and sank. I must have dropped it. I made yachts out of cabbage-tree bark and equipped them with paper sails. The tadpoles that appeared in the water from time to time doubled as whales.

We were taught country dancing one night a week in the hall. We danced the Dashing White Sergeant and Strip the Willow for the elderly people at Borradaile Trust in the town.

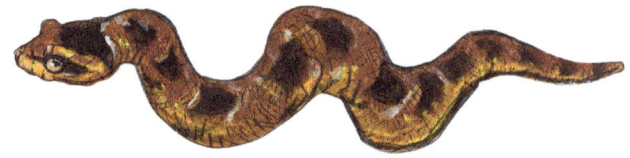

Saturday was the best day of the week. Monday and classwork was a long way off.

Each term there was what we called a craze. I have never understood to this day who initiated these crazes, but at the start of every term it would be marbles, or jacks, or something else. One term we made blow-pipes out of bamboo and shot one another with arrows made from thatch with pins stuck in the end.

At break each day we would happily entertain ourselves on the cement quadrangle outside the classrooms with a tennis ball. King started with all players standing with their right foot forming a circle, toes touching. Whoever had the ball dropped it vertically into the space between the feet and on its second bounce whoever's foot it landed on was ON. He had to grab the ball as quickly as he could because the rest scattered, trying to put as much distance between themselves and the boy who was ON. The boy with the ball tried to throw it at someone and if that boy was hit he became ON too. You could not run if you were ON so you had to throw the ball to someone who was ON. If the ball was not caught by someone ON and rolled on the ground, the other players could run and change their positions to get as far from those ON as possible. By using your clenched fist you could punch the ball away to avoid it hitting you, and you could tie a handkerchief around your fist to soften the blow.

Karlo required two teams, each team standing on either side of the fifth-form classroom block. One team defended the quadrangle, the other the soccer field behind. One team had the tennis ball. The

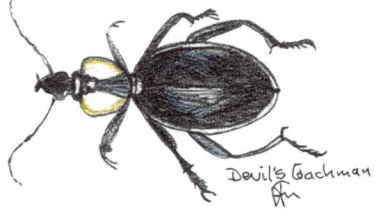

Devil's Coachman

strongest thrower would throw the ball over the roof and in doing so his team shouted, 'Karlo!' If the receiving side caught the ball they would run around the side of the classroom block towards the other team's position. Whoever had the ball pretended not to have it. He would try to hit a member of the other team with the ball, getting as close as he could before releasing it so as not to miss. If he succeeded, that person joined his team, and so it went on. With fewer catchers it became more difficult to catch the ball, so the balance of power favoured the bigger side until there was nobody left on the other side.

British Bull Dog was played on a sandy rectangle at the end of the quadrangle beyond the boxing ring. Two teams faced each other. One team called on a member of the opposing team to come forward. He attempted to weave his way through the ranks of the other team and reach the wall without being touched. If he made it through unscathed, the rest of his team could set out and try and make it through. If you were touched, you joined the other team.

Each morning after being roused from sleep by our matron, Miss Flood, we would have a cold shower to wake us up. As we got older, it became the greatest embarrassment to have an erection in front of all your mates, and particularly in front of the matron.

The dormitories were upstairs, the classrooms downstairs. After breakfast we made our beds and cleaned our teeth. We all had mosquito nets and these were tied up neatly. My net was pale blue. In our first year, the matron would line us up outside the lavatories and we would have to file in one by one. You were not allowed to flush the toilet until the matron had inspected what you had produced and

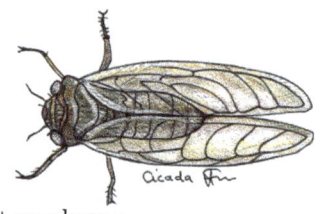

mark you off on her sheet. If you did not produce a sufficiency, you were sent back for a second try.

After I had been a boarder for a full year, Miss Preston wanted me to sing the first verse of 'Once in Royal David's City' in the new chapel, which had a thatched roof supported by gum poles treated with creosote to defy the termites. It was dark and very quiet inside. The smell of creosote and thatch is an unforgettable aroma. As senior boys, we would have to read the lesson each morning, and as I grew older, whenever a lesson needed reading for an official day I was chosen for my clear voice. For chapel on Sunday evenings, Canon Grinham would play Handel's *Water Music* to us on the black school gramophone as we filed in with the chapel bell ringing.

I had a very good ear. I taught myself to play the accordion when I was very young and also the harmonica. I tried learning the piano but struggled to read music. I took to the recorder and learned to play it very quickly. I am sure that if I had had a good teacher I could have gone far with music.

Our school library was full of exciting books and I read all the books by John Buchan and Rider Haggard. I also read Percy Fawcett's account of exploring the Amazon jungle and *The Hunt for Kimathi* by Ian Henderson about the Mau Mau uprising in Kenya. This was to be a warning about what we might expect from Zimbabwe's Liberation War that came a few years later in the 1960s and 1970s.

My favourite subject was English. I wrote long essays with stories that rivalled Rider Haggard for inventiveness. We were the generation born not long after the end of the Second World War, so many

books and comics related to the war, particularly the war in the air. The books by Captain W.E. Johns were popular reads: Biggles was our common hero. We could all tell a Hurricane from a Spitfire.

Our comics either featured aerial combat during the Second World War or 'cowboys and Indians'; the 'baddies' were the Red Indians. It was much later that I developed a strong feeling of respect for the poor American Indians, their appreciation of nature, and their abhorrence of the needless killing of bison on the prairies during the building of the transcontinental railroad. That respect was similar to what I felt about the Bushmen. The idea of being able to survive in the wild by making traps to catch birds and small animals became a new obsession for me.

Art then became an easy conduit for my imagination, and objects that fascinated me found their way on to paper: ducks, aeroplanes, and new buildings going up around the school. I won prizes in the National Institute of Allied Arts competitions. My rendition of the Nativity I still have to this day. The art room was beside the main hall and served as a make-up room for school plays. On the opposing side of the stage was the carpentry room, and this connected to the art room by a narrow corridor. A trapdoor in the carpentry room led you under the stage.

The art room was light and airy, with windows along two walls. Through the windows on one side you looked out on to the washing lines and on the other side on to the quadrangle, which was grassed and descended in walled terraces to the dining room, staff common room and tuck shop. Along three walls were cupboards, and we would rest our

Devil's Coachman

paintings on the top of them. On one occasion our art teacher, Gerald Coney, had us draw one another, and I used this activity when I was teaching art later on in Malawi. I realised how important it was to be able to draw properly and, as a student in London, I attended figure-drawing night classes at Saint Martin's School of Art.

When I was eleven, my parents again took long leave. For the very first time they flew. I flew from Salisbury as an 'unaccompanied minor' to meet them in Rome, stopping off along the way in Nairobi, Entebbe and Khartoum. The plane was a DC-6B. After Khartoum, one of the engines caught fire and we had to make an emergency landing in Cairo. We were all driven to a large hotel in the city. I saw a tank parked in the street and in the afternoon we were taken to see the Pyramids. That night we boarded the plane and flew to Rome, where I was to meet by my parents. They were not there to meet me. They had taken a taxi to the airport and it had got stuck in traffic. My mother was beside herself with worry and kept telling the taxi-driver to go quicker.

From Rome we caught the train and travelled along the Italian riviera. We stayed in a dreadful hotel in Genoa, booked through Poly Tours. The smell of sewage erupted out of the basin every time someone in the building flushed a toilet. In Nice I was very excited about going to the beach, but I was surprised to find it was covered in pebbles. For lunch mother bought us what she thought was a sandwich but turned out to be a baguette about a foot long; it cost the earth. Father was out of his comfort zone and didn't enjoy the Continent at all

and longed to get back to Scotland. My mother loved every bit of it.

In London they bought a Ford Zephyr and drove to Scotland where we stayed in the Marine Hotel in Nairn. I shared a room with my half-brother David, who had just finished his National Service.

Gilbert and Sullivan arrived at the school in the form of *The Mikado*. I was in the chorus, dressed as a Japanese courtesan with fan and heavily rouged cheeks. In *HMS Pinafore* I was Josephine, the Captain's daughter, complete with bonnet and lipstick. In the photograph, my muscular shoulders stand out. My role was seen to be very challenging, so, to preserve my voice, I was allowed to rest in the afternoons. My beau was Raiph Rackstraw, a humble sailor who went by the name of Harrison. I had to sing the song with one hand on my breast:

Sorry her lot who loves too well,
Heavy the heart that hopes but vainly,
Sad are the sighs that own the spell
Uttered by eyes that speak too plainly ...

The Rhodes and Founders weekend was a double public holiday. The junior boys did not camp out, but once you had become a Boy Scout, you spent two nights sleeping out in a tent at Scout Camp. It never rains at that time of the year, but there are frequent frosts and heavy mists. The campsite was on level ground by a small stream that flowed between granite boulders and had been dammed to create a small swimming pool – which made it even colder at night. I had my camouflaged safari tent,

ex-Second World War, with what I thought was a bullet hole through one side, though it was probably just a cigarette burn. It came in three sections buttoned together; zips had not been invented in those days.

On kitchen duty we had to chop up fruit for the fruit salad. Our hands, washed but still not that clean, stained the salad a delightful pink colour. We had 'illegal tuck' in our tents. This amounted to tins of sardines, which I never liked much, Vienna sausages, bully beef and condensed milk. We tried smoking: three inches of the dried stem from a Red Hot Poker stuffed with old man's beard and you had a potent cigar – which turned us all off smoking for the rest of our lives! We were often sick. Sun, too much smoke from the cooking fires, our ersatz cigars, and eating a mixture of sardines laced with condensed milk did it. I had a thick sleeping bag but we froze at night.

After two sleepless nights having eaten food cooked on open fires but also having experienced a glorious time, we trooped back to school smelling of smoke, with grazed knees and sunburned bodies, and with earth under our nails, to face hot showers, fierce matrons, and a change of clothes. Our beds with their clean sheets and soft mattresses were a joy after the hard ground and the biting cold of the tent.

At the end of every term, the tin trunks with our names painted in large letters on the lid would appear from one of the sheds behind the laundry and be dusted off. They would sit at the foot of our beds. This was the first real indication that the end of term was near. We had to lay out all our clothes in neat

lines on our bed to be checked. Our matron would appear at each bed with a clipboard and check that nothing was missing. If an item was not there, you were sent to find it and you missed your turn.

On the last day, the Northern Rhodesians had to watch the other boys being collected by their parents and taken home. We had to endure another night at school before we were driven to Salisbury for our flight home. The planes owned by Central African Airways in those days were Vickers Vikings and Viscounts. The tuck shop would be opened; there might also be a movie. The dormitories were very quiet. All the NR boys would be bunched together in one dormitory – which allowed us to bounce about on the stacked mattresses in the adjacent dormitories. The following morning we would don our smart clothes and pile into the school VW Kombi for the trip to Salisbury and the flight home.

My first headmaster was Canon Grinham. He was short, stocky, bald, stern, and with a pronounced hooked nose like a vulture's. He always wore a clerical collar. The school was run along the best Church of England lines, with chapel every morning and evening. My classwork was satisfactory in those days.

Canon Grinham retired in 1956 and John Paterson took over. He was much younger and came from St Andrew's Preparatory School in Grahamstown, where my uncle had gone to school. My mother's school, the Diocesan School for Girls, was its sister school. He introduced achievement symbols for 'mark orders': up to that point you earned stars for good work.

He also introduced caning. If you received an

X symbol for a mark order, it meant that you were not trying hard enough, and this qualified you for a beating. The names of those to be beaten would be read out in front of the whole school at assembly on a Monday morning. You had to visit the headmaster after lunch during rest period. That night in the showers, the red cane marks would be evident for all to see.

Paterson also brought in rugby. We played on one of the lowest fields in winter, and on occasions there was a heavy mist hanging over the field. As we trooped back to the school and hot showers, our rugby jerseys steamed.

I dreaded these assemblies and even considered jumping off a rock to break an arm to avoid the humiliation. My self-confidence plummeted. In any situation when I was tested I was reminded of this. I developed ways of overcoming the suffering, which was the normal adjunct to unhappiness and self-doubt. When you do not value yourself or your abilities, anything you create is undervalued.

When I started painting, I would often give my paintings away. I would paint a picture that came straight from my imagination. It had everything a good painting should possess. Later, I would look at it and find faults with it. I would change it. Not satisfied with this, I would make more changes until the original inspiration had vanished. It became a mess and I would throw it away or paint over it.

As I matured and became attractive to females I used this to buy the affection I craved. This often led to relationships in which all I wanted was the physical act because it was this that gave me what I craved. I could not commit to love.

Red bishop bird

On Sundays, three senior boys would form a colour party in front of the flagpole to hoist the Union Jack. Before the ceremony, the flag had to be rolled up carefully and the rope with the release toggle tied in such a way that it unfurled with a tug from the rope but did not come undone on the way up the pole. The boy in the middle held the furled flag in his folded arms. One Sunday Mr Grieveson, the deputy headmaster, was on duty. He was a gentle, kindly man with a short moustache. I was guard commander. I placed a handful of dried leaves into the folds of the flag while we were folding it. When Mr Grieveson tugged on the rope to release the flag, the leaves came floating down on to our heads in a cloud. We struggled not to laugh.

After roll-call you were allowed to go out with parents or friends until half-past four in the afternoon. Roller-skating was a craze we all enjoyed. Outside the classrooms were wide, smooth cement corridors, ideal for roller-skating. For some reason, we skated on a single skate, rarely on two. We also sat on one skate and had a skate on each foot. Someone then had to push you down the corridor. We used folded-up hats as cushions. I devised a way of skating on one leg, then kneeling down, resting the other leg over the first and using the second skate as a sidecar. I was the only person in the school who had managed to jump the stairs from the three senior classrooms using a skate and sidecar.

The tuck shop provided our first experience of using money. I would work out change by counting in the air. I could visualise the numbers as they would appear on a domino. It sold liquorice laces, which made your teeth go black, multi-coloured marshmallow fish covered

in icing sugar which you could stretch, and suckers and jelly babies covered in sugar.

It also sold model aeroplanes that were made of plastic and came in kit-form made by Airfix. The glue we used was Samsonite, and I can remember the smell of it to this day. It coated your nails and skin like a synthetic skin, so the only way to get it off was with your teeth. After gluing the whole thing together – the wheels were tricky – you painted it with dope and then stuck on the insignia, which were transfers. We could also buy balsa wood models that we flew on the quadrangle. These were mostly gliders. Some had large red plastic propellers powered by elastic bands.

I think Mother regretted sending me away to boarding school and tried to make up for it by sending me things. She was a very reliable source of letters and small treats. Little gifts appeared regularly in the post. From a magazine, she discovered how to make a paper aeroplane. She duly sent me the instructions and a model that she had made herself, just to show me that it was possible. I can still make them to this day. Paper darts, as we called them, were made by all of us in different shapes and sizes from old exercise books.

The school buildings were an oasis in a sea of green fields, and beyond them was virgin bush with ancient *Brachystegia* trees with thick, gnarled trunks. Nature was all around us. Occasionally, large poisonous snakes slithered into the school buildings, only to be spotted by one of the estate labourers and killed. Hares came out at night to eat the grass on the playing fields. Fielding on the outfield during cricket matches you became aware of their droppings – the size of Smarties in small heaps. You could also entice

camel-back beetles out of their holes by poking them with a blade of grass anointed with spit. Red-winged Starlings nested in the roof of a covered passageway between the art room and the laundry. They would eat mulberries, which stained their droppings purple. The eggs, which we were not allowed to touch, were very beautiful – palest blue with small brown splotches over them.

During a heavy thunderstorm one night, a lightning conductor outside the washrooms received a direct hit. The blast dug a massive hole in the ground.

A horse from the riding school fell into the sewer near the main gate and had to be shot. One term, the whole quadrangle was dug up because the pipe to the septic tank had become blocked. We were given a thorough haranguing by the headmaster at assembly for this: the offending item was a school hat – which had the offender's name on it.

The washrooms had a row of dwarf toilets along one wall with half doors and a urinal at one end. We would compete with one another to see how high up the urinal we could pee. The toilet paper came in small neat boxes called Blanco; it was shiny and stiff and not absorbent.

In our second year, Miss Hill was our form teacher. An exciting moment was when she gave us our ink pens, which had small rubber bladders for sucking up the ink from the inkwell that was in the right-hand corner of our desks; until then we had used dip pens for our letters home. These were Osmiroids and came in a large box. We could choose which colour we preferred – red, green or blue. The nibs were fragile. In a stout wooden cupboard, which was locked, were bottles of ink, blotting paper

and chalk. The duty monitor for each class had the responsibility of filling the inkwells.

Each classroom had a blackboard with a board duster. Along one wall were boards on to which posters were pinned. We chewed blotting paper to make pellets and shot them at each other using an elastic band stretched between thumb and index finger. We also tried to get the pellets to stick to the ceiling. Drawing pins were highly prized items: they could be placed on the chair of an unsuspecting individual who was called up to the teacher to have his book marked.

We were also taught Latin. I marvelled at the exploits of the Roman generals Tius Labienus and Marcus Aurelius Cotta.

The staff dreaded April Fool's Day: they had to endure a series of pranks with good humour. If a teacher loomed on the horizon we would say, 'Chips!'

School breakfast during the week was mealie-meal porridge, with a spoonful of brown sugar planted in the middle like a brown eye, followed by egg of some sort, then toast and marmalade. We were always hungry. On Sundays it was Maltabella porridge made from millet. Some days we had scrambled egg and bacon, with big gleaming pieces of fat. I would shovel the bacon into my handkerchief and take it outside for the headmaster's dog.

One Christmas I was given a Kodak Brownie box camera. In those days, cameras required film that came on a spool. When loading the film you had to be very careful not to expose it to daylight. The film was sealed with a paper sticker that had to be cut carefully. The tapered end of the film had to be fed gingerly from the spool into a roller in the bed of the camera the right way up. By pulling out the winder,

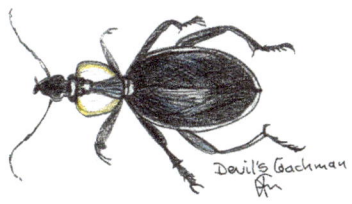
Devil's Coachman

the spool clicked into the other end. With the lid of the camera closed, the film was then wound on so that the figure 1 appeared in a small window. It was always a relief to see this as it meant that the film was winding on correctly.

I took photos of friends and teachers. Once the film was exposed you could give it to one of the teachers who was going into Marandellas. Black-and-white prints would appear a week later in a sleeve along with the negative in a tight roll secured with Sellotape. The film had either sixteen or twenty-four exposures. The Brownie had a viewfinder on the top that bent the light ninety degrees. A later Kodak used a smaller film, and that had a flash that used small flashbulbs that exploded when the shutter was pressed. These early cameras were entirely automatic, with no aperture or shutter speed controls to worry about. The lens was very wide-angle so that depth of field was enormous and focus was not an issue as long as you did not get too close to the subject.

I always had a sheath knife of one sort or another and carried these on my belt on Sunday walks to various kopjes on the estate.

A parent of a boy at the school had links to the Royal Air Force. Through his father, a Vulcan bomber flew low over the school at a pre-arranged time so that we could all see it. It had enormous delta-shaped wings.

Stanley Matthews, who played soccer for England, toured the country and coached the first-eleven soccer team. John Edrich and Bernie Constable, who played cricket for the MCC, paid us a visit and coached the first-eleven cricket team. I was in the first eleven for both cricket and soccer.

slender mongoose

Close to the estate was a riding school. I used to ride on Sundays because I rarely went out. The owners of the riding school had a classic Mercedes stationwagon that would appear at the school entrance and take us to the riding school. We would go for hacks along narrow paths through the woodland, and back at the stables we would eat molasses and bran. One of the horses was called Flicker. One of her ears was folded down, caused by a tick bite; she was grey, gentle and very popular. A small Shetland pony I liked was called Penny.

November the fifth was Guy Fawkes Day. An enormous bonfire was lit close to one of the sports fields, well away from the buildings. After supper, according to your age and perceived level of responsibility, you were given a tin containing an assortment of fireworks. There were always sparklers, always squibs on strings and a box of matches. Rockets soared into the night sky, courtesy of the duty master. One boy had a Roman candle shoot between his neck and the collar of his shirt while he was bending down. As he stood up, the firework became trapped inside his shirt and he was badly burned. There were no other accidents.

We were allowed to keep small pets. The pet room was a small shed behind the laundry. It contained the cages for our hamsters, guinea pigs, mice and rabbits. I was given a hamster. One of our teachers had brought it from a pet shop in Salisbury and I built a cage for it in Carpentry in readiness for its arrival. Hamsters are inveterate escape artists, and no sooner was it ensconced in its new home than it had detected a weakness in my craftsmanship. It was gone the following morning, and though I hunted high and low for it I never found it.

I was a member of the Bird Club, and one of my responsibilities was to feed three baby Eagle Owls. They had ear tufts and clopped their beaks if alarmed. They would blink at me suspiciously when I opened their cage and puff up their bodies to appear menacing. I fed them mince mostly, into which was added cotton wool as a substitute for fur and feathers in their diet.

I also had to feed a baby monkey. I gave it mealie-meal and bananas and I hated the damn thing. It showed me no gratitude and bit me if it could manage it. It made a terrible mess of its cage, which I had to clean out. I have never liked monkeys ever since.

I also started collecting birds' eggs and butterflies, and I was given a killing bottle that had cyanide in it. We became very observant as a result. If you were in the Bird Club you were allowed to walk on the estate without a member of staff, just as long as you had a companion. During our long break, if we had spotted a nest with eggs on a Sunday walk, we would dash out and try and bring the eggs back. You drilled a hole in one end then blew out the contents with a straw. We became good at tree-climbing.

During the rains, huge pink-and-yellow moths with false eyes at the back of their wings would be attracted to the security lights. They had furry bodies and branched antennae; they would be clinging to the wall the next day. Sometimes there would be longicorn beetles, which had long antennae, massive jaws and large eyes like motor-car headlights. If we could find two of them we would put them in a shoe box and try to make them fight each other.

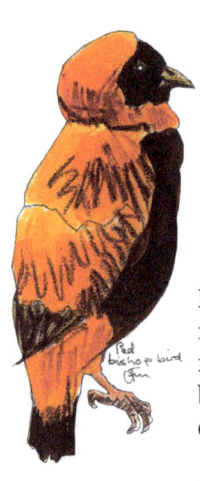

In my second year we started boxing. The boxing ring was under a cabbage tree at one end of the main quadrangle. The coach was a delightful fellow by the name of Agiotis. The leather gloves had a distinct smell about them.

I boxed against one of the Slack brothers in an inter-house match and he must have broken my nose because it bled profusely. The agony of being hit on the nose cannot be described. I won the 'best loser' cup for my bravery. It was only when I was working in Johannesburg several years later that I developed serious nosebleeds that would not stop under any circumstances. I had to visit the Accident and Emergency department of the General Hospital in Johannesburg for treatment, and it was only then that it became apparent that my nose had been broken all those many years earlier. It was repaired by one of the most skilled plastic surgeons in Johannesburg who had treated fighter pilots after the Second World War – Doctor Jack Penn at the Brenthurst Clinic.

When my mother saw how he had changed the contour of my nose she was shocked and insisted it be done again. Some of the cartilage was pared off. I chose to have the operation done under local anaesthetic as I felt embarrassed that the surgeon was doing the operation purely as a favour to Father, who was a fellow surgeon, and also so that it would not cost too much. I remember seeing the bill in which each ball of cotton wool and each swab was itemised.

We all had nicknames. Some were kind, some cruel; always well thought-out, though. Mine was an easy one: Mackie.

It was at this time that my academic record began to plummet. My mother had been religiously keeping all my school reports, but I have no record of them from then onwards. In the fifth year, when I wrote my Common Entrance exam, I was held back a year. My friends were now a year ahead of me. I developed a revulsion towards examinations of any kind, which even extended towards board games.

We played cricket in two terms of the year and football in the winter term. I played left half to begin with. The chaplain was an ex-professional soccer player and he coached the first eleven. His name was Claude Billington and he lived in a small flat at the top of the stairs between two dormitories. He always wore a cassock and smoked cigarettes from a cigarette holder. He wore tinted glasses. For one match we switched positions. I tried goalkeeping and became the first eleven goalkeeper ever after. I had a good eye and was fearless. In a match against the staff, I punched a shot over the bar, saving a goal.

In our senior year we became monitors and had numerous duties; one was bell-ringing. The school bell that rang during the day was a length of railway line hanging on a stand near the bathrooms. The chapel bell was a proper bell and was housed in its own little thatched house on the grass outside the chapel.

As seniors we were allowed early-morning swims instead of showers. We would don our costumes and dressing gowns and walk barefoot to the swimming-pool. In winter the water was freezing and it was a matter of a quick plunge and out.

At the beginning of a new term it was a thrill to see your name on the first-eleven cricket board.

I bowled slow off-spins which did not spin a great deal. I could also bowl leg-spin out of the back of my hand but I had no control over them – they either pitched beyond the wicket-keeper or halfway down the pitch.

In a home match against Digglefold School, the slogger came in when I was bowling. He was a huge Afrikaner boy by the name of Van Zyl. I bowled a very simple ball, well pitched-up on the stumps, which he tried to hit for six but missed and I bowled him middle stump. I surpassed myself by being a very good fielder and could throw down the wicket from the boundary. I also fielded in the slips and caught well. Batting developed only much later on in life when I had left school altogether and was teaching in Malawi.

Childhood in Lusaka

Our house in Lusaka was provided by the British government. It backed on to the European Hospital, and the mortuary could be seen from our back garden. I would watch ambulances arriving and see bodies wheeled in. We had a big garden that was not walled, as most houses are in Lusaka these days. The boundary along the main road was a fence, which I could squeeze through easily. Down one side of the property we grew mangoes, and along the back was a hedge of mulberries. On the front gable of the house was a metal owl screwed to the brickwork; this gave it the name of the Owl House.

My bedroom at the side of the house looked out on to pawpaws and mango trees. The mango tree at the back of the house, close to the staff quarters, had what we called kidney mangoes. They hung low on the tree and were difficult to spot: even when ripe they kept their green pallor. Their flavour was unlike that of any other mango I had tasted, and there were no strings in the flesh; they were delicious and very juicy. We grew a few vegetables in the garden – large red tomatoes with firm flesh, which I enjoyed with a generous sprinkling of salt. Mealies were my favourite for supper, which I had with butter and salt on my own at a table on the veranda.

The boiler for the bath water was next to my bedroom. I could hear the gardener lighting the fire each evening. I would put tin soldiers into the fire and watch them melt into shiny grey balls.

At Christmas it always rained. We had a Christmas tree. It went back to the garden in its pot and rooted itself. It was still there when I visited the house forty years later. It was customary for a

troupe of African dancers to appear at the house on Christmas Day in full tribal dress. They would dance and frighten me.

Shortly after marrying my father, my mother bought an enormous turkey and invited several friends for Christmas lunch. The house did not have a big enough stove to cook a really large turkey. Other friends were going away for Christmas and said, 'If you want to use our kitchen, bring the bird to our cook who is living on the property and he will cook it for you.' Mother duly obeyed these instructions and appeared at the house. She called and called for the cook but he was nowhere to be seen. He had gone home to his village.

In due course their garden boy arrived and said that he could cook the turkey. Mother was in a predicament, so she handed it over to him and said she would come around and pick it up the next morning. The following morning she arrived at the house, went to the kitchen and knocked, but there was no sign of anybody. She started calling. Finally there was a shout from the garden, where smoke was rising from a large fire on the lawn. The gardener had the turkey on a spit. It was excellent.

Johnnie, our cook, would bring the early-morning tea at 0600 hours to my parents' room. He was always punctual, reliable and very smart. One morning he appeared a few minutes late. He looked a little bit dishevelled, and my mother asked him what was wrong. He said he had had an argument with his wife. At this point my mother noticed that he was wearing his cook hat low over his forehead to hide a deep gash. His wife had hit him with an axe.

The second movie I ever saw was *The Wizard of Oz* with Judy Garland at the 20th Century Cinema

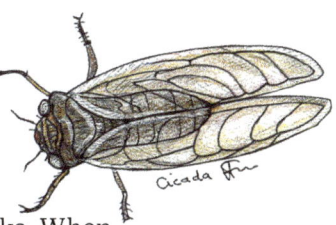

on what is now Katungila Road in Lusaka. When the witch appeared, I spent the rest of the movie under the seat with my eyes shut.

My first movie was *Where No Vultures Fly*, which we had seen when I was a new boy at Springvale. The hall had not been built then, so we watched it sitting on cushions on the floor in what became the staff room. After the first reel we were sent to bed, so I never got to see the movie through to the end, something I have regretted ever since.

One day, the Keith brothers came over to play. Their father was a doctor. I had my friend Michael Allan with me for the day and we played war games. The Keith brothers had to attack and try to capture our fort. I made smoke bombs using ash from the boiler wrapped in old newspapers. When I threw my first bomb it exploded, sending thick clouds of ash into the air over the enemy. Donny Keith started crying and my mother came rushing out to investigate. That terminated the conflict, which made Michael and me the conquerors.

Mother would take me to the Anglican church. One Sunday I felt faint and had to be taken out early. The next time, Mother gave me a packet of ginger biscuits to eat, which did the trick. Going home we passed the site for the new Anglican Cathedral, on which was a huge wooden cross; there was nothing else on the site. For some strange reason I believed that if you wanted to get married you walked about on the site and until you met your partner.

I had a Polish nanny, one of the ladies who were refugees from the war in Europe; they had bobbed hair and strong arms. One was an expert at embroidery and made beautiful curtains with hollyhocks on them.

When my parents went out to a function at night, I would lay booby traps across the doorway from the dining room to the living room so that when they came back I would hear a tin fall and know that they were back and feel safe.

My appendix became infected, and Father was summoned urgently from the Copperbelt, where he was working, to remove it. I can remember lying in bed in the children's ward feeling sorry for myself. In those days, anaesthetics were performed using ether. A mask was put over your face and you had to count aloud to ten. Just as you were going under, you heard a drumming sound that got steadily louder until you fell asleep. I also had problems with my teeth, which needed a general anaesthetic.

I learnt to swim at the public baths. There was a tuck shop that sold the same selection of sweets as our school tuck shop. The present-day Pamodzi Hotel is built on the site of the old municipal swimming pool. Mr Charles was the lifesaver and swimming coach; he taught me to swim. We started by standing on the edge of the pool and falling head-first into the water at the shallow end. He was not tall and had his hair cut short. He wore a black swimsuit with shoulder straps and was very tanned. I would cling on to his broad back with my arms around his neck and he would swim me out into the deep water. He wore sunscreen, which made his skin slippery.

We had such fun at the baths. At one end was the paddling pool. We invented games such as Shark: One person was ON and he had to defend the wall beside the springboard. The rest dived off the board and tried to touch the wall without being touched. If you were touched you became a defender. If you dived very deep, nobody could catch you. When

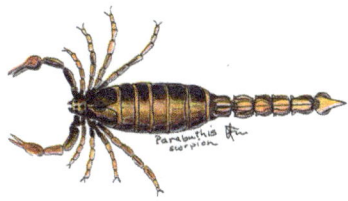

I was feeling very brave I dived off the high board. Just climbing the ladder and standing on the board was a very brave act. At Springvale I became the free-style champion.

My godfather, Bill Cherry, had a farm in Ndola on the Copperbelt, about five hours' drive away on the Great North Road. One weekend we paid him a visit. I had just been given my first bicycle, so the bicycle went with us. I remember the joy of being able to balance and pedal at the same time. My set of mini-bricks was stolen by one of the staff. It was recovered later and Mother washed it thoroughly with Dettol. While Father played golf, Mother and I went to the swimming pool. I was fascinated by the morning glory creeper that grew along the wall outside the baths: the flowers were midnight blue in colour and shaped like trumpets.

One Christmas I rode my bike all the way into town to the biggest supermarket in Lusaka – Kees Stores in Cairo Road – to buy my mother a present. I left the bike outside the store and it was still there when I came out. I cycled all the way home again. You could never do that in Lusaka today. I would ride along the paths near our house through the mealie fields and create jumps where the path went over an anthill.

In an Indian shop owned by the Dudhia brothers I spotted an accordion. I was given it for Christmas and I quickly taught myself to play it.

We always had a dog in the house, usually a Scottie. The first one in my life was Sally, who I would load into a straw basket tied to the back of my tricycle and ride around the garden. I had the normal run of rabbits and guinea pigs, and once a budgerigar that I called Tinkerbelle.

Me, aiming my .22 at Namwala beach.

Left to right: Father, Mother, Jean Jearey, me, David Jearey.
My camouflaged tent is on the right.

Standing, left to right: Jean Jearey, Jack Jearey.
Sitting, left to right: David Jearey, Father
Mother is sitting on the grass.

The breakfast table.
Left to right: Mother, Jean Jearey, Father, David Jearey, Jack Jearey.

Street, our gardener, showing off the head of a buffalo shot on the Namwala safari.

The school holidays were joyful times for me. My mother would devote all her time to me.

Father taught me how to make a catapult, and I roamed our garden and beyond with Street, our garden-boy, attempting to shoot birds. I looked like Huckleberry Finn and my interests in life were very much the same as his, though I didn't smoke a corn-cob pipe; that would come later. He carried a .40 Pennsylvania muzzle-loading rifle, while I carried my .22 Diana pellet gun; later it would be a .22 Brno rifle. His companion was Jim, mine was Street.

Street was a tall chap and always smiling. We spent a lot of time together. He taught me to make traps to catch rats and birds with birdlime. My interest in birdlime had dire consequences when I tapped into the trunk of a large euphorbia tree to extract the white sap. Some of the sap went into my eyes and sprayed on to my skin. In the morning, I couldn't see: my face was swollen and covered in blisters.

On Saturday afternoons, Father would meet up with Jack Jearey, a friend of his, and his son, David, and we would drive out to one of the farms outside Lusaka to shoot Guineafowl and Francolin. Street would come along as beater. These farms grew maize on a large scale, so we would form a line and walk through the dried maize. Any Francolin that rose was fired at. On one occasion, a bird flew down the line and both guns fired and missed. It was Street at the end of the line who eventually brought the bird down with a well-aimed throw of his knobkerrie.

As it was getting dark, we climbed into the cars and headed home. At a particular point on the road, the lead car would pull off and drive down a small sidetrack and stop. Grass baskets from the local market, carefully packed in advance by wives, would be brought out from the boot along with small folding canvas chairs. A soda siphon and glasses would appear, along with a bottle of Black & White scotch whisky, and a lemonade for me and Street. Cheese-and-tomato sandwiches, or ham with Colman's mustard, would follow.

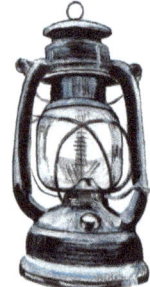

Father bought a share in an abandoned farm with an old farmhouse at Nega Nega, about an hour's drive out of Lusaka. He called it Inverue. We would spend very happy weekends there. It had no electricity or running water, and lighting was provided by Tilley lamps. To light them, you first filled them with paraffin and pumped it up using a small plunger. Then, you clipped a sponge soaked in methylated spirits on to the neck of the lamp. This was lit and, after a suitable wait, you put a match to the mantle. If you had not waited long enough, the paraffin did not vaporise and the whole thing caught fire. Father, being impatient, had this happen to him, and in his anger he threw the whole thing into the garden. The next time he tried, it worked perfectly.

There was a long-drop toilet in the garden, and Blue Waxbills would peck about on the path. Their call always reminds me of those days. One year there was an infestation of stink bugs. At night, as a precaution against mosquitoes, Mother would dress me in dungarees. The word entered the English language from India and refers to a type of coarse material; it was a precursor of denim. Most of the time I wore shorts. Dungarees had shoulder

straps, a useful pocket in front, and covered your legs. You rarely hear of them these days.

I had been given the Diana pellet gun for Christmas one year. I learned to shoot with it and was never without it. Street and I would go hunting birds, and any that I shot I gave to him. I carried the pellets in my mouth because if you carried them in your top pocket they fell out if you bent over. Bulbuls were what I shot most often. Lizards, sunning themselves on a wall in front of our house, were also targeted. I would throw empty tin cans into the air and shoot them before they landed. This skill remained with me for many years, and when I was doing a call-up during my army training years later, it earned me two beers.

My first victim with the Diana was a sunbird. These are tiny little birds that suck nectar from flowers using their long, curved beaks. The males have iridescent feathers, the females being rather drab by comparison. I put it proudly on Father's pillow.

The men would go out hunting after Guineafowl in the morning. On one occasion, Father tripped and banged his twelve-bore shotgun on a rock, putting a hole in the barrel.

The Kafue river was not far off. We would drive down to the neighbouring farmer and he would load us all on to a trailer and pull us down to the river with his tractor. At this point, the Kafue becomes swallowed up by marshes and reeds, which gives it the name Kafue Flats. During the rainy season, November to March, the river floods its banks in much the same way as the Nile does.

One Sunday, the three of us drove out to a farm belonging to one of Father's numerous Afrikaner

patients. The car was parked by the roadside and we had the whole farm to ourselves. Near the road was an abandoned hay baler. This intrigued me and I climbed up on to the seat and soon became fully engrossed. As it was getting dark, Mother and Father said they would walk back and get the car, leaving me to continue playing. They had misjudged the distance: by the time they found me, it was completely dark and I was in tears, convinced that I had been abandoned.

Hugh McKee was a good friend of Father's. He was a member of the Northern Rhodesia Legislative Council, whose members were elected and which operated much like a local government. He also owned Kees Stores, the big departmental store in Cairo Road. After the Second World War he had bought on auction the floats from a Sunderland flying boat in Durban. He had these sent up to Lusaka by rail and designed a houseboat from them, which was anchored in a lagoon on the Kafue river in what is now Lochinvar National Park. He also constructed a metal launch with an inboard engine that had a canvas canopy.

We would be invited for weekend outings. The drive down to the Kafue took less than an hour and the cars were parked at a boatyard just short of the bridge. Chugging slowly along to reach the houseboat took the better part of the day. I would fish for barbel from the houseboat using a night line. On the return journey, I would be given a big rod to fish for pike, trailing the line behind the launch. Father shot duck in the shallows and the launch would be anchored near the bank so that we could fish for bream. The houseboat had a flat roof that you could reach by a ladder, which, in the cool of the evening, was perfect for sundowners. We grew our own worms in whisky cartons and fed them with mealiemeal.

One holiday we travelled up to the houseboat and then went on beyond, taking tents and towing a small aluminium rowing boat. We saw herds of lechwe splashing through the shallow water of the lagoons. We were very close to Blue Lagoon, which was a sanctuary for lechwe. The launch had a raised platform midships, reached by a ladder, which I used as a lookout point for ducks and geese. In the lily-covered inlets along the river, African Pygmy Geese could be seen; they fed on the lilies. Occasionally I would spot a Spur-winged Goose.

I gravitated to using the .22 rifle. Its bullets came in orange and red boxes and were made by Kynoch. Father was always very careful with the number of bullets he gave me. Once I was allowed ashore with Street when I spotted a goose on a lagoon. We crept up to within range and, had it not been for a lapwing giving our presence away, I could have shot it with the .22. The lapwing flew around above our heads and the goose flew off. When the lapwing had settled I shot it instead.

The toilet was a grass enclosure downstream that was open to the skies. Father always took his shot-gun with him. One morning he brought down a goose from a sitting position.

When my father retired from surgery, he was invited to shoot duck, using the houseboat as a base. The rains that year had been particularly heavy, and the villagers who lived in the vicinity had to abandon their farms: their maize fields had become flooded. Duck in their thousands were attracted to the abandoned maize. The big launch was anchored to the bank, so we all proceeded inland using the small fibreglass dinghy with an outboard engine.

Father and I were dropped on to a submerged ant-

Lechwe at the Kafue river, Lochinvar conservation area

hill. The three other guns were positioned in a semi-circle on dry ground behind us. We were in the front line, unable to move, and every duck and goose that came past went over our heads. Father had brought only one box of cartridges and a full belt around his waist. In an hour he had fired off every cartridge he possessed. He had a spare box in the launch moored in the main channel some distance away. I volunteered to swim back to the launch and bring the spare box. I had my .22 and managed to shoot a flying Spur-winged Goose but failed on the duck. We had to stand for the remainder of the morning, unable to do anything until the others decided to call it a day and fetch us in the dinghy. We must have shot more than a hundred birds that morning.

One school holiday we went camping to Namwala, a small town on the Kafue river close to the Kafue National Park. The dining room was on the banks of the Kafue under mahogany trees, right by the water. The Jeareys came along with us. I had Street as my companion, and this time I would go off with him, hunting for doves, when Father and Jack Jearey went off while it was still dark, taking their fried-egg-and-bacon sandwiches with them. The women stayed behind. Their role was to cut the meat up and make biltong.

Father shot a hartebeest on one occasion when I was permitted to accompany them. He put out bait for lion, but nothing appeared. Visiting the bait one morning I was terrified that a lion would jump through the window. He shot a lone Spur-winged Goose that used to fly over the camp in the evening. One afternoon we went out to look for Guineafowl but without success. I had a

Elephant bulls will mix socially with females at waterholes.
Here, a very old bull tries to shove a youngster out of the way so that he can drink at a hole they have dug.

Zebra are very social animals and live in tight family groups

A huge flock of Quelea finches.

A Yellow-billed Stork arrives at a fish-out at a lagoon.

A large flock of Yellow-billed Storks circle, having eaten all the fish at a particular lagoon.

shot at a duiker but the shot went high. Later on, as it was getting dark and we were sitting having our sundowners, a flock of Guineafowl landed in the trees above our heads. Father managed to get one. The rest flew over the river.

One afternoon we drove upriver to a marshy area where sandgrouse came in to drink. Typical Namwala countryside has numerous anthills that are conical in shape and heavily wooded by comparison to the surrounding bush, which is flat and covered in tall grass. You can always find Francolin in them.

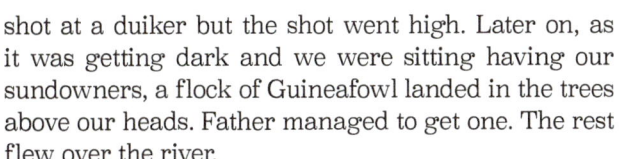

The villagers would use our beach from which to pull in their nets, which were made from the nylon cords taken from car tyres. The floats used wood from the sausage tree. I asked Mother if she could make me fishing net for me out of mosquito netting. It was like theirs in miniature; I caught tiny tilapia in mine. Upstream, the river narrowed and passed through rapids where there were many crocodiles basking on the sandbanks.

Father shot a buffalo bull, which was brought back to camp in the back of the Land-Rover. I would visit the staff quarters where most of the meat was hanging on wires to dry. It was a bit smelly. The hunter-boy had the scrotum of the buffalo and was scraping it down to make a tobacco pouch. When I asked him what it was, he tried to tell me that it was the skin from its knee.

I nearly trod on a large snake that slithered under a tin trunk at midday. I screamed. My mother thought I had been bitten, but it had passed over my foot. Father got the hunter-boy to pull the suitcase away before he blew it to bits with his shotgun. It was a cobra. One morning I found a small sand snake curled up in the warm ashes of our fire.

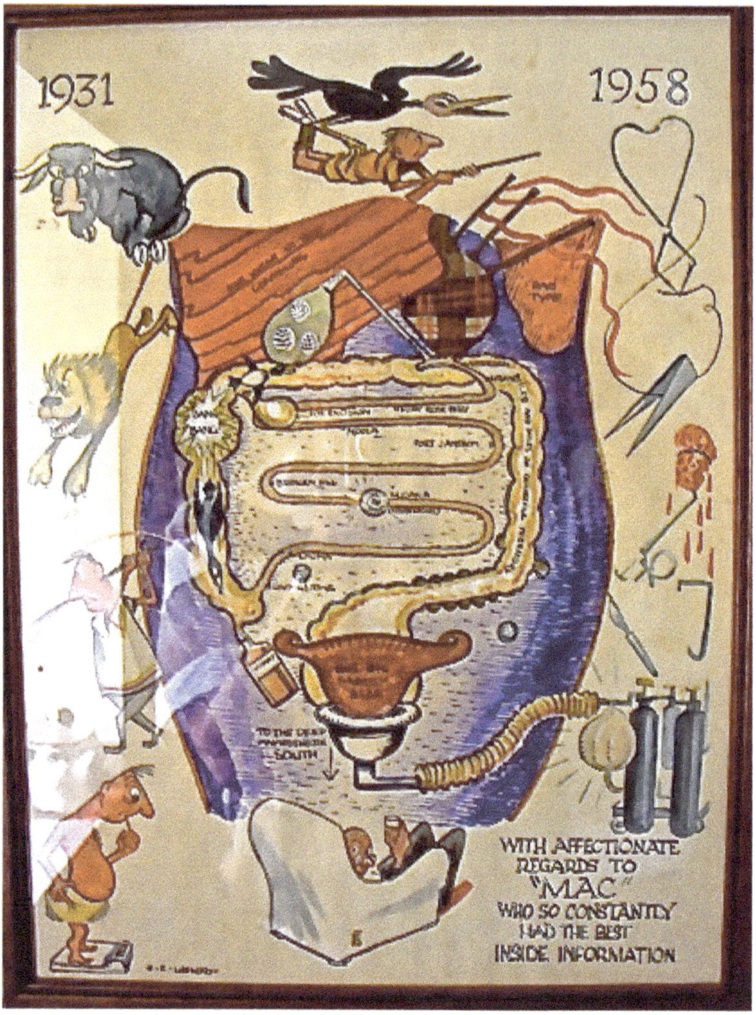

A painting given to my father when he retired from surgery in 1958.
It is a map of Northern Rhodesia in the form of the human digestive tract.

Father shot a buffalo bull.-

Moving South

Father retired from surgery in 1959 and received an OBE. Sir Humphrey Gibbs, the Governor General of the Federation of Rhodesia and Nyasaland, presented it to him at Government House in Salisbury. Father's brother, Peter, who was knighted, and a solicitor and director of several important Scottish firms, invited him to go on a hunting safari to the Luangwa Valley in Northern Rhodesia. Their Professional Hunter was Peter Hankin, whose camp I was to find much later on when I was operating walking safaris in the North Luangwa National Park.

My parents had never owned their own home. There was a scheme after the Second World War, introduced by the British government, in which small farms were made available to pensioners living in the colonies. My parents applied and were able to get two hundred acres of land in an area beyond Penhalonga in Southern Rhodesia called Odzani. It was on a mountain top on the edge of the Honde Valley and looked north past a landscape studded with granite kopjes. You could see the M'tarazi Falls and beyond Mount Inyangani, the highest mountain in the country. It had little agricultural merit but made up for this by having spectacular views in every direction.

My mother, who had no architectural experience, designed the house. Jack Bathurst-Brown, from Northern Rhodesia, who had also settled in the area, built it for them. They named the farm Braemoray after the grouse moor on the Earl of Moray's estate in Scotland where my grandfather had worked. They planted wattle and pine trees – the wattle to sell for its bark. They also planted fruit trees: apple, apricot

My father sipping his whisky and soda while being entertained by a traditional dancer from the village during his Luangwa Valley safari.
Peter Hankin, his professional hunter, is left of frame.

Overlooking the Luangwa river.
My father, on the right, sits next to his brother on their Luangwa hunting safari. Peter Hankin far left.

Flying termite

and plum. Mother grew flowers, particularly huge white and yellow chrysanthemums, which enjoyed the heavy red soil. We had our own chickens and vegetable garden. Water came from a borehole and was pumped into a reservoir above the house.

The air was fresh, bitterly cold in winter, the altitude about seven thousand feet and very invigorating. Thick fog would often rise up from the valley below and envelope us so that you could hardly see more than a few feet in front of you. There was no electricity to begin with, so we used paraffin lamps for lighting and cooked on an Aga stove that used anthracite. I had baths by lamplight. The room would mist up so that you couldn't see the windows. Moths would be attracted by the light and their shadows would be enlarged as they ricocheted off the walls.

On a shopping trip one morning we went up to the tea room on the first floor of Meikles department store in Umtali which had a veranda that gave you a marvellous view over the hills of Christmas Pass. I had a strawberry milkshake, and on the drive home on the twisting road to the farm I started feeling carsick. Before I could say, 'Stop the car!' I had to lean out of the window and be sick. The pink milkshake on our pale-blue 1961 Chevrolet Biscayne did not go well together. Once a week Father would drive into Umtali, which took about an hour, and play golf at Hillside Golf Course.

Father had hoped to continue his surgery in Umtali on a part-time basis; however, the hospital registrar didn't allow it. Not to be outdone, Father built a small clinic at the crossroads to Watsomba. Our maid, Diana, who was well educated and spoke good English, was the nurse and translator: 'snakes

The house at Braemoray in Odzani, on a mountain top at the edge of the Honde Valley.

The view from Braemoray across the Honde Valley.
Mount Nyangani, the highest mountain in the country, is in the distance.

in the belly' was a common ailment. Mother tried selling chrysanthemums and vegetables in Umtali but this wasn't sufficient to sustain them.

The eastern slope of the farm where the fruit trees grew was covered with ancient terraces and pit structures. The bush was very thick and impenetrable. Who built these pit structures and stone terraces and for what purpose? The pit structure is a circular pit lined with rocks about the height of a grown man. The floor is paved with rocks. Every pit structure has a narrow tunnel entrance that is roofed with flat rocks. In the centre of the floor of the pit is a drain hole. An early theory suggested that these were slave pits, and an even more fanciful idea was that they were designed to extract alluvial gold. It is now believed that the pits were designed to collect the dung from a species of dwarf cattle that no longer exists.

The farm had its own kopje, which stood right on the edge of the escarpment at one end of the property. From a rock on the kopje you could look down into the Honde Valley far, far below. I made a glider from balsa wood and my intention was to fly it off the top of the kopje. Carrying it without breaking the wings required care as it was a long walk. I then had to climb the kopje, which was covered in thick bushes. Eventually I reached a rock that provided an unhindered view of the valley below and was an ideal launching site. I pictured the glider floating down endlessly on the updrafts before disappearing into the distance. I launched it into the wind, but the wind coming up from the Honde Valley below was too strong and it forced the glider into a steep dive and it smashed on to the rocks. It was a very long and dejected walk back home.

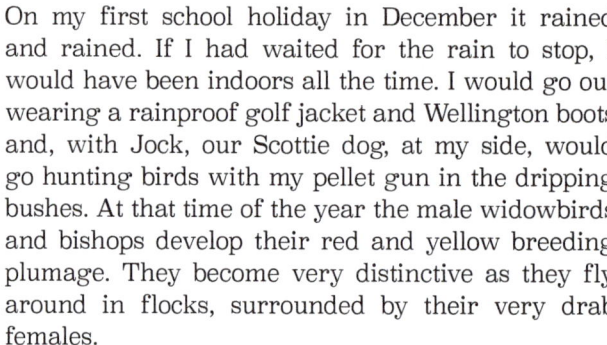

On my first school holiday in December it rained and rained. If I had waited for the rain to stop, I would have been indoors all the time. I would go out wearing a rainproof golf jacket and Wellington boots and, with Jock, our Scottie dog, at my side, would go hunting birds with my pellet gun in the dripping bushes. At that time of the year the male widowbirds and bishops develop their red and yellow breeding plumage. They become very distinctive as they fly around in flocks, surrounded by their very drab females.

One morning I met a forest cobra (*Naja melanoleuca*) on the road. Jock hadn't seen it and I was terrified that he would attack it. Our new cat, Tib, who had come down from Lusaka, spotted another one on our front lawn and ran from it with high bounds. The snake went down a hole and disappeared. We tried smoking it out but without success.

I picked a huge bunch of wild flowers for my mother as a Christmas present. There were wild arum lilies, orange gladioli, yellow irises, flame lilies (*Gloriosa superba*), ground orchids and pink proteas.

In the evening, flocks of Speckled Pigeons would fly over the house en route for their roosts in the rocks on a large granite outcrop behind the house. One evening I asked Father if I could stand out with the shotgun and try to shoot one. He gave me strict instructions not to put two cartridges in the gun. I waited patiently and nothing appeared. As it was getting dark, I thought I would take one shot at a swift, which were migrating in large flocks at the time. They are considerably smaller than a pigeon but twice as fast. I put another cartridge into the barrel to increase my chances. I chose a bird that was coming straight for me. I followed it and fired. The force of the impact knocked me off balance and, to save myself, I let go of the shotgun. It described an arc before landing on the ground behind me, facing me, whereupon the second barrel went off. The blast went between my feet and made contact with the outer edge of my left foot.

I looked down to see what had happened. Where the toes were, the leather of my sandal had been peeled back. My toes were a bloody mess. I screamed and began hopping back to the house. Father heard me and came and carried me indoors. Mother washed my foot and gave me strong pain-killers. I was rushed to the Umtali Hospital and underwent surgery that night. Several pellets were removed but quite a few remained. Removing the bandages was extremely painful: they had a coating of Vaseline but even so they stuck to the wound. The smell of rotting flesh remains with me to this day. It was a miracle that I suffered no long-term injury to nerves or blood-vessels. I was in hospital for a week and returned to school with my foot wrapped in bandages.

Zeddie, our cook, and his brother, Street, came with us to Southern Rhodesia. Zeddie's wife was expecting a baby. Mother knitted booties for the baby and gave them to Diana, our maid, to give to the wife. Shortly afterwards there were screams and the very pregnant lady came running down the drive pursued by Zeddie with a big stick. She was screaming for my mother to give her protection. Evidently it was very bad luck to give someone a present for an unborn baby. The fact that she might have had a miscarriage was not considered relevant at the time.

I was an avid reader of the *Sports Afield* magazine published in America and sold in Rhodesia. I used to write off for free catalogues. Advertised in the magazine was a taxidermy course offered by the Northwestern School of Taxidermy, Omaha, Nebraska. The course came as a Christmas present from my parents, complete with glass eyes. I still have them to this day. The pages are blood-stained. Father gave me all his old surgical instruments.

Living on the farm became impossible. The price of wattle plummeted when a synthetic alternative was invented to tan leather. The pine trees were very small and would only become economic at some time in the future; the same went for the fruit trees. Money was a major issue and political unrest was another. My godfather, Bill Cherry, who had bought a farm outside Penhalonga, had his pigsties burned down. A brick was thrown through the windscreen of the school truck as it passed through Mabvuku township on its return from an away rugby match in Salisbury.

My parents were fortunate to be able to sell the farm to our neighbour, John Colville, so we moved into Umtali, the third largest city in the country, which sits in a ring of hills close to the Mozambique border. It is a very pretty town, with avenues lined with flame trees and jacarandas. We moved into temporary accommodation near the showgrounds. The garden had a tall acacia tree that was full of weavers' nests.

The following year, my parents bought a house in Murambi on the lower slopes of the steep mountain-

side overlooking the town – the very first house that either of them had ever owned. Two houses up the road was virgin bush, full of Samango monkeys, baboons, bushbuck, and the diminutive blue duiker, which boasts more scent glands than any other antelope.

The house was on a steep slope and the garden was terraced. You felt as if you were in Switzerland, with tall fir trees bordering the property on all sides. In November, the flame trees at the bottom of the garden exploded into flower with the first rains, carpeting the ground with their scarlet petals. Paradise Flycatchers fashioned their tightly woven basket nests in the forks. By day, the harsh call of Turacos could be heard from the forest. In the evening, pairs of robin-chats challenged one another from the garden walls. At night, the galagos (bushbabies) cried like banshees in the fir trees.

Under the house was a garage and utility room, and beside that was a small room that became my workroom, where I painted, did taxidermy and kept my reference books. It had an upstairs veranda over the garage that had canvas blinds to keep out the hot afternoon sun. That was where Mother banished the lion skin and the table made from an elephant foot, relics of Father's Luangwa Valley safari with his brother.

Father got a job as tuberculosis specialist for the Ministry of Health. It was well paid and was more or less a mornings-only job. I was sad to leave Braemoray. I had had freedom and plenty of space all to myself. There were very few people of my own age in the area and I think my mother worried that I was not getting enough contact with other children, particularly young girls. I was extremely shy in the company of strangers.

I could cycle down the road and play golf at Hillside Golf Club. Going down was easy, coming up was a steep climb all the way. I went for long walks up the mountain with Kirsty, our Scottie. I caught a snouted night adder (*Causus defilippi*) on the road below our house and an egg-eating snake (*Dasypeltis scabra*), which I photographed and released.

Mother bought a grey Morris Minor Traveller, the car I learned to drive in. It was a small stationwagon that had wooden panels along each side and at the back. The back seats folded down, creating a lot of space for carrying provisions. It had a notoriously poor handbrake, which was to cause Mother a great deal of embarrassment on one occasion when she parked on one of the roads leading up to Main Street. She turned the engine off, put the handbrake on, but didn't leave it in gear. When she came out of the shop, her dear little grey car was nowhere to be seen. A pedestrian saw her plight and pointed down the road. It had gone through the plate-glass window of Grant's garage. On its journey in reverse, it had crossed a busy intersection. The car was unharmed and Mr Grant was not too upset. He didn't even ask Mother for money to repair the plate glass of his showroom window.

I, too, suffered similar embarrassment when driving a young lady back home after a party. She lived right at the top of a very steep hill. I stopped to let her out at her gate with the handbrake on and my foot on the footbrake. When I tried to get it into gear it wouldn't go. I had to reverse down the hill with my foot on the brake and the handbrake on. When I reached level ground, I took my foot off the brake and tried to get it into gear but it lurched to the side of the road and went down a steep bank. I had to leave it there and walk home.

When I finished at Springvale, I passed the Common Entrance exam and was accepted by Peterhouse, which was just over the main road that formed the watershed and the railway line linking Salisbury with Umtali. The uniform was navy blue. Long trousers for the first time. Many of my Springvale friends were there and also my long-standing friend from Lusaka, Mike Allan. He had been at Whitestone school outside Bulawayo.

Secondary school years

My academic struggles persisted after I moved to Peterhouse. Having been kept back a year, I was now older than the other boys in my class. We had to sit IQ tests and I would panic and be unable to write anything.

When I arrived at Peterhouse I was put into C Block, which was where all the 'thickies' were put. Being labelled a thickie became a terrible burden to carry; socially, we had very low status. In the second year we moved into Toyes rooms. These were small studies. You could hang photographs on the wall. I had a wooden box with a padlock that I had made in carpentry in which I kept all my treasures. We could make coffee. I had a small immersion heater along with a tiny radio on which, using earphones, I could listen to the LM radio hit parade (from Lourenço Marques) on Saturday mornings.

The boys sent to C Block were the smokers. Being a smoker put you into a special category. This was the category that did best with the girls. The members of the school rock band all came from my class. They also had a reputation as bullies. Through my ability to play sport, I was spared their influence. They belonged to the engineering club and worked on motor-car engines in their spare time.

Art was not given much importance in the school. We had a few mediocre teachers who did not inspire us to great heights of creativity. In my year, there was only one pupil for A-level art and he was a friend of mine: Keith Alexander went on to do art at university and had one-man exhibitions in New York. His work was strongly influenced by Salvador Dali.

There was a choir, which I avoided. The chapel

had a good organ. The quadrangle with its fountain and terraced lawn became an outdoor theatre and Macbeth was performed there with great success – even the galloping horses of Guildenstern and Rosencrantz were a live touch.

On Sundays I would go out into the bush with Michael Allan: the bush became a great escape from school work. One year we arranged to come back with Webley air pistols. I was in the rifle club. I brought up my Brno .22 rifle and won the Best Shot of the School award and was allowed to wear an old tie that belonged to Ian Ferguson, the Chemistry teacher, who took the club. He wore glasses, was a heavy smoker and drinker, and had a drooping moustache. He walked with a stoop.

I joined the Natural History Society, run by a geologist from South Africa, Peter Ginn, who was a bird photographer and later wrote books about birds and became a world expert. On trips into the bush I carried my hatchet on my belt. It had been made in New Zealand by Estwing. We would go on expeditions to collect specimens for the museum in Salisbury. We would take along a skinner to prepare the drawer specimens.

In 1962 we drove to the Kalahari desert in the school truck. One of the maths teachers had a Land-Rover. We located a San encampment and met a group of San. An anthropologist by the name of Hans-Joachim Heinz, Professor in the Faculty of Medicine at the University of the Witwatersrand, had produced a dictionary of the !Xoo tongue (also known as Taa) and was living with them. This was the beginning of my interest in the San, and also in the indigenous American Indians.

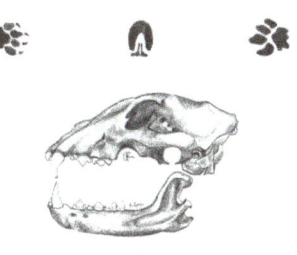

Living closer to school in Umtali, it was easier for my parents to come over and take me out on long-leave Sundays. Mother would prepare the food that I liked most: I had a special love for her sherry trifles. As well as sherry, they had nuts, wafer biscuits, a lot of cream, and glacé cherries on the top. On one occasion, the trifle had been placed on a tea trolley that was brought up to the table. As we were talking, we became aware that Kirsty, the Scottie, was being sick in the living room, and on inspection it became obvious that she had been helping herself to the trifle.

On another occasion we drove to the foothills of the Chimanimani mountains and camped above the Haroni and Rusitu valleys. This is a very special environmental region, with a tropical forest that receives a lot of rainfall from the mountains. One group went down into the valley for two nights while the other group stayed on the plateau. The villagers would catch fish by swimming down the river holding a net in front of them. We shot a green mamba (*Dendroaspis angusticeps*) and, in our mist nets, ringed several species of rare twinspots. At night, bats would get caught in the nets and were tricky to get out. They could also give you a nasty bite. I shot a Southern Banded Snake Eagle, which occurs only in that part of the country.

I got into an argument with a friend in my house who had been with me at Springvale. I secretly envied his good looks, his confidence and his brains. What had started as an argument developed into something more, something that the rules of our primitive social system could not deal with. The only way I could think of dealing with it without losing face was to challenge him to a friendly battle. It would be a *muzhanji* fight, as it was the time of year when the

muzhanji trees were in fruit; another name for them is *mahobahoba*. The fruits are the size of kiwi fruit and full of woody pips. They are edible, but there is not much to eat once the seeds have been removed. They are, however, ideal for throwing.

We each had to make up a team. The site we chose for the battle was one of the kopjes on the Springvale estate, which we all knew well as most of the group had been pupils at Springvale. It was not high, had a flat top and plenty of room for manoeuvring, but it provided good cover in the form of large boulders scattered here and there. We carried empty laundry bags with us that we filled with fruit as we went along. We avoided open spaces and kept to the trees so that we would not give our presence away to 'the enemy'.

We reached the kopje first and approached with caution to avoid being ambushed. Thus we could seize the high ground and be in a better tactical position. The enemy arrived late, talking loudly, and giving their presence away to us in a very unprofessional manner. Battle commenced once the rules of combat had been established. Phillips, who was on my side, got a direct hit on the nose and started crying. It was hard to say who won. I was not hit once but I did manage to inflict a good number of hits on the enemy. We walked back to school on good terms, the cause of the conflict already forgotten.

One Sunday, with Michael Allen and two others, I spent the day on the Springvale estate. To reach the estate you had to cross the tarmac road that connected Umtali with Salisbury. I had my catapult. It was a Late Leave Sunday, and we only had to be back at school in time for roll-call at 8:30 p.m. As we were crossing the road near the Tarisira bottle store, we saw several geese feeding on the grassy verge,

quite oblivious to the busy traffic. I decided to shoot one. I chose a small grey one. The stone stunned the poor bird and it began flapping madly, going around in a circle. I had my small hatchet and gave the bird a few hard smacks to the head. I picked it up and we all ran for the shelter of a nearby gum plantation.

At the time, there was a noisy beer-drink taking place at the store and we thought the shouting was directed at us, so we all raced back to school in a mad panic. I was holding the goose to my chest, and halfway back decided to jettison it. Michael Allan had stayed with me. The other two had disappeared. When we were nearing the school buildings, he pointed to my shirt and shorts, which were drenched in blood. We found a water tank and I gave myself a good wash. It was still early. Having calmed down a bit, we decided to go back and pick up the goose and cook it – which we did. We went down to a small kopje below the school and lit a big fire.

In the meantime I started plucking the goose. Geese have several layers of feathers, which makes them waterproof. The second layer is almost impossible to remove. A goose is a big bird and needs a lot of cooking. We put the whole bird on the fire and very soon realised that it would never cook. Time was running out so we cut it up into small pieces and went back to school and tried to eat it.

Philip Pascal had come over to Peterhouse with me. He was friendly with the Achesons, an American family whose son had been to Springvale with us. They had a beautiful ranch on the Wedza road, directly south and within walking distance of the school. Philip left a 12-bore shotgun and a pump-action .22 with them. One Sunday we walked over to the house with another friend and went shooting.

We came upon a dam that had a pair of black ducks on it. We crept up quietly and Philip had a shot at them with the shotgun and missed. As they took off, they flew past me and I brought one down with the .22. We tried cooking it by encasing the whole bird in wet mud. However, like so many bush techniques, you have to have a very hot fire and cook the bird for several hours. When it's sufficiently cooked, the feathers are supposed to fall out; however, there is no way to judge when that moment has arrived. We took ours out too early, half-cooked, feathers still firmly in place.

In the school holidays we would go up to the Troutbeck Inn in Inyanga and fish for trout. Inyanga is the region where Mount Inyangani is – the highest mountain in the country that we had been able to see from Odzani. It is eight and a half thousand feet (2,592 metres) high and straddles the border with Mozambique.

On other occasions we would stay at the self-catering cottages on the nearby Mare Dam. Mother prepared the food in advance. On one occasion we arrived mid-afternoon. Father prepared his tackle and went out to the lake, where he fished diligently until dark, catching nothing. Mother unpacked all the food, and then, with half an hour to spare, walked down to the water, caught a fish, and returned to the cottage to begin cooking supper. Father arrived cold and exhausted, and launched into a long explanation about the wind being too strong to cast and the fish not feeding. Mother said nothing. When he saw a big trout lying in the sink in the kitchen he was dumbfounded.

We spent one Christmas at Troutbeck Inn. If you had caught a trout, the procedure was to bring it to Reception to have it weighed, and there it lay on display on a large silver salver for the guests, coming into dinner dressed in their jackets and ties, to admire. One evening, a Swiss gentleman with a very bald head came in late for dinner looking very flustered. He came up to Father and pointed to his head. He had a trout fly embedded in his scalp with a short length of nylon attached. After dinner father had to remove it.

Those were magical times. The gentle splash as a fish rose to feed on a midge. The wood fires in the lounges. The smell of wattle. The cawing of ravens. The tinkle of tiny frogs in the reeds by the lake. The chill air at night, often with mist. The drum beaten each evening for dinner.

We played golf in the mornings. Major Herbert MacIlwaine, who had built Troutbeck and introduced trout fishing, appeared on the water each evening like one of the Valkyries in his green boat rowed by his gardener. When Father was not catching anything, the sound of Major Mac banging each trout he caught on the side of the boat was very demoralising.

Father tied his own flies. For fishing he wore an old tweed jacket with leather patches on the elbows and several flies sticking out of the lapels. He carried a shooting stick with him, with a fishing bag that had everything you could possibly imagine in it, a landing net hanging from his belt, and Wellington boots.

College years

I left Peterhouse before writing A levels as there was an age ruling that did not allow me to continue. A friend of ours from Springvale was in the same predicament. He had done his South African matriculation exam at a cram college in Johannesburg, so I was enrolled at Damelin College. Mother and I caught the train from Umtali and headed for Johannesburg, where we stayed in the Victoria hotel.

I lived in the YMCA on Rissik Street, and would walk through the station to the college each day. My mother had a nursing friend living in Johannesburg, and they would take me out from time to time. I would also catch the bus and go to the Zoo. At night, after seeing a movie in town, I would walk back to the YMCA across the Rissik Street bridge, hoping that someone would pick me up and give me a lift. Nobody ever did. I was eighteen and very lonely.

My half-brother, David, was working in Johannesburg for a year for a merchant bank, doing a locum for the manager. This gave me a chance to get to know him better. I spent weekends with him in his cottage in Rivonia. His secretary was Lois. She was ten years older than I was, of medium height, had a small bosom, shapely legs and a rounded bottom. She was interested in films and photography and art. She had blue eyes. We got on well together. She became the sister that I had never had. Older and wiser.

Damelin solved all my academic issues. The change of environment made all the difference; I don't know exactly what it was. I had always had a problem making sense of problems if they were presented to me on a blackboard. My mind went into a panic and I couldn't think. The college issued its own textbooks that explained all the problems clearly and simply, so you could work at home and make sense of everything quietly and in your own time. I passed seven subjects, taking three courses that I had never done before, and got into the University of Natal in Durban.

I could have done art. After much soul-searching, I chose architecture. I was too late to get a place in residence, so I lived out instead, and it remained that way right through my university days.

David was returning to London, so his relationship with Lois was coming to an end. He arranged to visit my parents in Umtali and spend a week with them. He brought Lois with him. This coincided with my long vacation. I was not expected home for the vacation so I decided to hitch-hike home instead. I had a project to complete – the painting of a Picasso music player. I spent two nights on the road, the first with a very kind family in Estcourt, the second with the family of a young student I met on the road whose parents lived in Chipinga.

My parents were taking David and Lois up to Troutbeck for a few nights. David applied himself exclusively to fishing, leaving Lois to her own devices. This played into my hands. I took her rowing in the boat. The following day I booked two recalcitrant horses to ride. They absolutely refused to budge, despite several kicks in the ribs. After a lot of persuasion we realised that if we faced them in the direction of their stables they would move. The stables were across the lake some distance away. They started off at a stiff gallop across the eighteenth green, down the fourth fairway, across the bridge, and up the fifth fairway until we reached

their stables, whereupon my horse tried to wipe me off on a low wattle branch. The gallop had taken up only twelve minutes of the hour at our disposal, so we dragged them back to the hotel and repeated the process.

Back in Umtali I bought Lois a black obsidian necklace. Each night after dinner she would come down to my studio to watch me painting. On the last night, I had the necklace ready and gave it to her. She hugged me, then kissed me passionately. We became locked in each other's arms. Until my brother walked in.

Lois slept in my bedroom and I had the settee on the veranda. After they had gone, the mat on my dressing table carried the aroma of her perfume for a long time. It was *Ma Griffe* by Carven; *griffe* is French for a claw. One review of the perfume said: 'It smells like the kind of perfume a good girl who doesn't yet know she is a bad girl would wear.' I fell in love with Lois.

Architecture was the toughest course to take. We worked every weekend to complete our projects. I could not cope with the volume of work and did not write the exams. I had my first emotional breakdown. My mood was one of hopelessness and despair. I switched courses and did a BA degree instead, choosing English and Psychology as majors, along with History of Art and Architecture. I got my degree.

I got an Asahi Pentax SLR for my twenty-first birthday. Lois sent me a card that said, 'The world is your oyster now.' I fell more in love with her.

National service

The Liberation War in Rhodesia had started. Incursions into the country by guerrillas trained in Tanzania, Mozambique and Zambia were on the increase. Army service was compulsory. I had not been called up, but I thought it sensible to get it out of the way. I had no fears of the army. I could shoot, I was a keen walker.

I qualified as a marksman. Shooting on the range was one of my few pleasures. We were trained to use hand grenades – Mills bombs. During a familiarisation course with them, one of us found, to his astonishment, an igniter set in the grenade he had been given to dismantle. This is what sets off the grenade when the firing pin is released. We had a lucky escape. Had it gone off, we would all have been killed.

I specialised in Signals because I thought I might as well learn something useful. After four and a half months, we were sent to Brady Barracks on the outskirts of Bulawayo. There was a lot to learn – Morse code being one of them – and again there was the pressure of exams. I had a degree; the instructors resented brains. At our end-of-course party, I let Corporal Voysey's front tyres down. We were drunk, and the next day were driven back to Llewellin Barracks to meet the others. Then we had a long drive, which took most of the day, in an open truck in the blazing heat to Wankie town, where we were barracked in an old Road Camp close to the railway. We all felt pretty sick by the time we arrived.

When I was chosen to be the radio operator on my first patrol, I had never seen a ration pack. Each pack weighed seven kilograms and was designed to

last twenty-four hours. At Brady Barracks we had not had any training in patrolling. Our mates who had not specialised in anything had had plenty of experience of patrolling and knew how to select from the 'rat pack' only what was absolutely necessary for a patrol.

The radio we carried on patrols was a TR 28 manufactured by Racal South Africa. I have a Canon printer today and it must have weighed about as much. In addition, you carried a spare battery. It was huge. The weapon provided for signallers was a Stirling Machine Gun (SMG), a sub-machine gun with a thirty-round magazine that fitted into the side of the weapon. It fired 9 mm rounds. The patrol was to last ten days and was to commence on the Matetsi bridge on the Bulawayo–Fort Victoria road and end at Pandamatenga on the Botswana border. In addition to the radio, I carried a gas stove, spare cylinder, hand grenade, two bottles of water, and spare magazines for the SMG; a magazine held thirty rounds.

When we got off the trucks and put on our packs at the Matetsi river I could hardly stand. All in all, I must have been carrying about fifty kilograms. I had the radio on my chest and the pack on my back. The SMG was on a lanyard around my neck, and it ended up swinging about under the radio. The release catch for the magazine was on the top. It was mid-afternoon. We stopped for the night while it was still light. It was only then that I realised that the magazine for my SMG had fallen off. I had to tell the Lieutenant about it. He promptly placed me on open arrest. We all had to go back and look for it but we never found it. Thankfully, the patrol was recalled a day later for other reasons.

Military training during national service at Wankie.
I am on the right.

A recent photo of me fishing on the lake at Troutbeck, Nyanga.
Photo: Shelley Hood

On my first weekend pass from doing basic training at Llewellen barracks, Bulawayo, 1970,
I had hitch-hiked up to Troutbeck, where my parents were staying for the Easter weekend.

Back at the base outside Wankie, I had to report to the command sergeant major, who was ex-SAS. He said he would send me back with four others in a Land-Rover patrol, to be paid for by me and those who had been with me on the patrol, to look for the magazine. If it was not found I would be on a charge. I reasoned that it must have come off as I was coming up a steep incline because then my knees would have been pressing against the underside of the radio and the SMG. We found the magazine in just the place that I had expected to find it. I was so relieved. From that moment on, any feelings that I might have had about enjoying the army were ended. I began counting the days until our release.

We were posted to a remote army base close to the Zambezi river and the Zambian border. Returning in the truck one morning, we spotted a small herd of kudu, made up of cows and calves, drinking from a small stream. The sergeant fired at a cow and she dropped. When we went up to her she raised her head and looked at us accusingly. Her enormous black eyes with their long eyelashes were filled with reproach. I will never forget that look. I never shot a living creature after that.

Our sergeant took us on a jungle range. He offered a beer to anybody who could hit a tin plate that he threw into the air. I hit it twice! The sergeant wasn't too pleased when I showed him the two holes.

Film school and teaching

When I left the army, l flew straight down to my graduation in Durban. My shaved head and suntan made me stand out from the other students. After that, I taught for a term at Whitestone preparatory school outside Bulawayo.

While I was at Whitestone, I submitted an application to do a film-making course at the London School of Film Technique. I went over on the last voyage of the *Windsor Castle* from Cape Town, and stayed in a bedsit in Whittingstall Road, Parsons Green. I made friends with students from Canada, from the USA, from Israel, and even a few from the UK. I did well, passing out with a diploma with honours. My script in our final year was one of a few chosen to be made into a film. It was about the relationship between a torturer and his victim. I directed it, but what gave me the most satisfaction was editing and scriptwriting.

Over Easter I spent a weekend with my Uncle Peter and Aunty Renee in Scotland. Their home on Hermitage Drive in Edinburgh was on the edge of a small stream. Uncle Peter had a Rolls Royce and a chauffeur who would pick me up from the station when I visited. Their garden smelt of freshly mown grass and the apple trees fascinated me. We stayed in the Dryburgh Abbey Hotel, close to the ruins of Dryburgh Abbey on the River Tweed, where my uncle fished for salmon from a boat with a gillie. He caught a salmon and gave it to me to take back to London; on the train, it rested in a special salmon basket on the rack above my head. I toured the ruins, where

Sir Walter Scott is buried, and took photos of the daffodils that were popping up, and did a drawing that I still have. I walked along the river and found, among the pebbles, a tile with 'Brian' engraved on the back.

I took Shelley, my Australian girlfriend, to visit my aunt in Nairn. We went fishing up to Loch Assynt and stayed in the Inchnadamph Hotel. I stayed in a caravan by the water's edge, some distance from the hotel. When the wind blew, the caravan rocked from side to side. I made a sketch of the loch with its wooden rowing boats tied to a jetty.

Back in Nairn, my cousin Sandra, who was working at Aviemore ski resort in the Cairngorms, picked us up and took us for dinner in Aviemore. On the way back, the winding road and seafood cocktail made me sick, and I vomited all over the walls of my aunt's newly painted bathroom.

To work in the film business in England, you had to belong to the Union. You could become a member only if you had worked in the profession for some time. I decided that, as South Africa was getting television for the first time, it was better to go there, so I went to Johannesburg. Through a school friend, whose father was big in South African Breweries, I was given an interview with an independent film-production company and was accepted. However, I would not start for three months. What was I to do in the meantime?

I found work doing part-time clerical work, and another film company needed someone to teach film-making. They wanted me to commit full-time and I broke my commitment to the first company,

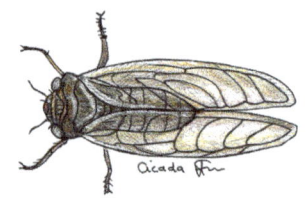

which I regret to this day. To work in television in South Africa you had to be bilingual in English and Afrikaans; I had never learned Afrikaans.

I started doing Iyengar Yoga in Johannesburg City Hall; this was my introduction to alternative healing. I went for an interview as a newsreader for the South African Broadcasting Corporation but I was too nervous and lacked confidence. In addition I couldn't speak Afrikaans. I met a Scientologist who made documentaries. He said I lacked confidence.

Out of the blue I got a job as Art Director on a German feature-film that was being made in Cape Town, in Gordon's Bay harbour, close to where my Uncle Charles was living. I stayed with him. Most of the film was shot on a fishing boat. The weather was dreadful: the time of the south-easters, the 'Cape Doctor'. I sprained my ankle hurrying down the ladder to the hold, carrying props.

When the film was completed and I was on the way back to Umtali for Christmas, I developed hepatitis. My parents were going to spend Christmas at Troutbeck. I joined them but was far too sick to eat anything. I spent a week in the Infectious Diseases Hospital.

I accepted a teaching post at Springvale School to face up to the demons that had beset me there when I was a pupil. The headmaster had been a Latin teacher and the Music teacher had been one of the matrons. I was head of the Art department, a housemaster, and the colts rugby coach. With the war on, it was very difficult to find teachers.

Eagle Preparatory School, up in the Vumba mountains on the border with Mozambique near

Umtali, closed in 1976. The pupils moved over to us, along with their headmaster, who had been a teacher at Springvale, and several of their teachers. Their buildings were used by the Elim Missionary Society. In 1978 there was a brutal massacre at the school, in which eight adults, men and women, and four young children were bayoneted to death, including one four-week old baby. The women were raped.

I was amazed at the difference between my generation and the new generation. During break we could always entertain ourselves; we never had to go to a teacher and ask for assistance. Videos had now become the means of entertainment. The Springvale estate was just the same, though. The groundsman, Patrick Gosho, was still working at the school; he had a house in the grounds. The grey Massey Ferguson tractor that towed the mower that cut the grass on the sports fields, and which we had been taught to drive as young Pioneers, was still operational.

With the war on, it was foolhardy to go on picnics into the bush. A teacher at Peterhouse was killed on a back road near the school. Driving down to the South African border, you had to travel in convoy: a jeep was leading with a mounted machine-gun, and there was another one at the back.

During the war years, most of the pupils at Springvale came from Zambia, which had attained its independence in 1964. The border between Zambia and Rhodesia was closed in 1973. At the beginning of term, a bus with our pupils on it would arrive at the border at Chirundu and drive on to the bridge over the Zambezi. Another bus would reverse on to the bridge from the other side and the pupils would leave one bus and climb into the other.

I organised wide games over the Rhodes and Founders holiday weekend. It was over those very same public holidays that I, as a Boy Scout, had spent time in my Second World War tent, eating sardines and condensed milk and smoking cigars made from Red Hot Poker stems stuffed with lichen. The demons that had haunted my school days had dispersed – for the time being, at any rate.

I lived in a small flat next to the library. Later, I lived in a cottage twenty minutes drive from the school on a farm belonging to one of the teachers. The farmer and his wife lived at the school and ran the Junior House. Before leaving for school each morning, I had to visit the pigsties and check that all was well. Shortly after I had moved on to the farm, there was a knock on my door at about nine o'clock one night. I pulled back the curtains cautiously, peered out through the glass of the front door, and saw Kenneth, the cook from the main house, standing there in his white tunic and cook's hat. I could just make out the pig-boy standing next to him. My thoughts immediately went to my responsibility towards the pigs. I opened the door and asked Kenneth what had happened. He muttered something about the box having broken. I visualised a sow having just farrowed rolling over and crushing her piglets: when farrowing they lie in a metal crate. I told Kenneth to go down to the pigsties and I would follow in my car. I found my torch and car keys and set off. The sky was a mass of stars. It was very quiet. The farmhouse was in total darkness.

The pigsties were beyond the farmhouse, and I saw Kenneth and the pig-boy waiting by the road. Instead of waiting for me next to the pigsties, they

were standing on the opposite side of the road, next to the path that led to the staff compound. I stopped the car and, pointing towards the pigsties, asked Kenneth to show me the sick pig. He didn't move. He shook his head. 'No bwana, it is the pig-boy's wife who is sick, not the pig!'

It turned out that the afterbirth had not appeared. I visualised having to enter a dark hut with a young woman groaning on the floor and having to press down on her stomach and get her to cough – the instructions I had been given by a doctor friend who had often had to treat such cases.

While I was wondering what to do next, the pig-boy went off to the compound, leaving me standing in the road with Kenneth. I could hear the pigs grunting in the background. In a very short time, a line of women appeared. They bent down to climb through a gap in a barbed-wire fence. The woman leading was the new mother, and she had her baby swaddled in her arms. Without any further instructions from me, the mother and three other ladies squeezed into the back of my two-door Renault 4 and the father climbed in the front next to me. All he said was 'hospital', and off we went!

Call-ups

Having done my army training, I was eligible for call-ups that lasted four weeks, the duration of our school holidays. On my first call-up, I was given a Bren gun to carry: it weighed nine kilograms – I weighed about seventy. I must have been one of the smallest individuals in the company and had never had any training on a Bren, and yet the army, in its inimitable way, decided that I was the most suitable person to carry it. There were six-foot-tall farmers who weighed 150 kilograms, but little me was the one who got nailed.

That call-up took us to the north-east of the country towards Mozambique. Along the border was a minefield with a high barbed-wire fence running on either side. Our task was to patrol along the minefield, and we chose to do this by walking along a narrow track a few metres from the minefield itself. We felt quite safe doing this until one day we spotted an anti-personnel mine sticking out of the ground directly where we were to put our feet. It had been washed out of the minefield by recent rains.

The tsetse flies were chronically persistent. Their bite is like a red-hot needle. Normally, once it gets dark they disappear. Not this lot. They were hungry and had not seen human blood for a long time. One evening, one of the guys in our stick became hysterical as they continued to bite him as he stood stark naked while having a wash from his mess tin.

One night we were woken to the sound of repeated mine-blasts. We leapt out of our sleeping bags, prepared for what seemed like a very concerted attack, and crept towards the minefield. There were more explosions further up the minefield, which

only added to our fears. When we could see what had happened, we realised that a herd of kudu had jumped the fence and set off the mines; as they ran, they exploded more and more. In the daylight, vultures came down to feed on the carcasses and exploded even more mines. It was real carnage.

In my second call-up, my thumb was crushed in the tailgate of a truck, which splintered the bone and was extremely painful. I spent the rest of the call-up doing camp duties at a small base camp nearby.

My third call-up was over Christmas. Once again, we failed to receive our Christmas goody parcels donated by several charities. I wrote to the *Herald* newspaper about this and thought nothing more of it. Much to my surprise – and horror – I was summoned to appear before the Commanding Officer of Fourth Brigade to answer questions about my article, which had embarrassed the top brass because they had lost a cheque sent to them to purchase Christmas parcels. They asked me whether I would retract my statement. I said I would, as long as the *Herald* printed a breakdown of all money allocated to the forces.

That seemed to be the end of the matter. However, the army always has the last laugh. As we were being disbanded at the end of the call-up I found that I was on the list for continuous call-up. This meant being in the army on a full-time basis. The chances of being killed or wounded were extremely high; many people suffered irreparable psychological damage.

As I was a teacher, I could apply to our local District Commissioner for exemption – which is what I did, and I was let off. If all else failed, I had planned to drive into Botswana and hand myself over to the British Embassy there.

Back in Umtali one Christmas, I met Moira Findlay at a dinner party with my parents. She was a nurse at Kariba General Hospital. Her sister worked for Norman Carr in the South Luangwa Valley National Park in Zambia. Through her sister I was able to work as a safari guide one school holiday at Chibembe Lodge. With the border between Zambia and Rhodesia closed, I flew to Zambia via Malawi.

Part Two

Life as a Safari Guide

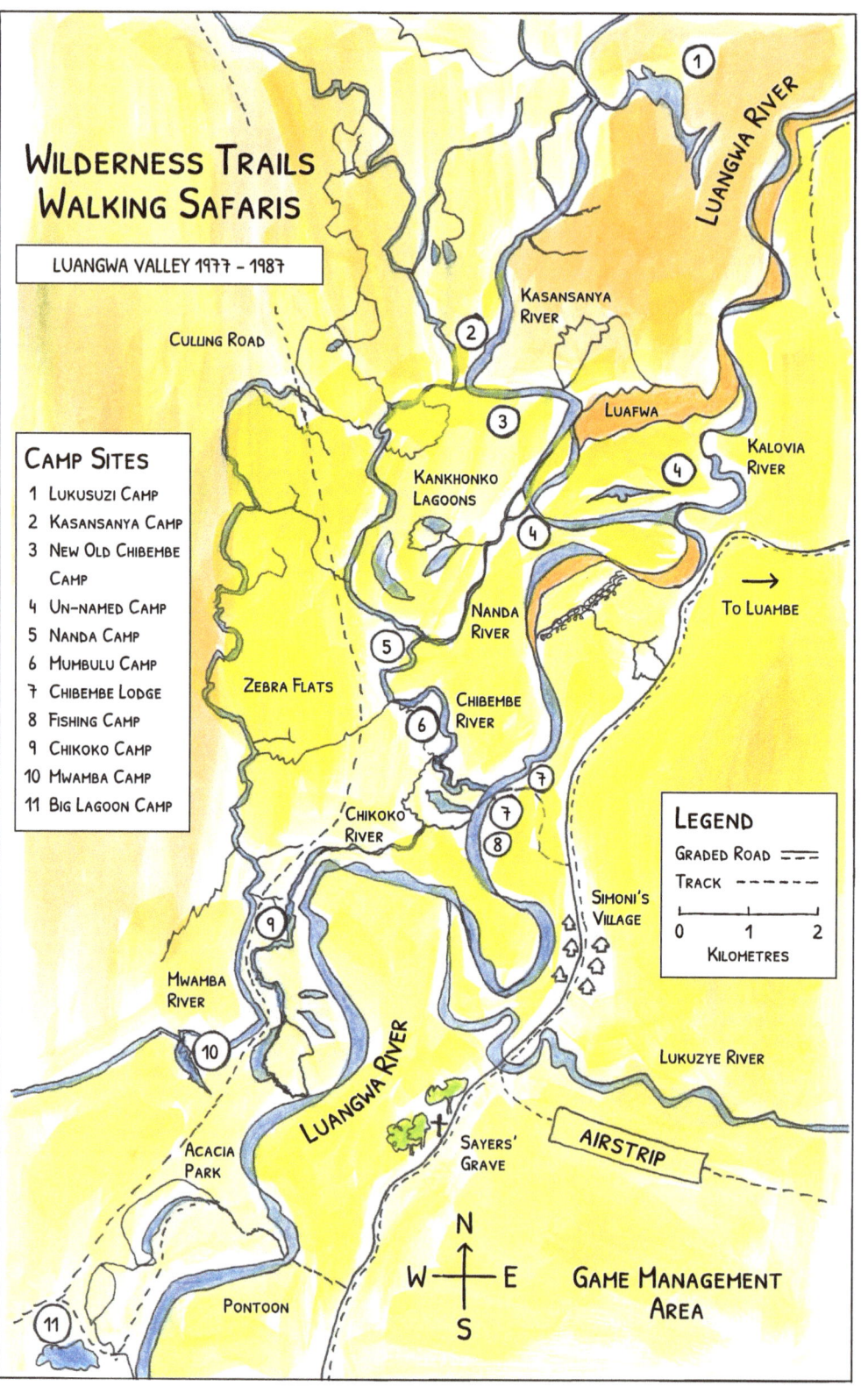

The Luangwa Valley

The Luangwa Valley is in the southernmost portion of the Great Rift system that starts in the Red Sea and includes all the great African lakes. The Rift is a fault formed along tectonic plates and resembles a bath tub. In places, the sides are nearly vertical, creating sheer escarpments that are a challenge to road-builders but not to elephants. The bottom is flat, and rivers that flow down the escarpments on either side collect to form bigger rivers and even lakes.

The Luangwa Valley takes its name from the Luangwa river, which flows down the middle of the valley and has its source in the north of the country, close to the Tanzanian border. It flows all year round but is dramatically affected by the rains, which begin at the end of November and continue through until March. At the height of the rainy season, the valley floor fills up like a basin, bringing fresh water to oxbow lakes and to grasslands. In the process, any roads that are not part of the all-weather system around Mfuwe – the tourist hub, where the international airport is situated – become flooded. Any tourist enterprise not linked to this all-weather road system closes down when the rains come, so this means that you have only six months of income: the rest of the year you make plans and take new bookings.

From early times, the Luangwa Valley has been home to wild animals in great profusion and of great variety. When I visited the valley for the first time, it was estimated that there were more than a hundred thousand elephant. The river system, with its lagoons and oxbow lakes, is home to thousands of hippo and abundant bird life. Many species of fish feed on the

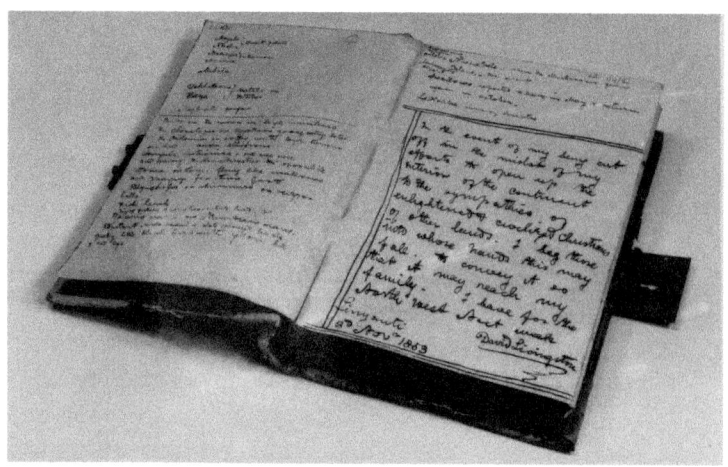
David Livingstone's dairy.
Photo: National Archives of Zimbabwe

David Livingstone is attacked by a territorial hippo while crossing the Luangwa.
Photo: National Archives of Zimbabwe

David Livingstone in the Bangweulu swamps during the rainy season after crossing the Luangwa Valley.
Photo: National Archives of Zimbabwe

Squeaker

dung of the hippo. The Portuguese had trading posts in the valley long before the British colonised the region. They were interested in capitalising on the ivory and precious metals. David Livingstone crossed the Luangwa river in December 1866.

The valley floor is flat. The soil consists of sediment brought down by the river, much like the Nile when it floods. The high banks are kept in place by the roots of trees, which anchor the soil so that it can resist the floods. Without this, the weight of water soon erodes the riverbank, cutting deeper and deeper into the bends so that eventually, like a loop of gut deprived of blood supply, it dries out and dies. This obsolete channel becomes an oxbow lake or *luafwa* – the local name for a stretch of river that no longer receives water. These *luafwas* are found along the entire river system and are soon covered in short, nutritious grass that is attractive to hippo, puku and other grazers. Hippo, which are extremely numerous, favour certain entry and exit points when they come out of the water to feed. These become deeper and deeper as the years go by until finally a new channel is formed.

The South Luangwa National Park covers an area of nine thousand square kilometres at an altitude ranging from five hundred metres to one thousand metres. The North Luangwa National Park covers an area of four and a half thousand square kilometres. The Bisa people, who lived on the valley floor, survived by hunting and fishing, exchanging the meat with the tribes living on the escarpment for other commodities. They had lived in the valley for centuries but, when the game reserves were created, they were moved out and settled along the margins of the valley, where they had to give up hunting

Tilapia

and learn to till the soil – something that they were both reluctant and unqualified to do. At village level, administration is carried out on a traditional basis by the chiefs, of which there are a number throughout the length and breadth of the valley.

Surrounding the national parks are Game Management Areas, where commercial hunting is permitted. The theory governing the existence of these areas is that, once the population of a particular species increases to an extent that it can no longer be confined within the park, the surplus will migrate into the hunting areas, where they can be shot.

Because of the steep escarpments on either side of the valley, access by road is very limited. Regular commercial flights during the tourist season bring tourists to Mfuwe. Small bush strips dotted about the valley, kept open mainly by the hunting-safari companies, extend the reach by air a little further.

On the eastern edge of the valley are two small towns. The closest is Chipata, called Fort Jameson before independence, which sits at the end of the Great East Road near the border with Malawi. The other, Lundazi, lies further north. Most safari companies buy their fuel and bulk goods in Chipata or ship them in by truck from Lusaka at the beginning of the season. Close to Mfuwe is Kamoto, a Dutch-run mission hospital.

Along the western edge of the valley is the Great North Road, which stretches as far as Tanzania; parallel to it runs the Tazara railway. The only town of any significance on the Great North Road is Mpika, from where two dirt tracks run down the escarpment into the valley. One ends up in the corridor between the North and South parks; the other comes out centrally in the North park.

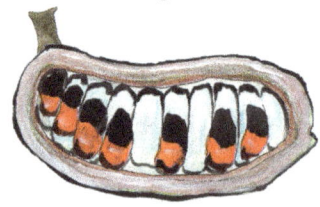

As well as the huge number of elephant in the Luangwa Valley, there was also a very healthy population of black rhino in the valley's catchment area. Thornicroft's giraffe occurs only in the Luangwa Valley. The only animal to be found in other parks and not in the Luangwa were cheetah. I began a love affair with elephant.

On my first visit to the Luangwa Valley, I flew into the original airport on the west bank of the Luangwa river. A pontoon connected with the main road system on the east bank; now there is a bridge, and the old airport no longer exists. I was picked up from Mfuwe lodge by Pat Grey, the lodge manager at Chibembe. We drove past Nsefu camp, which consisted of small thatched rondavels overlooking the river, and passed herds of zebra and waterbuck. Elephant were everywhere. There were so many animals; I couldn't believe my eyes. My first impressions of the park were overwhelming. The only accommodation for me at Chibembe was in one of the storerooms.

Zambia was doing well in those days. The price of copper was high and many expatriates were working on the Copperbelt. The Zambia National Tourist Board owned most of the camps in the South Luangwa National Park. The roads in the park were well maintained, and several pontoons on the river functioned efficiently and were well maintained. Most of the scouts employed at Chibembe lodge were old hands from the national parks service and several had been in the army before that, serving in the King's African Rifles in various areas of conflict.

On that first visit I became familiar with the

Male and female Thornicroft's giraffe. The male, in front, is darker than the female.

The black rhino grazing peacefully that I thought had been shot by poachers.

Black rhino mating on Chikaya Plain.

road system in the park and took clients on morning and afternoon drives. I met the artist David Shepherd and his whole family. They came to Chibembe each year and stayed in the A-frame chalet, which had enough beds for them all. David became famous for his spectacular paintings of Luangwa elephants. He also bought an old steam locomotive and had it shipped back to England from Mulobezi.

On one of my first drives, I passed a black rhino grazing beside the road and noticed that it had a big wound just behind its left shoulder. As we watched, it turned and I saw that it had another wound on the right shoulder. A little further on we saw a herd of elephant, and in their midst was a cow, lying down flat on the ground. It didn't move! Putting the two experiences together, I was sure that poachers were to blame, so I reported the rhino and the elephant to the Game Department.

Feeling very proud of myself, we drove back the way we had come and, much to my surprise and shame, the elephant family were still there but the one I had presumed had been shot was now back on her feet. The rhino was also in the same place and feeding contentedly. Back at camp, I learned that rhino can be the victims of sores caused by a burrowing insect. I also learned that, from time to time, elephant lie down on the ground and sleep. I later even found lion climbing trees. I spotted lion waiting in ambush on the Salt Pan. I watched spellbound as Lilac-breasted Rollers performed barrel rolls to attract a mate.

When it was time to go back to Rhodesia with the war still raging, I was very sad to leave. I had really enjoyed myself. I looked forward to coming back and to

Norman Carr holding Big Boy and Little Boy at the time he brought them to entertain the children in the European Hospital.

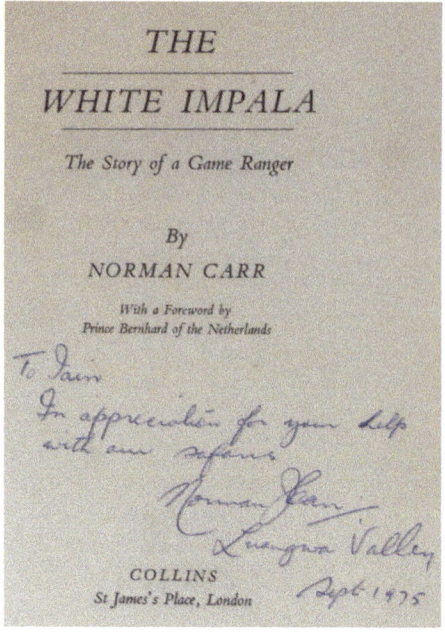

After my very first safari, Norman Carr gave me signed copies of two of his books when he was manager at Chibembe Lodge.

Norman Carr with a group of Italians on the pontoon linking Chibembe with the road system on the west bank of the Luangwa River. Ben Zulu is the pontoon chief. He later became boatman at Chibembe Lodge.

qualify to lead walking safaris. Walking safaris were the pinnacle of a guide's career. Norman Carr signed two of his books and gave them to me, along with enough money to buy a pair of Nikon binoculars in Lusaka. It had been a good beginning. I felt extremely excited. This really was what I wanted to do.

Norman Carr

Father had known Norman Carr for many years. Peter Hankin, the professional hunter on his big safari with his brother to the Luangwa Valley, had been a close friend of Norman's.

One morning during the school holidays my father called from the hospital. 'Send Iain over immediately. There's something he has to see.'

I knew my way around the hospital and ran to my father's consulting rooms. Norman had brought his two lion cubs, Big Boy and Little Boy, to the children's ward of the European Hospital. Norman walked with a stoop, an injury received from a wounded buffalo. He always wore a safari jacket with big pockets, khaki trousers and old veldskoens without socks. I can remember the cubs padding in ungainly fashion down the main corridor of the hospital after Norman. I held one of them in my arms. They were as big as two-month-old Labrador puppies and had fluffy coats. They would be reintroduced into the wild some years later when they were fully matured. He detailed their story in his book, *Return to the Wild*, and also in a documentary film.

Some years later, when he was living on land close to Mfuwe, Norman would bring his clients into Mfuwe lodge, pick them up each day and take them on game drives. I was staying in Mfuwe at the time and he invited me to accompany him on one of

these drives. He drove to a hyena den that had young cubs. He parked and waited. The cubs emerged one by one from the den and looked around cautiously. Norman's Land-Cruiser, like most safari vehicles, had no doors. He was wearing his customary veldskoens without socks. One of the cubs caught a whiff of his feet and walked over to where we were parked, went up to the driver's side of the Land-Cruiser and sniffed Norman's feet. He didn't move.

Norman Carr's daughter, Pamela, was a successful wildlife artist. Having grown up in the bush, she knew far more about the wild areas than even the most experienced safari guide. We used to see groups of Italian tourists visiting Chibembe. When the lodge was very full and guides to take game drives were at a premium, Pam would step into the breach. On one occasion, a safari vehicle was brought around from the workshop to Reception for the afternoon drive. An Italian group climbed aboard and waited for their driver to appear. Pam appeared and introduced herself as their driver, whereupon the whole group got out of the vehicle and went to another one with a male guide. This had nothing to do with Pam's ability as a guide: they needed someone with machismo!

My second visit to the Luangwa Valley was when I was teaching at St Andrew's Secondary School in Blantyre, Malawi. I flew to Lilongwe and was met by Norman Carr at the airport. He drove me to Chibembe in his locally assembled Range-Rover, which let a lot of dust in through the back door: the road from Lilongwe to Chipata was being graded at the time and there were many very dusty detours. This time I had a bed in the swimming pool changing hut. Norman took me out on short walks from the camp to introduce me to being a walking guide.

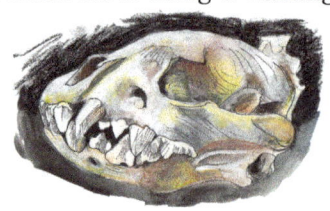

In those days there were no guide licences, and each safari lodge had its own in-house guide-training scheme. Norman would take you on a short walk, explain how the system worked, and see whether you were competent to take a group out on your own. Before this happened you had to go on several walks with an experienced guide. On my first walk with clients, I went with Patrick Ansell. His father had been a very influential zoologist and had written several books on the mammals of Zambia.

Chibembe lodge

Chibembe lodge was owned by Zambia Safaris, and they also had several hunting concessions close to the lodge. It had a huge cold room and a massive Lister generator to keep the meat cold for the lodge and for the hunting camps.

Chibembe lodge was an ideal location from which to spearhead walking safaris. It was outside the park but on the edge of its boundary, which was the Luangwa river itself: to get into the park, all you had to do was cross the river. Being so far north, the road system of the park barely reached it. Big Lagoon camp was the closest Zambia National Tourist Board lodge to Chibembe. The road system reached it and terminated at a pontoon crossing on the Luangwa river some miles south of Chibembe and before Chikwinda Gate. Therefore, Chibembe had, all to itself, a vast area of prime unspoilt safari country.

Several of the walking guides in those days were employed as hunters. Mike Wright was a veterinary officer. Archie McClaggan was a professional hunter. Clive Kelly was headmaster at a school in Chipata. Ishmael Osman belonged to a shopkeeping family in Malawi. During the busy season, guides were drawn

Patrick Ansell and group wade the Luangwa with me as an apprentice.

Patrick Ansell leads my first safari at Chibembe.

Patrick Ansell assists a client on the tree bridge used to cross on to the island formed by the Luangwa and Kasansanya rivers.

Mamba camp.
Patrick Ansell is the safari guide sitting at the end of the table for this, my first, walk apprenticed to him.

from wherever they could be obtained. Patrick Ansell's father was a well-known zoologist, and Patrick was a walking guide when I started working at Chibembe. Robin Pope was a walking guide and his parents lived in Lusaka.

Chibembe offered game drives, short morning and afternoon walks from camp, and a three- or four-night walking safari. The long walking safaris from Chibembe were the best way to experience the real African bush at first hand. I have seen nothing to equal it ever since, and I have guided in Zimbabwe and Tanzania.

During the period that I was associated with Chibembe lodge, night drives became extremely popular and they remain so to this day. The aim is to spot those reclusive animals that appear only after the sun has gone down. Often the elusive leopard can be seen along with his larger cousin, the lion. Kills take place and a good drive can be very exciting, especially when you are in an open vehicle.

On one night drive at peak season, when vehicles are at a premium, an experienced guide went out with a group of Italians and their tour guide. The tour guide sat in the front next to our guide. There was no space for a spotter, which is customary: the spotter manages the light and calls out when he has seen something interesting.

The vehicle had seen many summers and the battery was probably locally made and reaching the end of its operational life. The high-powered spotlights used for night drives draw a lot of power from the vehicle's battery, and the general rule is not to turn the engine off unless you are very confident of the state of your battery.

The spotlight picked up the eyes of a group of

lions some distance from the road. Much excitement. As was customary, the driver left the main road in order to get a little closer. He took the vehicle right up to the lions so that they were no more than a few metres from the vehicle. Suddenly they could see that there were also young cubs. Even more excitement! Then the driver chanced his luck. The excitement that he had generated clearly had gone to his head and he lost his sense of perspective. He switched the engine off. The light dimmed, and then went out altogether. Total darkness ensued.

Once the only light is turned off on a very dark night, you are immediately blind until your eyes become accustomed to the dark – and this can take some time. While it is happening, your imagination is conjuring up all sorts of exciting scenarios. I gather the silence was pretty tangible at this point. Lion don't generally associate vehicles with human beings. With a powerful light dazzling them, they are at a disadvantage, but when darkness descends they lose their fear and become inquisitive – especially young lions. They become playful and have been known to gnaw car tyres. One of the aluminium hand basins at Kasansanya camp had been chewed in this way.

From euphoria one moment, the mood in the vehicle shifted to hysteria. The driver tried to start the engine. The starter motor whirred for a few seconds, the engine spluttered, then stopped. The Italians held their breath.

In the dark you become very reliant on your sense of hearing. Every sound becomes amplified. The sound of the wind in the long grass or of a leaf falling to earth would not be heard with the engine running. With the engine off, those sounds take on a much greater significance.

The driver considered his options. A battery will recover sufficiently after a while to start the engine. He realised that they were parked on the side of a termite mound. If he could move the vehicle a few feet, it would freewheel sufficiently with its own momentum to get them away from the lion and out of danger and he could try starting the engine. He turned to the tour guide crouched beside him. 'Signore, would you please help me. All it needs is for you to get out and push the Land-Rover a few feet forwards with the help of one or two of your clients? Please!'

The request fell on deaf ears.

The driver got out very gingerly, closing his door ever so quietly so as not to intimidate the cats, and sidled to the back of the vehicle, pretending all the time that he was part of the paintwork. By leaning his back against the tailboard and using every ounce of strength he possessed, he got the vehicle moving and, with the help of the slope, was able to push it out of range of the inquisitive cats, who observed the whole business with some interest. After a little rest to calm his nerves and get his breath back, he tried the starter and, much to everyone's relief, the engine started.

In 1979, Queen Elizabeth II visited Malawi as a guest of President Hastings Kamuzu Banda. I was teaching in Blantyre at the time and stood on the road, as we all had to do, to watch the Queen passing along Chileka Road with President Banda in the black Rolls Royce, a present to the President from the British government.

A week later, I made my third trip to the Luangwa

Chileka Road, Blantyre. The queen on a visit to Malawi driving in state with President Banda to the airport in the Rolls Royce formerly used by the Governor General.

The artist David Shepherd with his family on one of their regular visits to Chibembe Lodge.

Valley and was in camp when Prince Andrew was a guest of Zambian President Kaunda, and he stayed for a few nights at Mwamba camp, one of Chibembe's walking camps. The Manager of Chibembe at the time was Phil Berry. Phil was part of the royal party, and his wife, Margaret, was running Chibembe in his absence.

She had heard that a group of poachers had accosted the driver of a grader that was grading the roads in the area. He had driven his grader at the poachers and one had climbed aboard and struck him on the head with a machete. This was the very first incursion of poachers into the Chibembe walking safari area, and Margaret was in a dilemma as to what to do. She realised that she had to pass this information on, but it had to be done very diplomatically because if Panji Kaunda, the eldest son of the President and a senior officer in the Zambian army, who was part of the group got wind of the incident, he would have brought in the army and the whole thing would have got out of control very quickly.

Margaret asked my advice. I suggested waylaying the convoy before it reached Mwamba camp and trying to get a word in with the Prince's bodyguard in private. We parked beside the road and waited for the convoy to arrive. As it approached, I walked out into the road and waved to Norman Carr, who was in the lead vehicle. He stopped and I had a few quick words with him so that I could identify which vehicle the Prince's bodyguard was driving. I asked if I could have a few words in private with him and he replied to say that as long as the incident was not politically motivated we need not worry.

At this moment Margaret asked the Prince if she

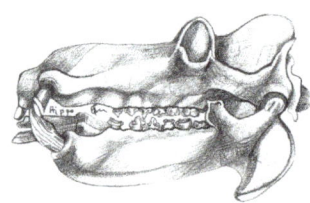

could take his photograph. His reply was, 'No, thank you. Maybe later.' Margaret never got her photo. We had gone to a lot of trouble to make sure that his safari was a success and the very least he could have done was allow Margaret to take his photo. I thought very little of Andrew then and my opinion hasn't changed ever since. The convoy carried on without anybody else being any the wiser.

Walking safaris
Norman Carr had been the first person to develop the walking safari as a concept. The idea of walking up to game was a novel approach – and to many sceptics it was absolutely crazy! I don't think it had been tried before in any of the safari areas in Africa. South Africa followed an orthodox approach to safaris, which was entirely by vehicle, and walking safaris developed on private conservancies only much later.

Norman had grafted his walking safari concept on to that of the traditional hunting scenario. As he was fluent in Chinyanja, when he retired from the Game Department after independence in 1964, he was able to keep close to the new people who came into the department and provide assistance and advice whenever they requested it. He knew the workings of the safari business both from the Game Department's perspective and as a safari operator; he knew it from top to bottom and inside out. Using experienced game scouts who had worked in Problem Animal Control became the norm. It became Game Department law that any walking safari in a national park had to have a game scout accompany it.

In Zambia, the way in which the safari system has developed owes a lot to the co-operation that existed

between the private safari sector and the Department; they worked hand in hand. Poor funding of the Game Department brought many problems with it. For walking safaris, this meant shoddy equipment – rifles that were not properly maintained and a lack of ammunition. To overcome this, safari lodges bought their own rifles and ammunition and made certain that the scouts allocated to them could shoot and had decent uniforms and boots.

In the 1970s, all the scouts who were posted to safari companies for walking-safari duties had worked for several years dealing with problem animals. Problem Animal Control entails being posted to villages close to a national park and dealing with animals that have had an adverse impact on the lives of the villagers. This would entail shooting crop-raiding elephant and hippo; it would entail shooting lion that killed their cattle. In fact, this gave them experience in dealing with all the animals that would cause problems on a walking safari. At that time all the scouts I had to deal with were very likeable people. Mwenda, for example, had been a soldier with the King's African Rifles and seen active service in Malaya and Madagascar.

A certificate I designed for all those who experienced a walking safari at Chibembe Lodge.

A typical walking group. Patrick Ansell safari guide, Bernard Mbao game scout, Keala Banda tea-bearer.

A walking group study hippo on a morning walk out of Kasansanya camp.

Walking-camp construction

The earliest we could reach the lodge from Lusaka after the rains was the first of May. This gave us just a month in order to be operational by the first of June when the safari season commenced.

Downstream of Chibembe lodge was the fishing camp. This was owned by one of the hunting companies and designed to provide accommodation for any off-duty hunters and their families. It consisted of six or seven grass huts with a kitchen and dining room. Our fibreglass banana boat, so called because of its shape, was moored just below the camp. To reach the national park and our walking-safari camps, we had to cross the Luangwa river by canoe.

In the run-up to the start of the season, several volunteer helpers would be invited to get the lodge tidy and working properly. The huge Lister generator had to be started, all the electrical wiring checked, the massive cold room cleaned and the walls whitewashed, the pool emptied and repainted, the chalet roofs re-thatched and the walls painted. Septic tanks that had capsized during the rains had to be re-dug and covered with branches and grass.

The vegetable garden was kept going throughout the rains by a small team who remained in camp as caretakers. They were provided with rations and malaria tablets, along with a good supply of fishing lines and hooks. The HF radio, which was our only means of communication with Lusaka and the outside world, had to be started, and the antennae hung up in suitable trees close to the Reception.

A month before the safari season began, a team of lads from the nearby villages would construct

Kasansanya camp from across the Kasansanya river where Moffat was the cook.

Kasansanya camp showing the dining room and the sweep of the river upstream of the camp

Lunch in the dining room at Kasansanya camp. Simon Bicknell, centre, safari guide apprenticed to me.

Moffat, the cook from Kasansanya, demonstrates his cooking facilities.

three or four trail camps from natural materials in the national park.

When I started taking walking safaris in the 1970s, a network of roads connected with the walking-safari camps that were functioning at the time. By the time I had stopped teaching in 1985 and was working in a full-time capacity as Walking Safari Manager at Chibembe, this network did not exist. The main reason for this was the absence of the pontoon that had been moored close to Chikwinda Gate. This pontoon allowed vehicles to cross into the park and connect with the road system there that originated at Mfuwe and stretched right down to the south of the park and as far north as Big Lagoon camp and Acacia Park.

On my first walking safari under the tutelage of Patrick Ansell, we visited three camps that no longer existed by the time I became Safari Manager. The first of these was on the site of the original lodge, and came to be known as the New Old Chibembe site. It was not far from the new site of Chibembe lodge but was across the river in the park itself.

Lukusuzi camp, the second camp we visited, was the furthest north of all the camps and close to a hunting camp. In the vicinity were two lagoons. One had the sinister reputation of being where local villagers would drown the second of any twins born: their belief was that a second twin could not have a spirit so it was killed by drowning it in this lagoon. The second lagoon was long and narrow and several very old *Borassus* palms grew on its banks. The camp was resupplied by road from Chibembe, and luggage and foodstuffs were carried across the river by porter.

The third camp was Mwamba, and it was close to the Mwamba river, from which the beautiful lagoon it

was built on received its water during the rains. This was the camp to which Prince Andrew was taken on his royal visit. The cook was called Nanzikani. He had a small marijuana plant growing outside his kitchen that I would always point out to him. He would grin.

Not far from Mwamba camp was Big Lagoon camp, one of the old camps that had belonged to national parks during colonial days and after independence to the Zambian National Tourist Board. It was later sold off, along with Nsefu camp, to Wilderness Trails.

As Safari Manager I was responsible for building three walking safari camps: Chikoko, Kasansanya and Mumbulu.

Kasansanya camp was right on the Kasansanya river, which by then was receiving most of the water that reached the Luangwa river. The national park boundary was the deepest channel of the Luangwa. The geological term for this is thalweg. This aspect of the ever-changing pattern of the Luangwa Valley river system meant that, if the main channel of the Luangwa dried up, the national park boundary shifted to the channel that was receiving the bulk of the water that was coming down from the Mupamadzi river in the north of the Park. This meant that what was once national park land was now part of the Game Management area, where hunting was permitted.

Kasansanya camp had everything going for it; it was my favourite camp. You could walk in any direction and never meet another walking group. You were close to Zebra Flats, which had lion. You were close to the Kankhonko lagoons, which always had a plentiful supply of birds and animals of all

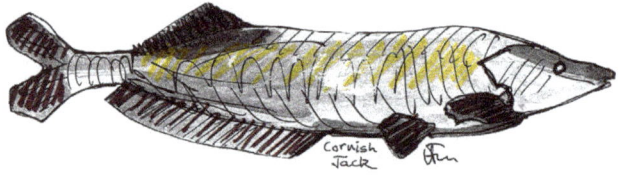

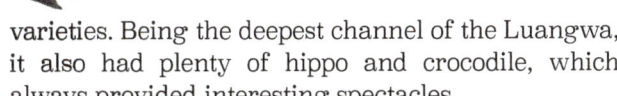

varieties. Being the deepest channel of the Luangwa, it also had plenty of hippo and crocodile, which always provided interesting spectacles.

One of the oldest walking camps I built was on the Chikoko river, which had water only in places. The camp was in a shady spot on the riverbank, looking out over Acacia Park. This was an area of parkland with enormous *Faidherbia albida* trees, which made it very popular with elephant, who would congregate at a certain time of the year to eat the pods.

The newest camp, and one that I personally sited, was called Mumbulu, after the Nile monitor lizard. The camp was right on the banks of the Chibembe river, near its junction with the Nanda river. It was very close to the Kankhonko lagoons, in easy reach of Zebra Flats, and an easy walk from Chibembe lodge itself.

All the bamboo for thatching was cut on the road to Chipata and brought in by truck. Leaves from the ilala palm were cut to be used as binding. The only materials you could take from the park itself were dead mopane trees killed by elephant, which were used for the uprights for the roof.

Making my first reconnaissance to each camp after the rains in the company of one of our scouts was an exciting time. The grass was tall. The game trails clearly defined. Birds were noisy and monitor lizards were mating. Many intra-African migrants such as the Woodland Kingfisher were still evident. On more than one occasion I arrived at the camp to find that the main shade trees had been washed away and were now at the bottom of the river. A new site had to be found quickly: this was the case with New Old Chibembe site.

The first thing to do was get a gang on to

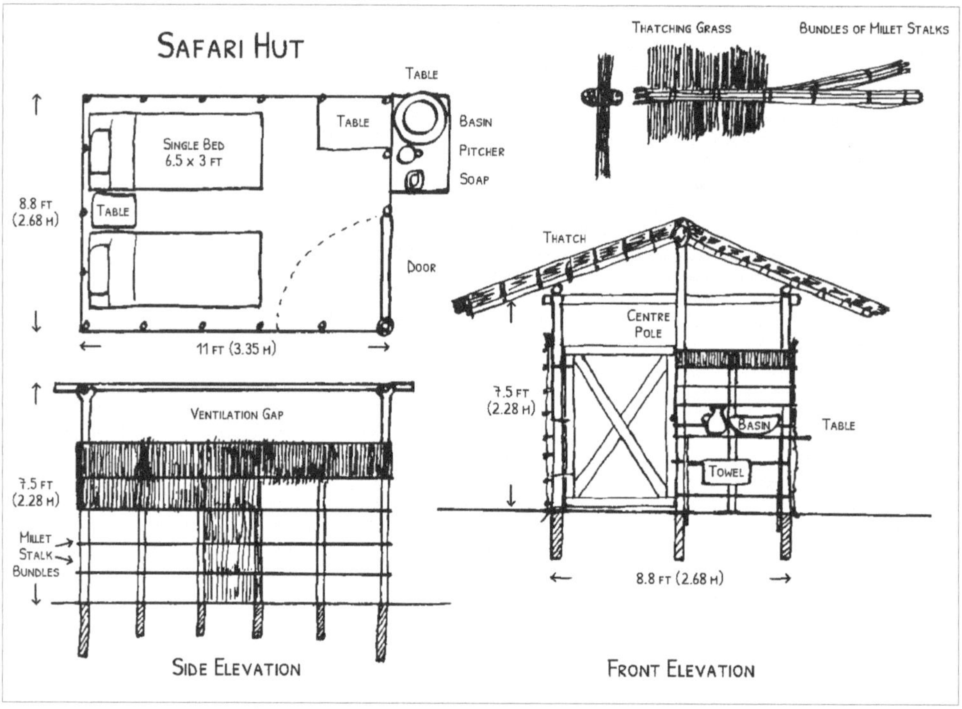

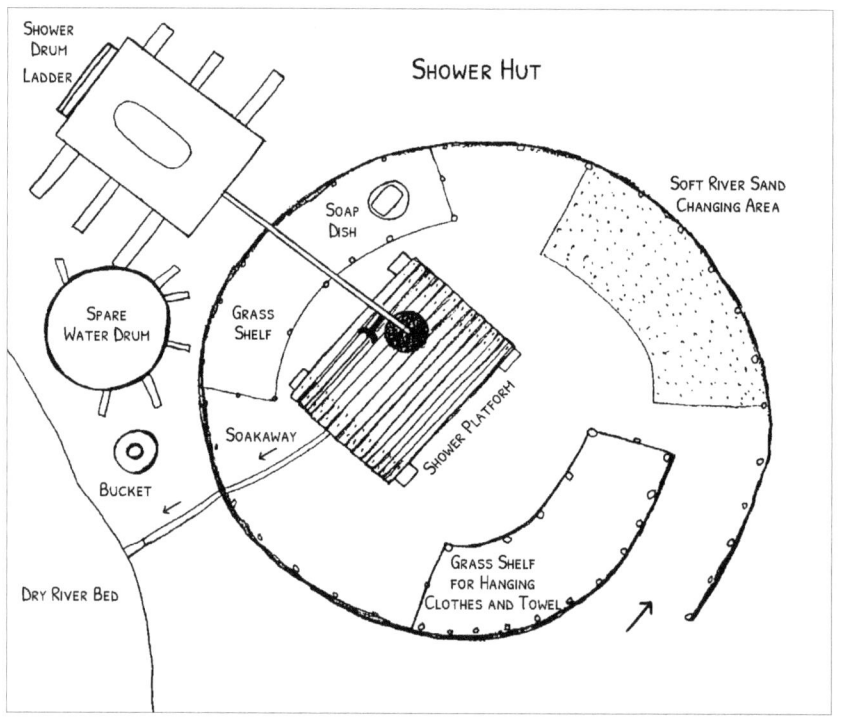

Designs for a safari hut and a shower hut

the site to cut the grass. Next, I would go out and site the huts so that each would get some shade after lunch for the snooze period but not be too close to the adjoining hut or to the dining room. The site would then be levelled and soft river sand laid where the huts would be constructed.

Alec was the camp construction supervisor. He came from one of the villages situated on the road between Chikwinda Gate and the lodge. He was about six-foot tall and skinny, so the dimensions for each hut were 'so many Alecs wide' by 'so many Alecs long'. The depth for the long-drop toilet was his height with his arms extended above his head.

The bamboos and palm leaves were carried in bundles on heads and first shipped over the river in the fibreglass canoe called a banana boat. Anybody who smoked carried a burning ember held in an old tin, as matches were not available. Before lunch, someone with a fishing line would try and catch a catfish: one would be cooked for the meal, the remainder carried home.

Once the camps were built, all the equipment for the three camps had to be carried across the Luangwa river by porters and then along narrow game trails to each one. Imagine what was involved in carrying a bulky gas freezer five kilometres along game trails that were also used by elephant and lion!

There were beds to carry, mattresses, drums for the shower, crockery and cutlery. All these were carried on the heads of youths from the nearby villages and who did not possess a pair of shoes or even a spare shirt. Everything was tied to poles and slung between shoulders. The bed frames were the most awkward, and the gas-powered freezer, with its bottle, was very unwieldy.

Alec paces out the dimensions for a new walking safari hut Kasansanya.

Young lads from the village take saplings they have cut near their villages to build the walking camp.

Isaac Zulu briefs the team of lads from the village who are carrying bamboo to build the walking camps.

Front row (*Left to right*): Alec, Keala Banda, Coffee. Isaac Zulu sits behind Coffee.

With the equipment installed, the three staff members were sent out and I would allocate the equipment to each one and get him to sign for them. Each camp had a prefabricated metal hut for the staff to sleep in, which gave them a feeling of security when the lion were moving through the camp at night.

It was my responsibility to supervise all these activities, and it gave me enormous pleasure deciding where to put each hut and making the dining room a place that would have a wonderful view of the river and the game that was attracted to it.

The distance from one trail camp to another was roughly the same. Each camp had four client huts and one for the Trail Leader. The dining room provided good visibility. The kitchen staff lived in a prefabricated tin hut adjacent to the kitchen, which afforded good protection at night from marauding animals. In each camp there was a shower with a drum and a long-drop toilet. These camps were taken down at the end of each season and all the equipment removed.

Each camp had a resident cook who would make bread every day, make pastries, and produce stews and roasts. They were unbelievable. Some of the old hands had been trained by District Commissioners. There was also a waiter and a 'bedroom-boy'. These three worked as a team and had to get on with one another. The only fancy equipment that the camp possessed was the gas-fired freezer.

I got to know a delightful old cook of the old school called Moffat. He was tiny – hardly five-foot tall – with a broad grin and a good sense of humour. His white uniform was always spotless and starched and he wore a tall cook's hat. I once interviewed him for a promotional video. When I asked him how long

The standard equipment for a walking hut: towels, soap, basin, jug of water, mirror, toothbrush mug. The sturdy door is made from palm stalks.

The shower at Chikoko camp, also a favourite for thirsty elephants.

he left the bread cooking in his oven, which was a hole in the ground, he would say one hour.

'But Moffat, you don't have a watch.'

'I know because it is my work!'

No further comment! In his kitchen, he showed me a tiny African Scops owl that was hiding among the creepers in the foliage above his head. The only modern gadget he possessed was a wind-up alarm clock.

These old 'bush cooks' could produce meals that would amaze any modern TV chef. Where I worked later in Tanzania there was a master chef named Naftal who had been trained by Hugo van Lawick–Goodall. There was nothing that he could not produce. In the tent where he did his frying he had a gas stove, but his oven was a metre-long pit in the ground, covered by a sheet of rusty metal. The hole was pre-heated. When the dish was ready to go into the hole, the coals were removed with a shovel. The baking dish was laid on a platform of mud clods so that the food did not overheat. There was no light out there. If you went to check to see if the dish was cooked, you could easily bump into an inquisitive hyena – or worse! He judged when the food was cooked by its smell. Fresh rolls were made daily in this manner.

Laundry was also performed daily. The iron was charcoal-heated. To keep the coals glowing red you first blew energetically through the small air vents, then whirled the iron around a few times – a bit like throwing a discus – and hoped that the handle didn't come off!

My third trip to work at Chibembe was when I was teaching in Blantyre. I drove in using my 1200cc lime-green Ford Anglia. I slept the night in a hotel in

Chibembe reception with several walking groups and their safari guides prior to departure.
Far left: Margaret Berry, acting manager, talks to an American client. Robin Pope is sixth from the left.

A fully loaded banana boat
with walkers crossing the Luangwa river
at the start of a walking safari Chibembe Lodge

Mwenda sits on the skull of an elephant
shot by poachers.

Lilongwe and was in camp by four in the afternoon on the second day. I drove in once more from Malawi and that was my last visit for a while.

Chibembe lodge, along with several other lodges, was sold off by the Zambian National Tourist Board and had been bought by a wealthy Zambian, Enoch Kavindele. He had given the management contract to a London-based company made up of old colonial civil servants who knew very little about running a company but who were fun to be with when they were talking of the 'good old days'.

They operated under the name of Wilderness Trails and were looking for people to run the lodge. I was approached by them to be the town manager for Wilderness Trails when I was teaching in Italy. This was not a job that I relished very much as I had no experience of office work. However, I saw it as a step in the right direction and one that would give me useful information from the ground up about how a safari operation worked.

The following year, I became Safari Manager at Chibembe lodge itself and ran it with Isaac Zulu. I recruited Trail Leaders through an ecologist who had brought a group through from the University of Kent in Canterbury. I also did occasional walks, all the safari work and the bookings. Isaac handled the workshop, the local staff, and all the maintenance of the lodge. He came originally from Zimbabwe and had no fear of snakes, which was very unusual because Africans are normally terrified of snakes. If one appeared in camp, he would simply catch it and release it far away.

With a full camp I would often arrange to have our drummers entertain the clients. The best drummer was Washen, one of our walking-safari 'tea-boys'. The lads always performed better with

Chibembe Lodge reception. *Left to right:* Gloria Mubaso, Petros Phiri, me and Wickes Helmboldt

Washen prepares tea on a walk.
He carries clean water, a tea pot, cups, tea bags, powdered milk, sugar and either biscuits or cake. He was also an accomplished drummer.

Game scout Coffee holds a Grey Crowned Crane chick found on a walk.

a few beers inside them to get them into the right mood while they heated their drums over a big fire beside the bar.

In addition to the drummers, the village 'witch doctor' would also appear. He was young, powerfully built, and wore a skirt of animal skins with rattles on his ankles and a head-dress of animal tails. As the drummers settled into a good rhythm, he would start gyrating and stamping his feet, sending up puffs of dust. The muscles on his stomach would ripple. The smoke rising from the fire sent light flickering over his glistening skin so that the tribal scars on his face, chest and biceps stood out clearly. Suddenly the rhythm of the drummers and the gyrations of the witch doctor meshed. The tempo went up several notches and the mood became electric.

Walking back to my cottage after the event, I heard the African Wood Owls calling to each other, the male more gruff than the female. Over the years I had learnt to mimic their calls, so I did this, and one of them swooped low over my head in protest.

When the generator was turned off and the lights went out, it didn't take long for the honey badgers to make their appearance. You could hear them scuffling through the grass, growling and grunting as they bumbled along in the direction of the kitchen – where they raided the dustbins. If the doors to the kitchen had not been securely fastened, they would find a way in and smash jars of marmalade and even gnaw into tins of baked beans. The mess in the morning looked as if a party of grizzly bears had been at work!

An enormous puff-adder was found in a disused pit that had once been a water-treatment plant. It measured more than a metre in length. This became

a local record when it was taken to the snake park at Mfuwe, where Phil Berry, our snake expert, looked it up in his record book.

At the end of the season we would have a Christmas party for the staff. Clothing donated by our clients during the season would be given out. Numbered lottery tickets were given to each person. The numbers were put into a box and pulled out one by one. The staff member whose number was drawn could come and pick up an item.

I arranged a tug of war between the camp staff and the outside staff – those who lived in the village and came in each day to the lodge to work. There were also games such as musical chairs.

On a trip to Mfuwe airport one morning, we passed lion beside a small stream. This was always good news because we knew the lion would still be there when we returned later with a jeep full of fresh visitors who had come up on the daily Zambian Airways flight from Lusaka. I loaded up my new group and headed for the camp. As we approached the stream where the lion had been in the morning, I slowed to see if they were still there. They were. I pulled up in the shade and turned the engine off. Another vehicle from the lodge spotted me, saw the lion and stopped opposite us.

We had been observing the lion, who were about twenty metres away, for a few minutes when they suddenly became very tense, put their ears back and looked very hostile. The driver in the other vehicle began waving his arms. I had no idea what was going on and presumed there was something coming behind me that I couldn't see – more lion perhaps.

So I started the engine and began to drive away. As I did so, there was a loud banging on the side of the vehicle and the other vehicle began hooting, so I stopped. One of my passengers had stepped off the back of the vehicle, without saying anything to me, which had spooked the lion, and I had left him behind. He was trying to catch up. He was an American journalist, and when he was reprimanded for behaving like an idiot, he simply said, 'In Kenya we were always allowed to get out of the vehicle!'

I was flying out to Lusaka from Mfuwe airport and had already been given my boarding pass. The incoming flight from Lusaka was due in a few minutes. Suddenly there were shouts of 'Fire!', and panic ensued. There was a general rush of drivers towards the car park, because burning petrol was flowing through the car park and threatening to set fire to the expensive safari vehicles there.

I went out to find out what was going on and to see if I could be of any assistance. One of the hunters, arriving in time to meet his new clients, had decided to refuel from a jerrycan and in the process caused a static spark, which had ignited the fuel. He had dropped the jerrycan, and burning fuel flowed on to the tarmac and headed for several parked safari vehicles.

All I remember after that is a vehicle reversing in a hurry, the driver misjudging the space behind and cannoning into one of the tall, metal flagpoles standing on either side of the airport entrance. His bumper snapped the flag pole. Out of the corner of my eye, I saw something falling towards me. Instinctively I raised my arm to deflect it, and the next thing I remember was lying on the cement with someone pressing very hard on my forehead. She was one

A family group gather together before crossing the Luangwa River just before night fall.

Two lion mating. While the female is on heat they will mate frequently.

of the tourists. Then the ancient airport ambulance appeared and I was lifted into the back and laid on a stretcher; an orderly, with a handkerchief that had belonged to the tourist, exerted a great deal of pressure on my forehead that caused more pain than the wound itself.

After a very bumpy ride, we reached Kamoto mission hospital, where a young Dutch doctor put several stitches in my forehead and bandaged it up tightly. I missed my flight and was picked up later by a vehicle from Chibembe, slightly concussed but none the worse for wear. Coffee, one of our game scouts who had witnessed the accident, couldn't believe his eyes when he saw me a week later. He thought I was a ghost!

At the end of the season at the end of October, the huts were dismantled and the grass removed so that it could not be burned by poachers during the off-season. Each year we tried to retain the poles for the huts, mopane logs that we had collected and cut to size. They were as hard as rock and very heavy to shift, but they would burn. When set alight, an entire tree would burn from tip to root continuously, taking as long as a week and leaving just a white-ash record behind on the ground.

The rains usually began towards the end of October, and it was always a rush to get the lodge battened down and all the equipment in the three trail camps brought back to the lodge, counted, checked and put away. After one particularly heavy rainy season, the storeroom where we kept the walking-safari equipment was flooded and the blankets and linen spoiled.

Aerial views of the Chibembe walking area during the rainy season.

Lukusuzi National Park

The Lukusuzi National Park, north-east of Chibembe, stretches up the eastern side of the escarpment and, at its most eastern boundary, comes very close to the main tarmac road linking Chipata with Lundazi. If the Lukusuzi National Park could provide scope for an activity during the rainy season, that would be worth investigating. I had ideas about white-water rafting and walking safaris during the off-season.

There is a dirt road that climbs up through the hills from the Luangwa. It goes through the park and meets the main Chipata–Lundazi road at the other end. The terrain is mostly miombo woodland, with a lot of granite and mountain acacia. I studied the map carefully and decided that it would be possible to be dropped off on the road that goes through Lukusuzi and walk down to the river. From there it was an easy walk following the river downstream to where we would arrange to be picked up.

I invited John and Carol Coppinger to join us; they were managing Nsefu camp at the time. We took Alec Zimba as our armed guard and several porters. Alec was another of those who had been in the King's African Rifles and had served in Malaya, Burma and Madagascar. At the time he was into his seventies and had recently taken on wife number three, who was sixteen years old. He was always perfectly turned out, never got angry, and was always jovial and tireless. He had his own rifle. At the end of one safari he described how he was looking forward to being with his young wife. He pursed his lips to show me how he was going to take her nipple into his lips.

We reached the Lukusuzi river by nightfall without any difficulty and chose an attractive

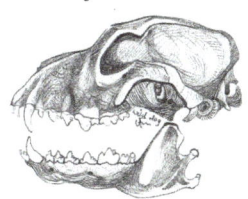

John and Carol Coppinger visit Lukusuzi National Park

There is very little water in the Lukusuzi river in the dry season.

This was our last night stop. The Lukusuzi river cascaded down a steep, rocky cliff, and we camped under the trees beside the water.

We found more than a hundred hippo in a rock pool on the Lukusuzi river.

campsite on the sand by the river in a circle of rocks. The Lukusuzi is a typical seasonal river. The river begins to flow when the rains come in November; water exists only in isolated rock pools when the rainy season ends. With their sensitive snouts, elephant can detect water under the sand, and they often prefer to take water by digging rather than straight from the pools in the rocks, which become heavily polluted as time passes. They are very particular about the quality of the water they drink!

The next day we were amazed to find hippo tracks far from any visible sign of water. There was no grass to be seen anywhere, so where they had gone to find grazing was a mystery. We followed one well-beaten track that led us in the direction of the main river and to a rock pool in the riverbed the size of a tennis court, where an amazing sight met our eyes. There must have been more than a hundred hippo, crammed tightly together like sardines. Their dung was metres high on the fringes of the pool. We took photos and left quickly so that we did not stress them too much.

We found the carcasses of two elephant families shot by poachers. We also spotted a pack of wild dogs. We walked all the following day and camped by a high waterfall close to a wild mango tree.

Miombo woodland does not support game in large volumes as the riverine area does. You find more of the solitary antelope that prefer rocks and hillsides, such as roan, sable and klipspringer; you would be lucky to find these on the valley floor. We found an elephant tusk in the river that we took back with us.

Despite its lack of game, the Lukusuzi has a variety of scenery unlike anything you will find down by the Luangwa river. The river is continually

Left to Right: A porter, Robbie, who worked at Kamemena Island as tea-boy, John Coppinger, Carol Coppinger, Alec Zimba.

Left to Right: Two porters, Robbie, John Coppinger, me, Alec Zimba.

John Coppinger inspects the bloated carcass of one of a family of elephants shot by poachers.

John Coppinger and Alec Zimba inspect the bullet holes in a tuskless female elephant shot by poachers.

changing character as it has to contend with the rocky terrain: there would be flat, sandy stretches with reeds along each bank, and then the river would change course and pass between granite cliffs. The trees there are predominantly mountain acacia.

Our rendezvous with the vehicle from Chibembe was spot on at midday the following day.

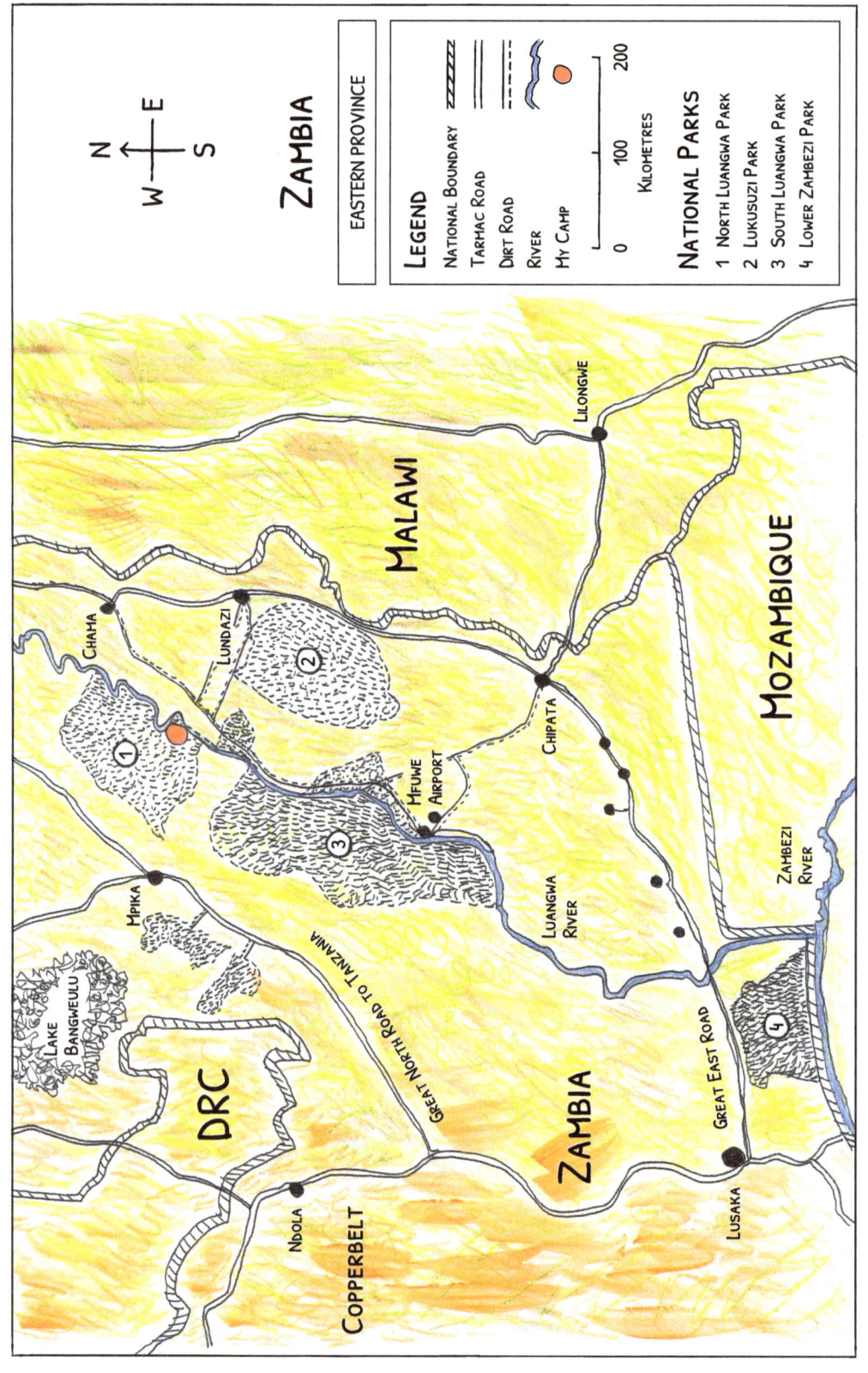

Interesting events from my diaries

May: The start of a new season at Chibembe

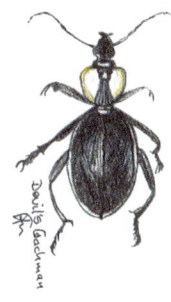

We drove up to the Luangwa Valley in two new Toyota Hiluxes, brought in from Botswana. Left Lusaka at 1.10 p.m. and reached Chipata at 9.30 p.m. to avoid the worst of the midday heat. I was driving one, Mark Evans the other. The tar road just before the Luangwa bridge was very badly potholed. The uniformed soldiers on the bridge were surly and officious.

We stopped at Crystal Springs motel on the outskirts of Chipata. We had T-bone steaks and Mosi beers, then carried on driving at 10.30 p.m. and reached the Musundile river, which was flowing strongly. The concrete bridge had been completely washed away. We drove back up the road a little and slept. It was midnight. I slept in the cab with my window closed and was bothered by only one mosquito. It was very stuffy. Richard, one of the waiters, was badly bitten around the face, sleeping outside.

We set off at 6.00 a.m. and had no difficulty fording the river. The road from then on was easy-going except for a few places where there was standing water on the road itself. Saw no sign of elephant apart from old droppings on the road. The grass was very high along the road verges. In the villages the millet was at least ten feet tall. Baobabs were in leaf most of the way along the road. The only animals we saw were impala, a few wildebeest, two eland and some warthog.

The Lukuzye river was flowing strongly just

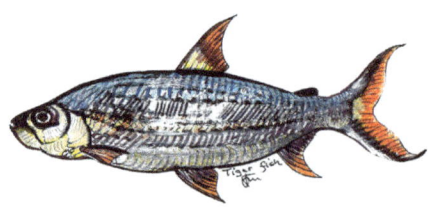

before the lodge but we crossed it easily as the bottom was firm. The road from the Lukuzye to the lodge was easy-going except where the Lukuzye had overflowed its banks and covered the road with soft sand and had formed into deep corrugations.

At Chibembe, Isaac Zulu, who had been at the camp for three weeks already, was there to meet us with his building crew at 9.00 a.m. The camp looked very tidy; the entrance arch into Reception had been newly thatched.

The small lagoon behind the camp was full of water and the stream that brought water into the lagoon next to the fishing camp was running. In the *albida* trees beside the lagoon, Grey Herons and Cattle Egrets were nesting.

During the rains, the Luangwa had cut the bank away next to the manager's house, exposing the roots of the sausage tree (*Kigelia africana*). The far bank of the Luangwa seemed much closer. The river had cut away a large swathe of bank there.

The fishing camp downstream from the lodge – where we had moored the banana boat for crossing into the park – was badly overgrown and all the huts had collapsed.

There were no signs of elephant in the lodge or on the far bank. The vegetable garden was in good shape already, with asparagus and tomato plants flourishing.

In the dried-out swimming pool were clusters of frogs and toads in a heap trying to conserve moisture.

I needed to get out to the trail camps to see how things were after the heavy rainy season. I took with

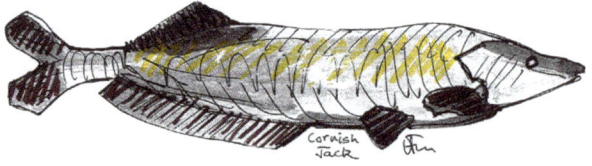

me Coffee, as game scout, and Washen, as paddler for the banana boat.

We set off from camp at 8.15 a.m. The banana boat was moored some distance below the fishing camp. Washen went into the boat first and positioned himself in the stern, holding the only paddle. Coffee waited for me so that I could sit on the seat towards the middle of the canoe; he sat in the bows holding a bamboo pole.

The boat was tethered by a length of twisted cable to a short bamboo stake shoved into the bank. The steel filaments had come undone and it was a mess.

Coffee untied the cable from the post and Washen swung the canoe into the current. When he felt we had gone far enough downstream, he turned the canoe into the main channel. Very quickly we were swept downstream and carried beyond the mouth of the Chibembe river and the sandy beach we were making for. I had presumed we were going to moor the canoe there, but Coffee had other ideas. He had decided, quite sensibly, that the only thing to do was to try to paddle up the Chibembe as far as the mouth of the Chikoko river before abandoning the canoe. This proved to be more difficult than imagined. The river was flowing very fast, carrying a considerable volume of water with it from the Kasansanya higher upstream – which was where we wanted to go.

Washen, with one paddle positioned right at the back of the long fibreglass boat, was not able to keep us going upstream against the current. Again we turned and headed for the Chibembe mouth, Coffee pushing with all his might on his pole and Washen keeping us head on the current. We started to make some headway and entered the Chibembe river, hugging the right bank.

As we neared the bank, Coffee was able to get good leverage with his pole. However, for just a second or two, the prow would veer into the bank and all Coffee's efforts could not prevent it from striking. Once the momentum of his polling was spent, we soon became a victim of the current and started drifting backwards. For a second time we found ourselves approaching the Chibembe mouth going in the wrong direction. Before our humiliation was complete, Coffee managed to gain a pole-hold and, with much urging directed at his paddler sweating in the stern, we once again moved forward, inch by inch.

At this point I was ready to leave the boat and walk: I was convinced that we would never get up the river in this manner. When I suggested this to Coffee, he would have none of it, so I settled into my seat and decided to wait and see what happened before making another suggestion. Surprisingly, Coffee and Washen had developed a technique that was proving successful: we were moving forward, although it was taking a lot of effort from both of them. It was a stinking hot day with the humidity right up and signs of thunderclouds all around. Very soon, Coffee's forehead was beaded with sweat and his shirt was soaking.

As long as Coffee could provide a good thrust, the boat moved forward. Sometimes he got the angle wrong, and by exerting pressure on his pole all he did was oppose the direction of thrust rather than assist it and the effect was like a break. Then, no matter how hard Washen puffed and panted, the boat moved backwards, and by the time they had got their rhythm again we had lost twenty yards. It was a hard struggle.

By heading for the inside of the bends, where the current was flowing slower, we eventually made it to our destination. The distance we had covered was not more than a mile – and it had taken us an hour of great effort to achieve this.

We moored on a flat beach across from the mouth of the Chikoko river. The short pole was thrust into the soft sand and the wire cable wound untidily around it. We pulled the boat clear of the water, just to make certain before setting off. Coffee was leading as usual, wearing my walking shoes that I had given him that morning, with Washen coming along barefoot behind.

The bush along the river was very thick. In the open, *Cassia obtusifolia* bushes were still very green and luxuriant: six feet tall, they blocked our path. We followed hippo paths that led us under the dark canopies of *Canthium zanzibaricum* bushes, through which very little light penetrated. The ground under these bushes was sandy and clear of any other growth.

I kept a good look out for large animal shapes lying under the bushes that could be sleeping hippo, but there were none to be seen. At this time of year, there is always sufficient water in the pools and lagoons to provide refuge for those individuals who live solitary lives away from the main river.

We set course for the Kasansanya. Our route took us along the swollen Chibembe river, which was carrying a lot of water.

Where the Chibembe met the Nanda river, we headed inland, skirting the Kankhonko lagoons. Up to this point we had seen only one elephant – a young male drinking from a small lagoon to our right. As he was my first elephant of the season, we stopped

to watch. He continued drinking, undisturbed by our being there, and we left him content in the knowledge that he was safe in our presence.

Our route led us to the right of the largest lagoon over recently flooded black cotton soil that was heavily pot-holed by elephant and hippo footprints. On the edge of this area we entered higher ground covered with tall, tussocky grass the colour of corn. As Coffee was about to step over one of these grassy clumps, a large black snake began thrashing around inside in a desperate attempt to escape. I moved to my right and Washen followed my example. Coffee didn't move and allowed the snake to dash away in a flurry of gun-metal coils. From its semi-erect hood and large size, it was obviously a cobra. Its girth was as thick as my wrist and it was about four feet long. It seemed to satisfy the requirements of a black spitting cobra (Naja nigricincta woodii).

We then headed towards our tree bridge, which provided access on to the island formed by the Luangwa and Nanda rivers. It was at least four or five feet under water and it would have taken another three to four weeks for the level to drop sufficiently. On we went, on a direct line for Kasa-nsanya following the Nanda river in order to see if there was another place where we could cross, but none presented itself.

We reached the point where the Nanda leaves the Luangwa. From there we could see our New Old Chibembe site, where a surprise was waiting for us. The huge tree that provided all the shade for the huts had collapsed into the river, its roots in the air revealing the gaunt framework of the huts sticking out starkly in the harsh sunlight.

On we went, noticing lion spoor in the sand on

the bank of the Kasansanya. No Skimmers were evident at their usual nesting spot, presumably because the island hadn't formed with the water level so high.

I couldn't get over the amount of greenery that was around. On all the exposed dambos, tall *Cassia* bushes, still very green and full of pods, covered the ground; in places we had to fight to get through. This, combined with the heat and humidity, made the going very hard.

June
Dawn 5.20; Wake 5.30; Sunrise 6.00. Set off 6.30.

An all-German group was going on to Malawi after their safari with us. In the group was one man who stood out immediately when we mustered at Reception before setting off. Despite my instructions the night before about not wearing white clothing, he was wearing a floppy white cotton baseball cap. It didn't suit him at all. In addition, he was carrying a white plastic shopping bag in one hand and an old clockwork Bolex movie camera in the other. The bag contained a wide assortment of medicines that were given away free by pharmaceutical companies. This was the clue to his identity: he was a retired physician from Heidelberg University. The drugs were give-aways.

The temperature at this time of year can reach well into the 30s during the day. He was wearing black leather trousers that tucked into calf-high boots, a long-sleeved leather jacket over a thick, long-sleeved shirt with a vest underneath. As well as those, he had a red scarf around his neck that covered his neck to the tip of his jaw. I looked at his

outfit and told him that he was going to be pretty hot later on. He shook his head.

'Ah, don't worry. I have done my homework. Sleeping sickness, there is no proper cure. Not so? In this valley are many tsetse flies. Not so? What I am wearing is to make it impossible for a tsetse fly to penetrate my skin and give me the disease.'

'But tsetse flies can bite through the tough hide of buffalo with no problem,' I said.

'That is living tissue. I am covered in processed hide. That is the difference.'

We set off. His plastic bag kept catching in the bushes and made an unpleasant rasping sound that frightened off the animals. With both hands full, he couldn't support himself when he stumbled on uneven ground so he fell frequently. He never saw a thing because his eyes were always on the ground ahead of him. When we stopped for tea mid-morning, he fell asleep on the ground from heat exhaustion. By that time the rest of the group had had enough of him. Their group leader realised this.

In the evening, when we sat around the fire and chatted, nobody spoke to him. It was evident to me that all his life he had never had to deal with other members of the public on a equal basis. He lacked all social skills. I tried to talk to him and make him feel more comfortable, but it was not easy.

Before the group set off for Malawi, this unfortunate individual was sent home – a unanimous decision of the whole group.

This was a group from the United States: two retired couples and a young Hispanic fellow from the Bronx in New York, whom I shall call Diego. Of the

married men, one was an architect who specialised in designing nuclear power stations, the other had been in charge of security at the Los Angeles Olympic Games. Diego was the oldest child of six and the only one to have made it to university. He ran the family business. He was very proud of his BMW motorcar, which, he said, had 'ground effects'. When I asked him what 'ground effects' were, he told me that there was a method of dropping the suspension and lowering the car's centre of gravity to make it more sporty. I was impressed.

Another thing that stood out about him was the fact that he wore bright-blue contact lenses. This gave him rather a bizarre appearance for someone who naturally had dark-brown pupils that matched his dark-brown complexion.

That evening, when I summoned the group to dinner, I noticed him standing in front of the mirror outside his hut, carefully removing the lenses. The next evening I had devised a plan. I asked him if he wouldn't mind showing the camp staff how he did this; he said he would be happy to do so. The bedroom attendant's name was John; he was a very simple fellow who had spent most of his life living in one of the villages along the road to the airport. While it was still light, I invited the cook, the waiter and John to witness the removal of the lenses.

Diego went through the routine as planned. When the first lens was removed John was aghast. His eyes were wide with astonishment and he was shaking his head in utter disbelief. When the second lens came out, he just couldn't take it. He turned tail and bolted back to the kitchen amid screams of amusement from the cook and the waiter!

During a tea stop on Kankhonko lagoon a herd of buffalo approach

An elephant uses her back legs as brakes as she goes down a steep river bank …

… and then holds on to a root to slow herself down as she slides down the bank.

A huge herd of buffalo late into the dry season approaches.

July
Dawn 5.20; Wake 5.30; Sunrise 6.00; Set off 6.30; Breakfast: egg and bacon

We arrived at the Kankhonko lagoons and observed a family of elephants feeding beside the water. The group consisted of old females, immature females, and one adult male with very imperfect tusks.

We continued along the Nanda river, which was fuller than usual. We watched another family group of elephant feeding on the steep bank of the river. They were unaware of us as the wind was right. One was carefully feeling along the lip of the bank with the tip of her trunk, searching for small herbs; she bent her front legs in order to get low enough. Once the wind changed, they all spread their ears, turned their heads from side to side, picked up our scent, then scurried off, tails sticking straight out backwards, heads up. Suddenly they stopped, raised their trunks like periscopes, and settled down again to browse.

I was surprised to see places along the banks where elephant had gone down to the water. The bank was extremely steep and in places nearly vertical to the water six or seven feet below. These elephants must have slid the last few feet, dragging their back feet like anchors to slow them down.

We came upon a huge herd of buffalo scattered over a kilometre deep and spread 180 degrees wide. Some were lying down under the trees with only their ears and horns visible; these appeared to be the rear guard of the main herd. They all were very powerful, with heavy bosses. The bulk of the herd was more to the right under a large fig tree. Most of them were standing, some on top of a big termite

mound. They were distinctly silhouetted against the bright sunlight on the tall grass behind them.

As we moved slowly to our right behind some *Combretum* bushes, a group of adults came inquisitively towards us, trying to get our wind but unable to do so: we were well screened by the bushes. They eventually stopped about forty metres from us, noses pushed forward parallel to the ground, nostrils flared, ears sticking down sharply from below their big, black horns.

The wind must have changed direction because the cows and calves under the big fig tree suddenly became alarmed and dashed off. The others joined them, slowly at first but coming more and more frenzied as the numbers increased. Soon the crush of bodies between the available gaps in the bushes and trees were so full of pushing, rubbing bodies that it was like a solid carpet of surging round shapes.

Flocks of Oxpeckers fluttered overhead, descending on to any backs that provided a stable platform for just a moment. The dust from the hundreds of bodies formed a dense cloud that rose up slowly above the trees. The thunder of the hooves on the dry earth, the twitter of the Oxpeckers and the occasional grunt and groan from the terrified animals drowned out all other sounds for several minutes.

As we moved over the ground where they had been minutes previously, we saw fresh cowpats on the pale grass and the dry ground was deeply imprinted with familiar crescent-shaped hoof prints.

Depart main camp: 8.10. Arrive Chikoko: 11.10

We arrived at Chikoko Camp just after eleven o'clock, having set out from the main camp at 8.10 a.m.

The water was very shallow where we had moored the banana boat after crossing the Luangwa. The boatman had to get out at the end, pulling us up to the sandy promontory. He had a very distinctive hairstyle composed of elaborate, tightly wound spirals, which made him look rather feminine.

The walk to the camp was extremely slow and difficult to control. In the party was Sybil Sassoon, a world renowned traveller and bird expert. Every bird was studied in microscopic detail. At the back of the group was the Deputy Director of Eco Safaris, Peter Moss. The game scout became fed up with the slow pace and walked ahead. This problem was sorted out that evening, and I also told the tea-boy to whistle if anybody fell behind. The next day, he would not allow anybody to fall behind – even one member of the group who had a cine camera and wanted to film the entire group from the back. I had to give special permission so that this could be achieved.

On the way to the camp we spotted four giraffe: one big, dark male, two females and one calf. We also spotted some enormous epiphytes growing from the branches of tall *Diospyrous* trees lining the Chikoko river that looked like enormous poppadoms. The fan-shaped leaves lying on the ground looked like tobacco leaves.

As we neared the camp I realised we were in for an amazing spectacle. In the distance we could see an abundance of Fish Eagles and Yellow-billed Storks circling. This undoubtedly indicated that a 'fish-out' was taking place in the lagoon in front of the camp, which proved to be the case. Once we had settled in and were seated on the chairs, we faced the lagoon

and watched the spectacle that was taking place.

We counted eight Fish Eagles, about a hundred Yellow-billed Storks, several Marabou Storks, and a few Hadeda Ibises, Hamerkops and Spoonbills.

The Marabou Storks have bright red patches behind their heads and huge sock-like protuberances hanging down below their beaks. They fished the water by stabbing into it with their broad beaks, making a lot of noise in the process. The yellow-bills, on the other hand, stood stock still, probing the water with one foot while holding one wing extended like an umbrella so that they could see below the surface, and stabbing suddenly when they felt a fish. Whenever a bird produced a fish it was pursued by its neighbours, and more often than not the yellow-bill dropped its prize, particularly if pursued by a Marabou. The fish were all barbel and each probably weighed about a quarter of a pound.

All the while this was going on, others were arriving, some of the yellow-bills making a sharp descent from a great height and angling their wings with a sound like a jet fighter going overhead. The noise was incredible: the squabbled-over fish after they were caught, the cries of the Fish Eagles, and the swooshing sound of diving yellow-bills. The Marabous had the advantage with their larger beaks and longer legs.

A group of satiated yellow-bills gathered in a flock on the grassy bank and watched the antics of their fellows. By the evening, most of the birds had moved on to another fishable lagoon. The remainder took off at a given command with a loud beating of wings, filling the sky with their black-and-white pinioned wings.

One evening

I was sitting beside the Kasansanya river, facing upstream, and waiting for my clients to go through the shower routine. This took a while, as the shower drum had to be re-filled each time. The sun had recently set but the water glowed orange and a Wattled Lapwing called as it was disturbed by a hippo that was emerging from the water to feed. I saw a large group of baboons ambling along towards the camp. They were grouped together and moving quickly, aware that they needed to reach their roosting spots before darkness had descended. I thought they were rather late to be moving, and their purposeful manner suggested that they were also aware of this.

Suddenly, one or two started barking loudly. Others took up the cry, and very soon pandemonium broke out and spread very quickly through the troop. The cause of the disturbance was unclear. Because it was nearly dark and they were far from home, suddenly coming upon our camp with its lights and strange sounds must have been adequate cause for their panic. A few decided to resolve the problem by climbing a small tree that grew on the outskirts of the camp. However, when a troop of more than fifty baboons tries to climb the same small tree, a lot of pushing and pulling takes place, not to mention barking and screaming from the younger ones who found themselves in a frenzied squash of bodies. The area around and below the tree was a grey, seething mass.

It didn't take long for one or two of the older baboons to see that there was no real cause for panic and they drew some away from the tree. Their

On a cold winter's morning hippo like to come out and sunbathe.

Elephants wade the Luangwa.
A photo taken when I drove the air crew of Prince Andrew's flight to Mfuwe airport on his visit to Zambia.

example was soon followed by the others, and very quickly the panic passed and all was quiet again.

Afternoon walk from Kasansanya

We had walked downriver to a shallow bend to study the hippos: there were at least a hundred, all packed together, shoulder to shoulder, where the water was just deep enough for them to stand. It must have been about 4.30p.m. We were watching one group of hippos to our left when suddenly, above the din, I heard a Black-headed Heron making a very loud metallic squawk as it flew past us.

I trained my binoculars on it and noticed that it was watching the sky above very intently. To do this, it had to twist its head in a most amazing manner so that it appeared that it had no head at all: the eyes were facing straight upwards and only the back of its head was visible. At the same time, I heard a sound like a jet fighter coming down in a steep dive. Looking up, I saw a small white-and-black shape plummeting down vertically: it was a Martial Eagle with its wings half-folded. It was coming down at an incredible speed.

As it neared the ground, two Egyptian Geese sprang into the air. The eagle made for them but missed at the last moment. He swooped up in a loop and, using what little height he had, he made another weak attempt at the geese – probably more out of frustration than anything else – but they evaded him. The eagle turned and flew gracefully away and came to rest in a tree not far off. What an anti-climax for such a dramatic dive! Had it not been for the heron providing sufficient warning, one of the geese would not have survived.

The kitchen staff at Mumbulu laying a sheet of corrugated iron heated with embers over their bread pit.

A walk to Kasansanya

Alec Zimba game scout. Moffat tea-boy. Clients family from Lusaka. Departed Chibembe at 7.45 a.m.

President Kaunda had paid a visit to Mfuwe to inspect scouts from National Parks and had then flown off to Addis Ababa for an OAU meeting. I had been in Lusaka for a dental appointment and had difficulty getting a flight to return to Mfuwe. During this period poachers had been active along the Mwamba river and out on to Zebra Flats.

We passed through our newest walking camp, Mumbulu, named after the Nile monitor lizard that were common there. They like to lie on the branches of the sausage trees that grow over the river; when disturbed, they drop straight down into the water.

Not long after crossing over the log bridge on the Chikoko river, we spotted nine kudu – one half-grown bull, some adult females and two very young calves. We carried on and reached Mumbulu camp, where I checked to see if the fridge was working all right. It was. Another group was due in there for lunch that same day.

We continued on to Kankhonko lagoons, where a splendid surprise was in store for us at our tea spot. Behind the lagoons, moving in stately procession, were six giraffe. They were coming towards us. To our right was a large breeding herd of eland. Two young bulls were fighting one another, sending dust up into the air with their efforts. One eventually pushed the other back so that it had to reverse for thirty yards, at which point the loser broke away and ran off, still pursued by the victor. The breeding herd numbered about forty-five.

We had tea, occupying our time

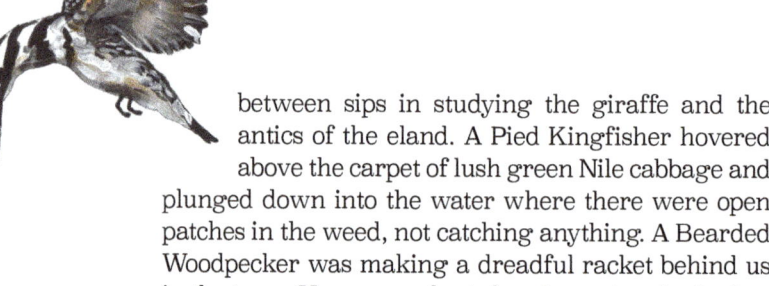

between sips in studying the giraffe and the antics of the eland. A Pied Kingfisher hovered above the carpet of lush green Nile cabbage and plunged down into the water where there were open patches in the weed, not catching anything. A Bearded Woodpecker was making a dreadful racket behind us in the trees. He never relented, so I wondered whether a mongoose might have been having a go at his nest.

After tea we carried on, heading towards the Nanda river. Emerging from the protection of some bushes that grew along the banks of the lagoon, a small group of elephant made themselves known to us. It was a family group and I was concerned about the direction they would take if they got our scent. If we blocked their exit from the lagoon it could be dangerous: the lagoon formed one barrier and the river another.

I checked the wind, which was blowing from right to left. This meant that, if we moved to the left of the elephant, they would not be able to smell us, so we headed towards the Nanda downwind of the elephant. We reached the river, which had very steep banks, and moved along the riverbank towards the elephant that were feeding peacefully twenty yards in from the river. We got to within forty yards of them and stopped behind a clump of bushes that gave us protection from them if they decided to charge. The wind kept blowing steadily, carrying our scent away from the elephant.

They kept moving slowly towards us until they were alongside us and not more than twenty yards away. I whispered to everybody that, if the elephant were to charge, the best thing to do was to go down the steep bank and stand on the narrow beach by the water. At that moment the wind changed

direction and the elephant smelt us. They all raised their trunks and swivelled their heads from left to right, trying to get a positive scent fix – looking rather like tanks trying to locate the source of hostile fire on a battlefield.

Then one of the young bulls got a good whiff of us. Fear had probably added its flavour to our scent. This convinced him that it was time to move and he bolted off, his tail sticking out horizontally and his legs moving like pistons. The others caught his anxiety and they, too, began running, but only for a short distance. Then they formed into a defensive laager, the youngsters in the middle and the adults on the outside, facing outwards. I thought that this was a good moment to retreat, so we slipped away quietly without causing the elephant any further anxiety.

Our route from then on followed the Nanda river until we reached a dry tributary, which we followed before branching off through the woodland towards our camp. On the way we spotted a solitary bull elephant, not quite fully grown and with only one tusk. We also picked up some ripe berries, called *muchenja* in the local Nyanja language, from the *Diospyros* trees. We reached camp at 12.15 having had a very interesting morning.

During lunch I noticed many vultures out towards the west of the camp. Hundreds of them were wheeling about and others were making for the spot from all directions. At 3.30 we had tea and decided to investigate.

We left the tree line and headed out across an open space with occasional bushes here and there and the odd mopane tree sticking out of the undergrowth. On every tree there were vultures. In every direction in front of us we could see vultures, hundreds and

hundreds of them. We made for some trees that held the greatest concentration of birds. Then we smelt the unmistakable odour of rotting meat. The thought that had been growing in my mind all along was that this was the work of poachers and that we would be about to find a dead elephant. As we approached the thicket, a great number of vultures burst out of the bushes ahead of us; others on the trees also took off with ponderous wing beats.

Thirty yards away I could see the prone form of a large, grey animal. The tail end had been opened up. The sides were streaked with white. It was under the densest bush facing outwards. It was a solitary elephant. At the same time as the tusks had been removed, the trunk had been hacked off. Hyenas and vultures had stripped the flesh from its face and neck. The rest of the body was reasonably intact. The stomach was distended and the legs were sticking out at acute angles like a child's stuffed toy. Its tail had been removed, and its ears hung down pathetically on either side of its head. The skin underneath the ears was waxy and smooth and dark grey in colour; the skin uppermost was rough and hairy and showed traces of a recent sand bath.

July
Canthium zanzibaricum in flower, along with the sausage trees. *Feretia auriganescens* finished fruiting. Muchenja in fruit but not ripe; the same for the tamarind. Baobab in fruit. Marula finished fruiting. Sausage trees and *Combretum microphyllum* about to come into flower.

Male vervet monkeys chasing one another

around, competing for females. Eland have young. Kudu mating. Eight hyena eating a dead hippo. Buffalo in large herds on Zebra Flats. Impala rams still chasing after the females and making a terrible groaning sound. Young zebra visible.

An Egyptian Goose taken by a croc on Kankhonko lagoons. Another mother with a string of goslings was calling anxiously to her young from the grass on the shore. She hopped on to a log so that she could keep a better eye on them. The small lagoon at Kankhonko drying out and the smaller crocs are walking through the grass towards the main river.

A young Martial Eagle stooping on a flock of Guineafowl and missing. Some Southern Carmine Bee-eaters have arrived. White-fronted Bee-eaters are already nesting.

August
The vervet monkeys at the lodge have started giving birth. They all produce them at the same time. The babies form small playgroups, watched intently by their admiring mothers. Their teats are positioned on their chest, like those of humans. When the babies are very small, they are carried clinging to the mother's fur on the underside. As they become more confident, they ride on her back like jockeys. Females without babies become very jealous of mothers with babies and try to kidnap them.

A female warthog on Zebra Flats with a single piglet. The piglets spend the first weeks of their lives underground in burrows. When they are old enough, they come to the surface and follow the mother around; by this time, they can sprint as fast as she can.

Five elephant were shot by poachers on Zebra

Flats. It was a family group, entirely wiped out. The matriarch was small; the youngest in the group was about nine years old. One female had been chopped through the spine with an axe to paralyse her; she had evidently struggled after being initially shot. All the tails had been removed. No signs of bullet holes. The foot pads from one elephant had come off and were lying around on the grass like dinner plates.

We met an anti-poaching patrol of four scouts, armed with .303 rifles and FN automatic shotguns, and four bearers. They had tracked the poachers after they had shot a buffalo. As they came towards us they disturbed a lioness. They looked a rag-tag bunch, poorly equipped and motivated by who-knows-what? I could not help admiring them and their efforts.

The temperature is in the 30s but the humidity, fortunately, not that high. If the present temperatures continue it will be unbearably hot by the end of the season.

Walk from Old Chibembe site
We heard elephants trumpeting, which meant either human beings or lion. We changed direction so that we could get a clearer picture of what was going on. There they were, standing under a large sausage tree and very agitated. Three fully grown elephant bulls, ears extended, trunks flapping about, heads swivelling from side to side. Tea-boy Gibson was sure there were lion around.

As we got closer, Gibson, who had very sharp eyes for his age, spotted lion running helter-skelter away from the elephant in all directions. The young bulls spotted the lion and started chasing them. The lion took off into the long grass. Now and then one

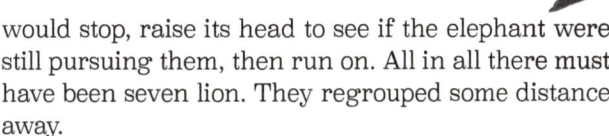

would stop, raise its head to see if the elephant were still pursuing them, then run on. All in all there must have been seven lion. They regrouped some distance away.

The lion must have been snoozing under the sausage tree. The elephants had the same idea and that was what had caused the ruckus.

While we were watching the lion from our tall anthill, another elephant appeared and walked past us very close, his attention on the lion.

Morning walk from Mumbulu camp
In the small lagoon close to the mouth of the Chibembe river, a young crocodile was sunning itself on the back of a large hippo. The hippo was totally unconcerned. It remained there while the hippo began wading out into deeper water until it spotted us.

In the afternoon, we walked down the Chikoko river in the direction of the main camp and reached the point on the river where there is some standing water and a very impressive stand of *Diospyros* trees. Coffee, our game scout, turned from the path we generally use and made a circuit towards the dry riverbed.

Suddenly, out from under a *Canthium* bush sprang a lion, which ran away in large bounds, shortly followed by another with a small mane. As they disappeared from sight, the baboons in the neighbourhood began barking energetically. We then spotted the kill – it was a big waterbuck ram, half-eaten and with a deep gash in its throat.

The next morning, we returned to the kill, walking very cautiously, but the lions were not to be seen. The kill had been dragged into the open,

Two young elephant bulls disturb lion resting in the shade of a sausage tree at midday during a morning walk

I spotted this leopard on one of my first game drives. It ran off the road and hid.

A leopard I photographed on one of my first game drives in the Luangwa National Park.

This leopard crossed in full view of a herd of puku during an early walk from Chikoko to Mwamba camp.

and all that remained was some meat on the legs and ribcage.

Walk from Chikoko to Mwamba
I spotted a leopard soon after leaving camp. It was lying fast asleep on the sandy bank of the Chikoko river and did not hear us approach, giving us a splendid view. Baboons some distance away spotted it immediately and gave their loud alarm calls.

A walk out to Zebra Flats
This was a walk to investigate the carcass of an elephant shot by poachers. As we approached the edge of the grassy plain, we spotted a large number of vultures that seemed to be coming in from all directions.

We headed for the biggest concentration of birds and soon spotted the carcasses, festooned with vultures. There were four dead elephant – another small family group wiped out: three smallish cows and a half-grown adult. Their heads and the tails had been cut off. Pieces of the ears had been cut off for shoes. The smell was overbearing. The carcasses were swollen with gas as the vultures had not been able to gain entry – that would have been the task of hyena and lion. We were all disgusted by the sight. The tusks would have been very small indeed.

We moved off towards a big fig tree on the edge of the plain and had tea. There were signs that a big group of lions had drunk from a pool, and there were also rhino droppings that had been scattered in the usual way. As we were walking away, we came on a zebra that had been killed by lion. It had been picked clean.

Cook Nanzikani prepares breakfast at Mwamba.

Relaxing at Mwamba after an afternoon walk.

September

Wherever there were sandy beaches along the Nanda river we saw signs of crocodiles. The females were laying their eggs about thirteen feet above the waterline and protecting them by lying on top of them. Crocodiles also regulate the temperature of the eggs by urinating on them if it gets too high. Honey badgers had dug up two nests and the broken shells were visible around the excavated hole: their footprint with its five toes was unmistakable.

The smaller of the two Kankhonko lagoons was drying up and small crocodiles were attacking the fish in waves. Whenever a croc went for a fish, there was a splash and a swirl of a yellow tail, and other small fish would leap into the air. At the far end of the lagoon, a congregation of Pelicans, Yellow-billed Storks and Saddle-billed Storks was developing in readiness for a fish-out.

Several puku were grazing fifty yards from the water and suddenly started making their alarm whistle. I checked out the area with my binoculars but could not see any sign of a predator. Alec Zimba, our game scout, who was sitting on a log some distance to our right, pointed excitedly. There was a lion that had got up from behind a tree and was moving towards the water. He lay down and we couldn't see him any more. We got up to have a better look but he saw us and ran off.

Chibembe to Kasansanya and Chikoko.
Moses game scout. Laston tea-boy.

We watched a family group of elephant on the old road that passed behind Chikoko camp. An adult male appeared and we became sandwiched between the bull elephant and the family group. The bull

A group from Connecticut, USA.
Claire Helmboldt is immediately behind me, with Laston, tea-boy and Moses, game scout.

On a walk, Moses introduces the ladies to a local viagra tree, which we later
tried in our tea. Moses stressed that women were not supposed to take it.
The tree is *Drypetes gerrardii*, and it had already had
a considerable amount of its bark removed.

was keen on joining the females but in the process became aware of us. He charged us and kept coming for about twelve minutes. Laston was running, we were running, and Moses took up a position towards the rear, where he started making threatening sounds. After a while, the elephant gave up, but he stood there, trying to make us out, head swivelling from side to side.

We spotted three giraffe as we approached Kankhonko lagoons. They were eating the flowers from an old sausage tree. They ran off in a cloud of dust and took with them about thirty zebra and a dozen eland.

We had tea at Kankhonko lagoons and watched a young bull elephant drinking about forty metres away from us. He proceeded to toss sloppy mud over his back and shoulders and under his chest. A warthog was having a mud bath close by.

After tea we headed for camp on a direct route, walking briskly as it was very hot indeed.

October
Mumbulu–Mumbulu–Chikoko
Game scout: Moses. Tea-boy: Laston

Clients: John and Susan Harrop from Wales, Brian and Janette Semmens from London.
We wake at 5.00 a.m. and start walking at 5.45 after tea and coffee, taking breakfast with us. The weather started out overcast and pleasantly cool: the first night was cold enough to require a second blanket on the bed.

We saw two warthog mothers with tiny babies in tow. Also saw two wildebeest and a roan antelope at Kankhonko lagoons. The smaller lagoon was nearly

I rescue a buffalo calf from Kankhonko lagoons with the assistance of a group from the UK.

Kankhonko lagoon covered in Nile cabbage after good rains.

dry, the water in the bigger lagoon very low and treacherous for animals trying to drink, particularly buffalo.

The day before, a group had tried to rescue a young zebra without success. I had sent a message to the staff at the camp to kill it – which they did, and they had the meat hanging up to dry outside their quarters.

Queleas in their thousands were drinking from the lagoon.

On the first morning out from Mumbulu, we passed between the first and second lagoons. At the big lagoon, we found two buffalo stuck in the mud at the edge – one an adult, the other a yearling. Both were submerged up to their cheekbones in soft, glutinous mud. I saw little hope in trying to rescue the adult, but asked my group if they would like to have a go at rescuing the young one. They were keen to do so.

The calf was a young bull; his nose was facing away from the bank. I asked everybody to collect dry branches until we had a good-sized pile on the bank. The buffalo was lying in a narrow channel with harder mud on either side.

We started by building a platform all around him. The mud was the consistency of porridge and very sticky. We started digging the mud out from around his back legs and throwing it on to the bank. After a while, we tried pulling and heaving, but he was soon sucked back in. In no time at all, the heavers were covered in mud up to their armpits – Laston even had mud on his head. Moses looked on, gun in hand, and managed to keep pretty clean, all the while prepared for an intervention from a source unseen. The ladies were bringing more logs all the time.

After an hour of heaving and shoving, we had his head and chest on dry ground and his back legs out of the sticky mud; a bit more heaving and pulling and we had him out.

At first, all he could do was lie in a heap, his eyes rolled back in his skull revealing red lids, expecting the worst, his legs sticking out at the back, chest heaving. With help from Laston, I managed to raise his torso off the ground and support his chest so that he could straighten his legs and get the blood circulating again. Soon he was standing, his sides heaving while he got his strength back.

His brown shaggy coat was smeared with mud up to his ears; his pathetic, limp little tail was drooping from the back. He had long, sturdy legs and stumpy horns about four inches long with blunt ends. Suddenly he tossed his head in an attempt to gore me and I knew then that he was going to live. He staggered off on his stiff legs, only to trip on a log and fall over. We lifted him up again, and at that point decided to leave him to get on with it. We returned to camp for a wash and a change of clothing. As far as we could know, he survived and made contact with the herd.

That night was a full moon, and it was hotter. Lion began roaring towards the Nanda confluence. Hippo started grunting loudly as the lion began moving in our direction. I was standing outside my hut and saw a waterbuck galloping past the camp followed by two lion who were trotting at a brisk pace. As they passed the camp they looked in our direction. We could follow their progress from their roaring as they went down the river. The first group starting roaring and were answered by a second group, so we had stereophonic sound. Then there was silence,

followed by more hippo grunting, whereupon we expected the first group to come past but they avoided us altogether. They passed under a tree full of roosting baboons, who began barking madly.

Before dinner we heard leopard grunting and impala snorting. The leopard continued with his deep, panting sounds for some time. Two hyena appeared on the bank opposite us, looking for what we thought might have been the leopard's kill; they searched backwards and forwards for quite a long time.

Early the following morning, Janette got the shock of her life when she saw, through the window, a large elephant that was feeding from a bush right next to their hut.

On the way to Chikoko we saw eland and kudu drinking from one of the pools on the river, along with buffalo, elephant and at least a hundred zebra.

Kasansanya camp
First light 5.30. It is generally cool early in the morning but extremely hot after 8.00. There are clear skies until 4.00 p.m., but after that, clouds appear and a wind gets up.

It is 6.30 on a crisp African morning and the sun is just beginning to squeeze itself over the earth's dark rim like a blob of blood oozing from a pricked finger. It is hugging the trunks of the skeletal mopane trees as it rises, throwing them into sharp relief. The gentle light softens and flattens, running shapes into each other like a watercolour, the colours pastel, a range of pinks, blues and violets, colours of the Cape Turtle Dove.

I am standing on the high, sandy bank above the Kasansanya river waiting for my walkers to get ready for their first early walk since coming to

Africa. Below me, the river steams as the sun's weak rays barely reach its troubled surface. To my left, a hundred yards downstream, I am attracted by the harsh staccato cackle of a Guineafowl to a solitary mopane tree that stands defiantly on the edge of a jaggedly eroded riverbank. As I watch, the first bold ones flutter to the ground to begin their long day of foraging. They are followed closely by the rest of the flock in a discordant emptying of the tree, which proceeds slowly at first and then quickly gathers pace as the fears of the remainder are overcome by the confident calls of those on the ground, who are already scuffling through the dry soil for food.

From another clump of trees I can hear the barking of baboons as the dominant males challenge the new day before they, too, follow the example of the Guineafowl and descend to the ground to begin their wanderings in search of food.

While this has been going on, my party has emerged from their huts, bearing cameras and binoculars and dressed in attire suitable for walking. After a quick cup of coffee, taken from an enamel pot kept warm in the white embers of the previous night's fire, we are ready to set off. Coffee, our game scout, has joined us, looking smart and efficient in his dark-green uniform. With him is our tea-bearer, expertly balancing on his head a wooden box, also dark green, that contains our sandwiches and what he will require to make tea for us later on in the morning. We greet him, and then I take Coffee aside and discuss our route for the morning. He had also heard lion roaring just before dawn and agrees with me that they have almost certainly made a kill. We decide on a course that will give us a good chance of coming on them.

As we leave the camp, the nip in the air is fast disappearing. The sun has freed itself from the pull of the horizon and is rapidly losing its redness to the clouds above our heads – all the more reason for us to be off and walking or else the lion will seek the shade before we can spot them. Coffee stops momentarily to prod the powdery sand with the toe of his boot. The small puff of dust that this produces hangs motionless in the cold air before dissolving.

The country we are walking through is mopane woodland that has suffered severe elephant damage. This is evident from the tusk marks on the trees – vivid gashes in the living bark where the elephant has thrust a tusk to prise off a piece sufficient to get a trunk-hold. If this is successful, the next step is easy. Long strips of bark are torn off and, if the animal is skilful, most of the bark will come away in one piece. It is rather like peeling an orange in one piece – easy once one gets going but difficult if the strip breaks. I am sure elephant are aware of this. If a tree proves to be too tiresome, an elephant will simply move on to another one. If that does not yield anything, out of frustration he will try and push it over. They have no scruples about destroying a tree simply to reach some ripe pods that are out of the reach of its trunk.

We are now walking along a game trail that follows the bank of a dry river. It is the favourite route for many animals heading for the main river in front of the camp. Suddenly I spot a dark, indistinct shape ahead of us. Coffee is studying a family of elephant off to our left and hasn't seen it. I give a low whistle and point ahead. He stops and, following my gaze, whispers 'Hippo!'

At that moment the hippo emerges from behind some tall grass and is immediately recognisable. He is a big, solitary bull, returning to the water after a long night's grazing. He hasn't seen us yet and is proceeding towards us at a slow pace along the same path that we are travelling on. He reminds me of a bad-tempered, paunchy old man making his way home from his club having been disturbed by a telephone call from his wife while he was snoozing after a big lunch.

Before anybody in the group can make a noise or take a photo, I put my finger to my lips and motion them to follow me towards a dead tree to our right. Coffee walks slowly away from the path, keeping himself between us and the hippo.

The hippo comes to within forty yards of us before Coffee interferes. By now we are safely hidden by the tree. Coffee has waited for this before cocking his rifle. At the sound the hippo raises his head and spots us. From a slow, swaying amble, he breaks into a stiff-legged trot, eyes fixed on us. This quickly shatters the image I had had of him earlier. Instead, I am aware only of the massive jaws, capable of crushing like fruit boxes the iron-hard hulls of native canoes, and of the beady, fear-crazed eyes in their little bone turrets, which at that very moment are intently fixed on us.

Camera shutters clatter behind me. My attention is directed at the hippo and what he is going to do next. Coffee holds his ground and does not shout or threaten but, with gun at the ready, he is ready to fire a warning shot and then, if necessary, an aimed shot. For my group, this is their first encounter with a dangerous animal, and the successful handling of this episode will decide whether the days ahead will be anticipated with excitement or dread.

Fortunately, the hippo does the

sensible thing and heads for the river. I can feel the tension in the group ease perceptibly. Coffee lowers his gun and uncocks it. Despite his cool handling of the incident, I know that he was as apprehensive as I was. Far from being the docile, comical characters of the mud hole, a hippo is ferocious when provoked and a very fast runner when cornered. They don't like being caught out of water and, if surprised while sleeping under a bush, usually attack; if one is unprepared, the results are usually fatal.

We crossed the *luafwa* – the dried-up section of an oxbow lagoon – and found lion tracks. On the other side, I spotted a lion in the bushes; two others were with it. They were under the *chibembe* (*Canthium zanzibaricum*) bushes. Having spotted us, they went further into the bushes; we could hear baboon barking, so they had seen them as well.

We left the *luafwa* and walked around behind the *Canthium* bushes, hoping that the lion might exit from the other side. We stopped and watched, but there were no signs of movement or disturbance of any kind. Then we heard footsteps on dry leaves and, looking under the bushes, I saw three young lion watching us from a low branch. They were lined up as if they were posing for their photograph. They stayed like that for some time before jumping down and vanishing into the shadows.

Later on, I found a Natal Mahogany tree about twenty feet high with the claw marks of a leopard on a branch about seven feet above the ground.

On a sand island by the Kasansanya river we found nests of either Skimmers or Lapwings. One had two eggs, the other, four. There was no sign of the birds around.

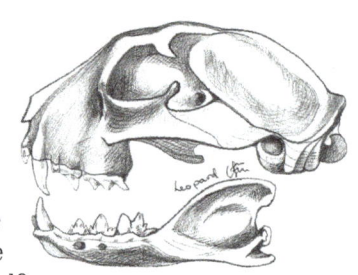

Walking along the vertical edge of the riverbank we disturbed a Nile monitor lizard that was sunning itself on the sand. It scuttled towards the lip of the bank, paused to sum up the situation and, with nowhere to hide, went over the top and down the steep bank towards the fast-flowing water beneath.

On the opposite side of the river, a large crocodile was cruising like a submarine with its conning tower raised. It spotted the movement, accelerated, and headed straight for the spot where the lizard had thought it could make a surreptitious entry into the water. As the lizard launched itself off the bank, the croc caught it and, with a ferocious shake of its head and a splash, it crunched the lizard in its formidable jaws before submerging. All that remained were a few bubbles.

Further on, immature crocs were also catching Quelea as they came down to drink. A quick snap and a splash and it was all over.

Animals are forced to drink regularly. I spotted several very large crocs cruising about opposite the camp: something was attracting them. As if from a signal, six or seven of them were concentrated in a small area. A smaller one appeared on the surface holding something in its jaws. There was a brief argument, then it submerged. All one could see of the big ones were the knobs above their eyes and the double serrated ridge along the base of their tail – it reminded me of the submarine Nautilus in Jules Verne's *20,000 Leagues Under the Sea*. They moved so effortlessly – so deadly, so single-mindedly, so calculating. One of them must have pulled an animal into the water because, a little later, an enormous croc with **bulging sides** emerged to sun itself and,

as if on cue, all the others dragged themselves out of the water and lay motionless, side by side.

Morning walk along the Luangwa
We saw a dead hippo, floating on its side and surrounded by dozens of crocodiles; the water was seething with them. Their yellow heads changed the colour of the water around the bloated white carcass of the hippo.

Occasionally, a big croc would force its way through or over the others to shove its snout and cheeks into the enlarged anus of the hippo, only to emerge with bloody jaws and a chunk of red meat that it would swallow by tossing it up and back like a heron swallowing a fish.

What was amazing was to see the other hippos clustered around their dead companion as if nothing had happened.

A walk from the Kalovia river to Kasansanya
We had not seen the pride the night before, although we had looked for them.

We were crossing the *luafwa* where it joins the Kalovia and had almost reached the hard ground when I spotted a lion moving towards a round bush. Others appeared from down in the river and soon we were able to count fifteen lions in all – five adults, the rest immature. We walked so as to cut them off but they spotted us and went across the river instead. We saw them on the opposite bank very distinctly and suddenly out of nowhere four hyenas appeared.

October. Rainy season imminent
The weather windy, humid and very hot. Big storm clouds forming towards mid-afternoon. The wind keeps the temperature down.

Spotted a Bat Hawk flying overhead that had obviously been disturbed by our presence.

First impala lamb spotted.

A morning walk from Kasansanya camp to Zebra Flats

The first shower of rain had fallen during the night and the ground was pocked by raindrops – a perfect surface for distinguishing fresh lion prints. There was a special feel in the air, a freshness. The bird calls sounded louder than usual simply because the air was clean.

We followed a single hippo track out towards the Chibembe river. I planned to hit the edge of Zebra Flats, then skirt along the boundary, keep to the trees and swing back to the Kankhonko lagoons, circle around them, and return to camp along the Nanda river.

We reached the Chibembe river and waded across as it was very shallow. On the other side, I noticed, very clear in the soft sand, fresh lion tracks: one very large male and a smaller adult. Coffee, the game scout, was half-hearted about following them, but he realised that I was very keen so we followed them. I think he felt that there was little point in going after them as there was an enormous wilderness out there that could hide any number of lion.

The tracks seemed to be following the riverbank and heading due north. We continued, our minds on other things, when I suddenly spotted the form of a big lion straight ahead of us, lying in the sand in the middle of the river in full view. I pointed him out, and by the time all the group had understood what I was pointing at, the lion had heard us and stood up. He turned to face us, recognised us for what we were,

and sprinted up the river. I motioned to Coffee and we followed at a slow trot, trying to reach the bend of the river, which would give us an uninterrupted view down the straight section ahead of us.

The lion covered the distance a lot quicker than we did, and soon it was about 200 yards away and still going hard. Just as I was about to call a halt, a big lioness, accompanied by an adult male with a small mane and another female also fully grown, appeared out of the grass. Then, would you believe, yet another female appeared. They all looked at us for a few moments and then disappeared into the grass with angry flicks of their tails.

We carried on, slowly now, and found where they had been lying in the sand. We studied the impressions their bodies had made – the grooves where their tails had been and the deepest impressions where their paws had dug into the soft ground.

We reverted to our original course and reached a suitable anthill to observe Zebra Flats. We could see herds of zebra in the distance, a few elephant, and a mother warthog with young. She was not at all concerned about us.

Moving on, we had covered only two hundred yards when we noticed vultures coming down behind where we had just been. We turned back and there on the ground were a few vultures picking at something. It was the remains of a male impala; all that was left was the skull and horns. Nearby, there was a leg with just the bones intact and some skin, and a little further on another leg bone, the pelvis and a shoulder blade.

From the spoor it was clear that lion had done the deed. They must have killed at some time during

the night because hyena had also been involved. We found where the lion had sprung their ambush and where the animal had died. All that remained was a small area of blood-stained sand and some partially digested grass.

Having killed and eaten, they would have walked towards our camp to have a drink and had returned to the same place, where they had collapsed on to the sand for a siesta, which was where we had found them.

I was convinced that it was this group that had been visiting our camp at night. I was pretty certain that it was the male that we had heard roaring and the half-grown female who were responsible for chewing the aluminium wash-hand basins that we had put on a wooden table outside each hut.

That afternoon, a big thunderstorm covered the sky and it looked as if rain was a strong likelihood; the night before it had not been not quite so obvious. As the rainy season was about to commence, we could expect rain every day. This was the last walk of the season and we would have to hurry to get everything packed up in time, otherwise we would not be able to get out because all the rivers between us and Chipata would be full.

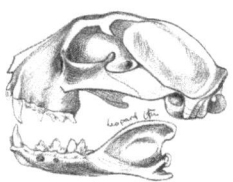

Meeting lion and leopard on walks

We were on a morning walk from Chibembe lodge into the national park. It involved a brief walk from the lodge to the Luangwa river and then a short ride across the river in the fibreglass banana boat, trying not to annoy the hippo that basked on a submerged island at the mouth of the Chibembe river, which joined the Luangwa at that point.

I waited at Reception for my walkers and introduced them to our game scout and the tea-boy. The latter carried a wooden box on his head that contained a brown enamel teapot, two litres of filtered water, a packet of teabags, some sugar, powdered milk, a jar of instant coffee and a packet of biscuits. If we were lucky, the kitchen might have added some cake left over from the dinner the night before.

My walkers were a retired German couple in their sixties. I had chosen a route following the Chibembe river upstream. My aim was to try and see as many species of animal as possible in the three or four hours at our disposal. The walk from the lodge to the boat took about ten minutes. Even though we were not yet in the national park there was often a chance of seeing something interesting – a herd of waterbuck grazing on the river bank, an elephant, even a lion. One always had to be on the alert, however. The feeling that camp was near gave one a false sense of security. There were often lion close to camp.

At the start of any walk I made a point of tuning in to the morning sounds, in particular to alarm calls on this short stroll to the boat. An alarm call from an antelope or baboon or monkey could indicate that a predator was still on the move and we therefore

had a good chance of seeing one. I would also look up into the sky for signs of large raptors because vultures circling could often indicate the presence of a kill. However, vultures need thermals to gain height, and these have not had time to form early in the morning. The path followed the riverbank and passed under tall *Faidherbia albida* trees and through a small grove of *Trichilia emetica* trees. The grass was tall on both sides of the path.

The boatman was waiting for us and we made the crossing. Hippo eyed us as we went into the deeper water. The boatman paddled the canoe on to the hard sand of the opposite riverbank and we climbed out. Off we went. Animals were plentiful and my species score was looking good, though we hadn't seen any predators.

I spotted a sausage tree that was covered in bright-green leaves and a mass of huge crimson flowers and decided to have a closer look. We wandered over and I picked up a few of the large velvet blooms that were scattered about at the base of the tree. The tree was a particularly fine specimen – about twenty metres tall with a broad, straight trunk and branches that grew out horizontally rather like the spokes of an umbrella. A hippo had scattered his dung at the base.

While taking all this into account I noticed fur on the ground – baboon fur. There were tight clumps of it scattered around the base of the tree. There was also some fresh blood on the ground and on the bark of the tree. I showed this to the couple. While I was doing this, Laxon, the tea-boy, whispered something to me. I stopped talking and looked to see what he had seen. He didn't say anything. He just raised his eyes and looked up into the crown of the tree. There

was an excited look on his face. I peered up through the branches and saw a dead baboon, lying on its back in a fork. The fur had been licked off its belly. I pointed this out to the two Germans. They were excited and moved closer to me to have a better look.

I looked back at Laxon to congratulate him. Instead of looking pleased he shook his head and indicated a point even higher up. Peering through the foliage again I got the shock of my life. There, directly above our heads in the crown of the tree, was a very large, very agitated leopard. He was planning his escape route, trying to decide whether to come down the trunk and risk landing on our heads, or to leap out from where he was. He was pretty high up and risked hurting himself.

I knew that I had to make a decision – and quickly. The leopard was about to act. If we stayed, he might land on top of us. But by staying, we might see, for just a fraction of a second, one of the most elusive and most spectacular animals in Africa, right up close. It was an opportunity that would not present itself again. I decided to stay put.

The leopard made his move. He jumped out from the top of the tree in a golden parabola that took him well clear of us. He hit the ground hard, and all the wind came out of his lungs in a sudden gasp that was part growl. He collected himself and was off in a few enormous bounds. We never saw him again. The German couple looked very shocked: they couldn't say anything for some time.

We moved away from the tree and sat down on a bank in the shade to see if the leopard came back; he didn't, so we went back to camp. My scorecard now had a leopard on it – not something that happened very often!

I was with a family group from the Copperbelt – a mother and father, their two daughters and son – and another father and his son. He was a veterinary surgeon; his son, at school in England, was out on holiday. A full house. Locals were always the most difficult to manage because, since they lived in the country, they felt they knew it all. I much preferred people from overseas because they had no illusions and were prepared to listen to what they were told. The scout with us was Mwenda, the one who had been a soldier in the King's African Rifles.

When I had been introduced to the group at supper the night before, I realised that there was a problem. The eldest daughter was very overweight and I could see from her body language that she was uncomfortable with herself and not happy to be on safari. She wouldn't look me in the eye while I was giving my briefing. Her mother asked me how long the walks were, and I tried to reassure her that all would be well.

We were due to spend two nights at Mwamba camp. This was the most isolated of all the walking camps and on the banks of a very pretty lagoon that filled during the rains and received water from the Mwamba river; it was dry most of the year except for a few isolated pools.

The walk from the lodge to the camp was uneventful, but the staff at the camp were excited because the group that had left the camp in the morning had fired a warning shot. From the porters who had brought the luggage out, we learnt that they had come upon lion on the road and that they had young cubs with them. That was exciting. I didn't

pass this bit of news on to the group as I did not want to frighten the mother, who seemed nervous enough already.

For our afternoon walk, I chose to walk towards a bigger lagoon in the vicinity that had hippo, and there was a chance of seeing elephant as well. We spent more time at the lagoon than we should have, so we had to take a shortcut back that led us through a series of thickets where visibility was very poor. It not the best thing to have done.

We came through one of these into a clearing, and there in front of us were three lionesses and several small cubs. One lioness came towards us immediately and the cubs took off after one of the other females. The game scout stood his ground facing the lioness. We slowly retraced our steps, keeping our eyes on the lioness to see what she would do next. Mwenda was watching her all the time and retreating, his rifle at the ready. The whole episode was over in a few seconds, yet it seemed a very long time. We all reached the outer circle of bushes and waited for the scout to catch up with us. Then we formed up again and started walking quickly back to camp, which was by then only a short distance away.

Back at camp, the mother of the two girls came up to me immediately and implored me not to go anywhere near the lion for the walk the following morning. I told her that I intended going in the opposite direction and the chances of seeing lion would be negligible. She believed me, and we had a pleasant evening with a good meal after a hot shower.

The following morning we were up early and out walking just as it was getting light. We followed the dry riverbed of the Mwamba river and saw many

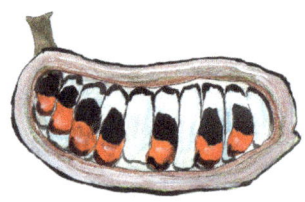

elephant and some giraffe. The tension of the night before had disappeared and all seemed well with the mother and her daughter, who was being very brave but not enjoying the experience one little bit. She walked with her eyes glued to her feet, seeing nothing and hearing nothing.

We stopped to have our tea break at a point on the river where there were some pools in the sand that elephant had dug. We had a pleasant break, sitting in the shade of a big tamarind tree that grew out of a tall termite mound and sipping the tea that our tea-boy had made on an open fire using dried elephant dung and grass. There were some slices of sponge cake from the night before as well. It was all very pleasant and relaxing. The vet, who had spent every spare moment climbing trees, shinned up the tamarind tree and scanned the bush for game.

When we were thoroughly rested, we started back to camp. We came on a very big bull elephant, spent some time getting close to him, and went on. It was then that I spotted something a long way off that with a tawny coat. It had a long body. It was not an antelope. Too big for a baboon. The only thing it could be was a lion. I pointed it out to Mwenda.

The lioness spotted us at about the same time and charged without thinking twice about it. From nowhere, another lioness appeared, joined the first, and together they came for us. We retreated to a tree and stopped, hoping that the lions would also stop, but nothing of the kind. They never slowed a bit; if anything, they accelerated. We retreated a little bit further and stopped, but still they came on.

They were now very close. The vet was trying to find a tree to climb but without success. I whispered to Mwenda to shoot. A lioness presents a very small target head-on. If he failed to kill her outright, she would be enraged on top of all the other emotions that had prompted her to charge in the first instance. I pulled the German bayonet that I carried on my belt around to the front.

By now the lionesses were so close that even if Mwenda fired and brought one down, the other one would be on us just from her momentum alone. If he wounded her we would have two big angry cats on top of us, creating havoc with tooth and nail. Not a pleasant way to go! What would I say to the mother if we managed to get out alive after all this? How could I possibly explain to her the circumstances of another encounter with lion so soon after the first?

The wait for the shot was unbelievably long. Mwenda was kneeling. His left elbow was resting on his left knee to give himself maximum stability and a steady aim. All his army training was centred on this one shot. He had summed up the situation in much the same way I had. His target was extremely small and moving fast across the ground. Quite impossible in the circumstances. The shot when it came was a huge relief. There was a very loud bang. The shot was a good one. Definitely aimed to kill. And he missed. But only just!

The shot went under her belly and threw sand in her face, the force of the shot spooking her sufficiently without wounding her. She ran on for a bit, slowed and stopped. Her companion ran a bit further and also stopped.

'Whew!' The relief that flooded through the group was unbelievable.

'Let's get out of here,' was all I could think to say. We retreated quickly in single file in case the lions changed their minds. On the way we passed the

old bull elephant, still feeding contentedly and unconcerned by the noise of the .375 shot. We reached camp and everybody headed to their huts in silence to gather their wits.

On this occasion, we left camp just as it was getting light and headed for Zebra Flats, a large expanse of grassland along the Mwamba river. The river did a series of tight loops, and during the rains the water overflowed and flooded the very flat countryside, producing long grass that was very attractive to zebra and buffalo. As we left the mopane woodland, the Zebra Flats stretched ahead of us to the horizon.

As soon as we stepped out from the trees a lion started roaring to our right. It was answered by another one a long way out on the plain. This went on for a few minutes, then stopped. It was obvious that the lion doing the calling was trying to locate members of its own pride. If we could make contact with that one then it might lead us to the others.

I started walking in the direction of the lion that had roared first, hoping it would call again. It did. While it was calling, we went as fast as we could towards the sound, and when I felt we were close enough, I stopped behind a dead mopane tree that gave us some cover. I got out my binoculars and started a very thorough search to try and locate this lion. It took a little while. The light was poor but I eventually spotted the lioness before she stopped calling.

As soon as she had received a reply from her mates, she started walking towards them. I let her go and followed her through my binoculars. The grass was short and there was no other vegetation

to hide her as she loped along. She walked without stopping for about twenty minutes and then dropped down into the grass. I made a careful note of the exact spot, using a particular tree and some bushes as markers. With these firmly placed in my mind, we set off. There were nine people in our group: six clients, plus myself, the tea-boy and the scout. Almost a cricket team. Surely the lion would see us and run away long before we got even close. There was no cover – the grass we were walking through was knee-high.

The sun was up now and it was starting to get hot. There was no shade as we set off in single file across the plain with just the very distant marker in the tuft of grass that I had in my mind to guide us. As we went along, I kept keeping this in sight in case the lion decided to move. On we went. It got hotter and hotter, and I began to worry whether the whole exercise was a complete waste of time. I am sure that my clients were thinking exactly the same.

My marker was less than a hundred meters away. I told everybody to hush. We moved forward more cautiously. We were heading towards a patch of tall grass shaded by low bushes. I stopped, raised my binoculars and had a really good look. I got the shock of my life. I could make out the ear of a lioness. She was facing away from us and lying down.

I turned to my clients and pointed, nodding my head at the same time. The lion were about forty metres away at this point. The doctor from Lusaka couldn't see them. She took a step to one side and left the line. That did it. One of the lionesses saw the movement, sat up and growled. Three others woke up and turned to face us. I told everybody to stand still. The first lioness growled and swished her tail.

The scout cocked his rifle. The hard metallic sound was enough. One lioness bolted, and so did her three friends. We watched them disappear into the long grass. It was as if they had never existed. We started walking back towards the shade. I halted under a tree and then we started talking excitedly.

Walking from Chikoko camp to Kasansanya camp, one had to cover quite a lot of territory and in the process pass through Zebra Flats. At some point I heard a baboon making its alarm call a long way in the distance. I always respond to alarm calls from baboons because they have very good eyesight and roam widely. The game scout with me was Mwenda.

After walking for about half an hour, we reached a grove of mopane trees that fringed a large expanse of open grassland. At this stage in the dry season, the grass had been trampled down by buffalo and elephant so was now quite short and visibility was good. Vultures were spiralling down to perch on a dead mopane tree on the far side of this expanse of grass. I was convinced that somewhere there must be a kill. The challenge was to find it before the lion spotted us and vanished: it was getting hot, and lion like to move off into the shade after feeding while it was cool. Once they leave a kill, vultures very quickly polish off what remains.

The baboon that had been calling was sitting in one of the mopane trees that we could see on the far side of this grassy area. We were well hidden, so it was just a matter of spending some time scanning the area with binoculars to see what was upsetting him.

I spotted some tawny shapes clustered

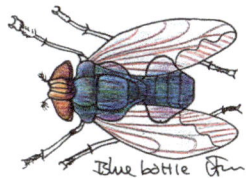

around something in the middle of the grassy area. They were lions and they had killed a young buffalo. As we moved closer to the edge of the trees, we disturbed a leopard who had smelled the meat and was being inquisitive. He growled as he bounded off.

We watched the lion feeding as best we could. I knew that as soon as we left the trees they would spot us and run away; we had to be patient and wait to get the full benefit of this amazing spectacle. When everybody had had a good look, I signalled to Mwenda that we should go and have a closer look. The instant we left the trees the lion saw us and scattered.

There was not much left of the kill: the hide was bunched up in untidy parcels, the ribs stripped, the stomach contents pushed to the side. It was hot and smelly and a myriad of blue-bottle flies were buzzing about. We took a few photos and left. No sooner had we gone than the vultures descended en masse.

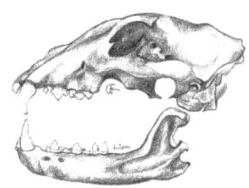

North Luangwa National Park

Wilderness Trails was bought by a big London-based company called Hayes and Jarvis. They were professionals and had a thoroughly modern approach to running an operation, which differed markedly from that of my former bosses. They owned lodges all over the world. In the opinion of Dick Pitman, who was sent out to make the necessary changes, there were too many managers at Chibembe. I was demoted from 'safari manager' to 'safari guide'. He believed that if you were a guide, that is what you should be; you couldn't be both a guide and manager. I realised it was time to move on.

I resigned from Wilderness Trails at the end of 1988. I was sorry to leave Chibembe. Some of my happiest moments had been spent there. I would miss the companionship built up over many years – the guides, certain characters who had been there from the moment I started, the kitchen staff and the ground staff.

What was I to do next? The walks at Chibembe had given me a passion for walking safaris. Very few operators did long walks, the sort I had in mind. For walking you need rivers – rivers to provide water for drinking and also to support wildlife. Animals are always near water. So are birds.

I had no capital to buy vehicles or a permanent camp. Vehicles are expensive both to buy and to run. I was good at building camps. If I could find an unspoiled area with good game and that had safe walking opportunities, that was what I was looking for. If I could rely on porters to carry the equipment, on small portable tents, and had a comfortable base camp with a good standard of finish, that would suffice.

Access would be an issue, but if there was an airstrip close by, we could bring our clients in by charter like the hunters did. We could also bring in supplies each time a charter flight arrived.

A friend of mine was trying to sell his business. The local currency, the kwacha, was worthless, and many people who had kwacha were trying to get rid of it in a hurry. The sale of the business didn't go according to plan. I used what capital I had, and my friend pledged what kwacha he had, as well as some of his own precious hard currency, so that I could qualify for an investment licence. I had no knowledge of running a business – I was not a businessman by any stretch of the imagination. This money was enough for initial exploration and an investment licence only – I would have to find another investor very soon. My friend also provided a Land-Rover and office space in Lusaka, so I had all I needed to get started.

Good communications were vital. I needed to have two or three VHF radios that we could carry while out walking and have in a vehicle with two HF radios to connect with town. The camp needed a generator, a good deep-freeze and a fridge for the bar. Showers could be managed along the lines of Chibembe, with solar panels for lighting. It also needed a spectacular view, with animals during the day, and had to be permanently on water, with good shade during the day. It needed to be close to an area with animals that one could walk to, and have the possibility of a long walk with varied terrain. I just had to find one.

I had heard fabulous stories about the North Luangwa National Park. It was referred to as a natural wonderland, unspoiled and teaming with game. I knew that Peter Hankin, the professional hunter for my father on his last safari, had been there. He had given up hunting and had been operating photographic safaris for a few years before he was killed one night in his camp on the Mwaleshi river.

An emaciated lioness had come into the camp the night before and eaten the sugar off the dining-room table. The following night she returned. Peter slept in a tent, some distance from his staff quarters. He was fond of his whisky and slept with the flap of his tent unzipped. The lioness had entered his tent and pulled him out; she had hardly any teeth at all. He screamed for help but his staff were too terrified to come out of their tent and start the Land-Rover to shoo the lioness off. He died, and his body was found the following morning. Adrian Carr, Norman Carr's son, arrived, found his remains and shot the lioness.

The following year I found the remains of his camp. All that was left was the toilet drum, sticking out of the ground, and the trees under which he had pitched his tents. The river had moved at least three hundred metres from its original course. I based Johnnie Pascoe, one of the characters in my novel, *Cleopatra's Journey*, on Peter Hankin.

The problem with the North is access: there are virtually no roads into the park. The western Muchinga escarpment is very steep. Two dirt roads come down the escarpment from the Great North Road in the vicinity of Mpika, one to the north and one to the south of the town. The one to the south of Mpika joins the corridor between the North and South parks. At the top is a memorial to Mary Gough, an ecologist who studied elephant: she had a camp on the Mupamadzi river and had died mysteriously.

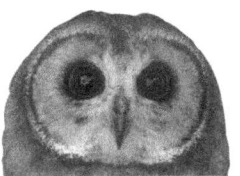

The character of Amanda Stockdale in *Cleopatra's Journey* is based on her. This road is of little use, as you still have to cross the Munyamadzi river, which flows parallel to the road. It is broad, fast-flowing and deep. Even then, you have the Luawata hunting area before you reach the boundary of the North Luangwa park.

The road to the north of Mpika eventually reaches Marula-Puku, the Owens's camp, in the park itself. On the main road you pass the turning to Shiwa Ng'andu and Kapishya Hot Springs, the stately home of the eccentric Sir Stewart Gore-Browne. His grandson operates safaris at the top end of the Mwaleshi river.

From the eastern escarpment you can reach the park off the Great East Road from the town of Lundazi. This, again, is a bad road, and when it reaches the valley floor it becomes very wet and marshy. The problem with an approach from Lundazi is that, once you reach the Luangwa river, there is no way of crossing it except by driving across at a shallow, sandy point. To find such a place requires local knowledge, which I didn't have at that time.

On my first approach from the eastern escarpment, I headed towards Lumimba Mission, where there was a Dutch missionary by the name of Father Van der Pol. He came from Friesland in the Netherlands and was a very strong and resourceful person who spoke the local languages and knew the people well. At that time he must have been in his seventies and was the only white person at the mission. In his bedroom was a narrow iron bed, the sort you find in hospitals, covered by a mosquito net. Each evening at 6.00, he

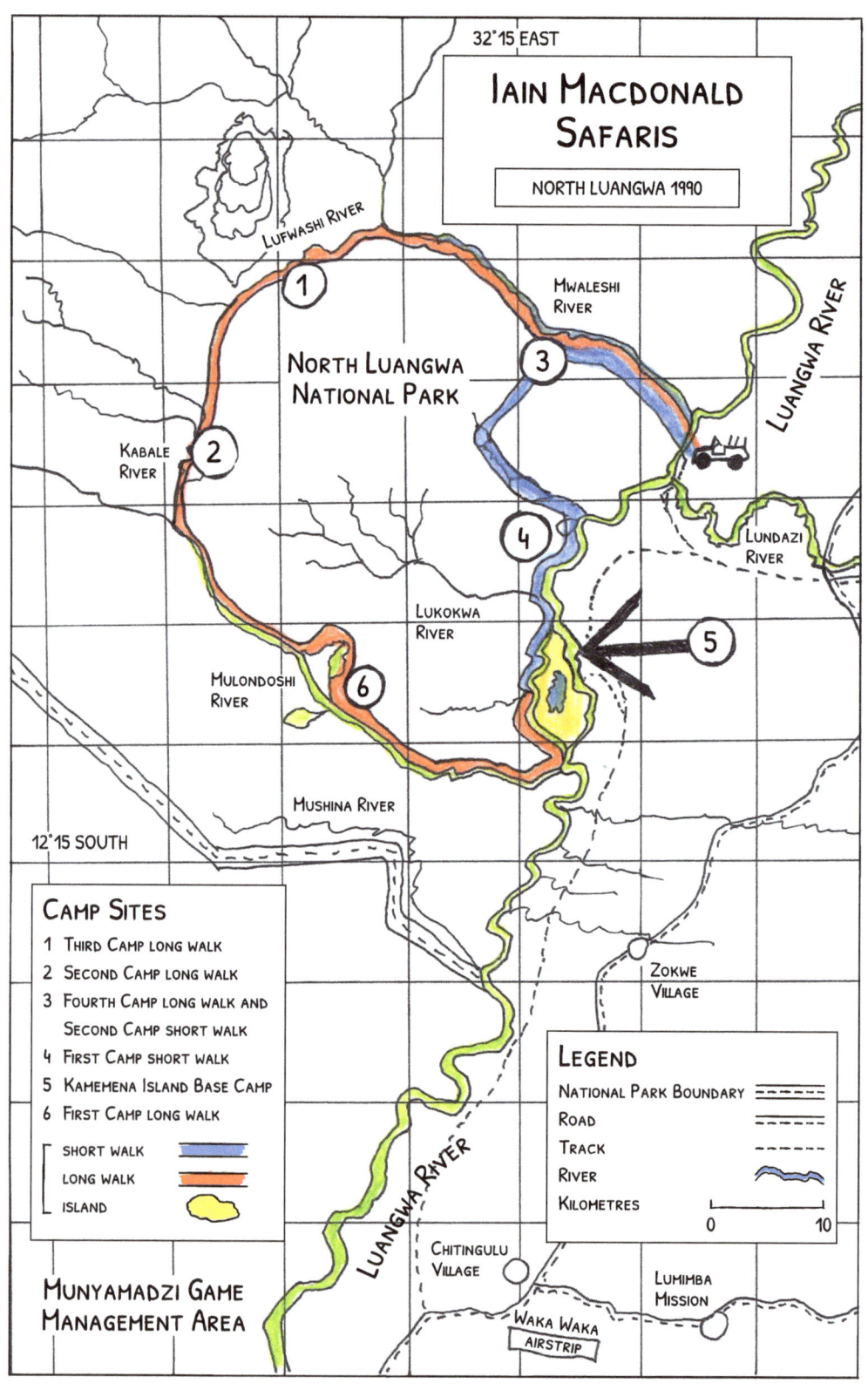

locked the doors of his house and they remained locked until the morning service.

I pitched my tent under a palm tree outside the residence. In the morning I discovered that the palm tree was the roosting place for hundreds of small insectivorous bats, who had showered my tent all night with their droppings. The mission had a few pawpaw trees, lemons and tomatoes.

The Father had a white Mercedes 4×4 truck that he used to buy the people provisions during the rains. The rainy season was a very hard time for the villagers because the roads became impassable and food was scarce until their crops were reaped. He gave me useful information about roads and access, and was able to recommend reliable people to work for me.

A year later, men from the village approached his house before he closed the doors for the night. One carried a rifle, the others machetes. One struck him on the head with a machete, another fired a shot at him with the rifle. The shot went through the roof. He wrestled with his attacker and managed shake him off before running out and into the church, where he rang the bell for help. In the process, he had been partially scalped and a flap of skin was hanging over his eyes. He was bundled into a vehicle and driven to a clinic where he was stitched up.

The thieves had been convinced that he had a stash of money hidden away. He received medical treatment in the Netherlands and returned to the mission the following year. Everybody knew who had done it; he pardoned his attackers. In conversation, he told me that in all the years he had been in the area he felt that his presence had not made the slightest difference. The people were still as superstitious as ever.

On my second visit, it was the first of May. I drove up from Lusaka to Chipata, where I did some shopping at the market and then proceeded north towards Lundazi. It was getting dark and I wanted to get away from the environs of Chipata before stopping for the night. I drove for an hour and, seeing what I thought was a grove of natural forest by the road and no sign of any village, I left the road and parked under the trees.

I pitched my little tent and lit a fire. I cooked a meal that I shared with my driver. He slept in the Land-Rover and I went to bed. I was just falling asleep when there was a loud shot and voices. I was too tired to bother about it so went back to sleep. In the morning, a group of villagers came along and apologised for shooting at us with a shotgun. They had thought we were cattle rustlers.

I borrowed a game scout from Chanjuzi scout camp and drove to the Luangwa river along a hunting track. I had an idea for a camp from the map.

The Land-Rover wouldn't start when it was hot, so the secret was not to stall. It stalled crossing a rocky riverbed. All my efforts to get it going again came to nothing. We left the Land-Rover where it was, lit a fire and made tea. My driver suggested wrapping my wet underpants around the condenser to cool it – it worked!

We got to the very spot I had in mind, an island, but how to cross? The river was about two hundred yards wide and deep in places. Crocs were visible along the banks. I parked the Land-Rover on a steep slope on the river's edge. When we got back to it I

let it freewheel down the slope before engaging the clutch. Fortunately, it started before we ended up in the river!

On the way back to Lusaka, we spent a night at Chanjuzi scout camp. I pitched my small tent with its mesh windows in a grassy patch not far from a tap. The place was swarming with mosquitoes. I doubled up on the malarial tablets I was taking, but when I got back to Lusaka I went down with a very bad dose of malaria. There were three types of malaria parasite in my blood. I recovered quickly after a course of tablets.

There was a good airstrip nearby called Waka Waka that was used almost exclusively by the local hunting operators. Chakolwa game scout camp was also nearby. Mobil Oil had recently cut a network of tracks through the whole valley when they were prospecting for oil, which were very useful for safari guides in areas without roads.

Mark and Delia Owens

Mark and Delia Owens were two Americans who had worked in Botswana putting radio tracking collars on lion and hyena. They had written a very readable book, *The Cry of the Kalahari*. They had set themselves up in the park to do research on lion using radio collars. I met them through the Luangwa Research and Development Project.

Mark had a single-engined aeroplane that he flew from an airstrip outside his camp, Marula-Puku, on anti-poaching sorties. On my first visit, he flew me over the park, looking for potential sites. They had been very successful in getting the backing of the Frankfurt Zoological Society with the long-term

An aerial view of Mark Owens's camp, Marula-Puku, in North Luangwa National Park.

Phineas burns poaching racks left by poachers

aim of reintroducing black rhino into the park. The buildings of the camp are made of river stone, and it sits on a small tributary under marula trees, from which it gets its name. Puku browse the shore line.

Mark was very keen to get safari operators into the park as a deterrent to the poachers who had been operating there for a long time with very little interference from the authorities.

Using information gathered from maps and flights with Mark Owens, I steadily built up a picture of where I would like to be. From the air I had spotted a beautiful lagoon full of hippo; there were good shade trees, too. It seemed to be an ideal spot. What made the site even more interesting was that it was on an island formed by the Luangwa splitting into two. Several large rivers came into the Luangwa at that point and they would provide good walking opportunities.

First, though, I needed to find it on foot. The only way was to try to reach it by walking south from the Mwaleshi river that meets the Luangwa river, which meant coming in from Mpika on the Great North Road.

I reached Marula-Puku camp in the afternoon, hoping to spend the night with the Owenses, only to be told that they were not there but were expected very shortly in their small aeroplane. The only problem was that there was no vehicle to collect them: one had gone for repair, another had been taken out and had not returned. The usual story.

I went back to the airstrip and met the plane and drove them to their camp. They had two American friends with them. Our Land-Rover was full of our camping gear, so, once we had loaded all their

luggage, Delia and their two visitors from America, Mark had to sit on the bonnet.

The next day I borrowed a game scout from Mark and drove to the confluence of the Luangwa and Mwaleshi. The grass was very long: it was like driving through deep water. I could not see where to go. I got the scout to sit on the roof with a stick, which he pointed either to the left or to the right to indicate where I should drive. If he took the stick away altogether, it meant that I had to stop because there was a big hole. We passed lion in the long grass.

We reached the Mwaleshi–Luangwa confluence and camped. The next morning we waded the Mwaleshi river and walked along the Luangwa, heading south until we reached the point where the river split into two, forming the island on which the lagoon that I had in mind as a campsite was. It was too late to investigate any further so we walked back to the Mwaleshi and slept by the vehicle. The following day we drove back to the Owenses and out to Mpika.

I realised that access would have to come from the Great East Road. I visited the regional headquarters of National Parks in Lundazi and got a very good game scout by the name of Phineas. He was with me all the time I was operating in the North park. I drove with him from Lundazi and, by following a hunting road that ran parallel to the Luangwa river and using the cut lines left over from the Mobil Oil exploration, I reached a point that was adjacent to the lagoon I was looking for.

Phineas and I waded the river. After that it was easy to find the lagoon by looking for the vivid green of *Trichilia* trees. It was full of hippo, and had very good shade, with duck aplenty in the water and on the bank.

A short walk from the camp and you reached the other branch of the Luangwa. The water acted as a boundary fence – like a medieval castle with a moat that made it easy to defend. The site had a grove of tall *Trichilia* trees, which are the best trees for shade as they do not shed their leaves and make a mess. By the lagoon were also several very tall *Faidherbia albida* trees. Although not great shade trees, they provide ideal roosting branches for large birds such as Fish Eagles.

Phineas remarked how beautiful the site was, and his comment finally decided me. This would be my base camp. I named it the Kamemena Island camp, Kamemena being the local name for the wild gardenia, *Gardenia thunbergia*; there were many growing around the camp.

I decided to build the sleeping huts under the *Trichilia* trees. The camp would have four client huts, two senior staff huts, a kitchen under an albida, a storeroom and a bar/dining room. The bar/dining room would be close to the water and under another tall albida.

Year one
I built the sleeping huts with ideas from *The Marsh Arabs*, a book by Wilfred Thesiger. The Arabs in the Tigris–Euphrates valley built enormous structures out of reeds called *mudhifs*. They bound the reeds into long bundles, one end being buried in the ground and bent over so that it met the opposing bundle. They were then bound together to form a perfect arch. A large building would have a row of twelve of these bundles, each of similar girth to a human's.

The height of a very large *mudhif* would be at

least fifteen metres and could seat twenty people sitting side by side along the walls. In width they are eight metres from wall to wall and the roof and sides are covered in matting. The front wall is made of very intricate basket-work. The design has not changed in five thousand years, and early examples are visible in stone carvings from Sumer. Gertrude Bell sent back the first photographs of *mudhifs* in 1920.

Instead of reeds, I used millet stalks, which are abundant in the fields after the millet has been reaped, bound together with palm leaves soaked in water.

My friend had failed to sell his business. He gave me what kwacha he could lay his hands on, but it was much less than I needed. It would not be enough to keep the operation going until I started generating income. I needed to find someone else to invest in my business.

I tried everybody I knew but to no avail. Eventually, an expat accountant whom I had approached to prepare a feasibility study found the figures attractive and agreed to finance the operation, but only as long as it made money for him. He also found someone else who was involved in farming and local politics who came on side.

My plans to fly my clients up to Waka Waka were scuttled when the price of aero-fuel doubled overnight. I was forced to arrange to fly my clients on regular Zambian Airways flights to Mfuwe.

I visited Harare in Zimbabwe and bought bedding and linen and crockery. I bought a small Honda generator in Lusaka and a Minus40 refrigerator from South Africa. I flew to London to buy radios and then on to New York to do some marketing.

Getting over the water on one side of the island was difficult at the beginning of the dry season, but as the water level dropped it became easier and easier. We found a shallow part that we marked with sticks.

Getting off the island on the north side required a boat, and I ordered a banana boat from a factory in Lusaka. Banana boats are long and heavy. How to carry it around? I designed a structure on the roof of our Land-Cruiser to which we could attach the boat without having to have a trailer.

In Lusaka I designed toilets and had them made out of galvanised iron at an Indian metal-working place. The banana boat arrived with other equipment from Lusaka.

Year two

Accommodation for my senior staff was on the bank of the river behind the kitchen so that it would be a short walk for the kitchen staff at night. The remainder of the staff lived over the river beside the road into the camp.

I built an airstrip with our porters so that Mark could land and convey messages to us. I gave him one of our Yaesu VHF radios; another I left at Chibembe lodge so that we could connect with them in terms of booking our clients when they arrived by plane.

I built a beautiful oven out of clay using the design from a book published by the Intermediate Technology Group in London; it had been tested in Guatemala.

I brought with me some of the staff from Chibembe that I had got on well with and who lived in the area:

Amber and Robin Harland, my first client, make the crossing from Kamemena Island to the mainland at the start of the long walk.

Amber sitting with Simon Barnes, a bird enthusiast from the London *Times* newspaper, on a North Luangwa walk.

Phineas, always smart and confident.

North Luangwa walk.
Left to right: Robin Harland, Robbie, Phineas and me.

At the end of the first long walk with Robin Harland and the team.
On the sand (*left to right*) are: me, Amber, Robin Harland, Peter Carlson.
Behind, on the log (*right to left*): Alec Zimba second from right, Phineas third from right, Robbie fourth from right..

Tax Ngoma, who was reaching retirement age but was a very experienced cook; Simon Zulu, who was a very good gardener; and Richard, a waiter from the walks. Others I found from my labour gang, who came from the local villages.

Lameck Phiri was a driver with a lot of local knowledge and expertise; he serviced the Land-Rover. Lameck had worked for a hunting company and knew everybody. Driving through the villages, he chatted to people he met along the way, so what should have been a quick trip took twice as long. He told me of a woman who had been pregnant for eighteen months. She had obviously had a miscarriage but had cleverly hidden the fact from her husband. She became pregnant again and gave birth successfully the second time.

I wanted Simon Zulu to grow vegetables on the east bank of the Luangwa river: as we were so far from any market, vegetables would be hard to find. I met up with Peter Carlson, who had come on a walk with me at Chibembe lodge. He was from Australia, where he had a business leasing out equipment to pop groups and was happy to provide technical assistance and companionship. He was also a good walker and keen on the bush.

When we started getting the camp up and running, Amber, my young Irish caterer, found a python wrapped around her toilet seat. It must have been living in the pit during the rains, and when the toilet drum was placed over the hole the following year it could not escape. Amber got the shock of her life when she raised the lid and had every reason to suffer from incontinence ever after!

Simon Barnes, a correspondent for the London *Times*, visited us in his capacity as bird enthusiast

The Bolnick group from America wade the Mwaleshi on a morning walk that took all day. Phineas is leading.

Returning to camp on the Mwaleshi river after a walk.

Our camp on the Mwaleshi river.

Alec Zimba leading the porters on a North Luangwa walk.

and not as sports writer. He reminded me of a 1960s hippie with his long hair and beard. He came equipped with Timberland boots and a burning desire to find a Bat Hawk. We found one for him.

Wherever we walked in those early days, we came on drying racks left by poachers. A popular spot was at the mouth of the Mulondoshi river at the southernmost tip of the island. If you stopped to rest under a tree when out walking, a Hooded Vulture would soon alight in a tree close to you. They associated food with people – and the only people they would have encountered to develop this relationship would have been poachers.

One of our staff out fishing spotted a group of poachers camped under a grove of trees on our side of the island and within walking distance of our camp. I realised we were in a difficult position. We could not become too aggressive, but on the other hand we needed to establish our territorial rights. We decided to attack them one early morning. In the encounter, our waiter caught one of the poachers, though the others escaped. As we were walking away, I turned to check whether we were being followed and saw a head looking at us from above the grass. I fired a shot over his head and he ducked smartly.

We took the poacher to National Parks, but instead of being grateful they were quite the opposite. They wanted to have as little to do with him as possible. Having discovered where he came from, they told us to take him to Mpika, his home area. This was quite impossible, so we just left him with them, having done everything we could.

Initially, with no real knowledge of the area, it was difficult for me to know where to start. The only way to get to know an area is to walk it. There were no roads, and no one who had any knowledge knew where it was best to go. Phil Berry, who had done a lot of anti-poaching work, had positive things to say about the Mulondoshi river, though there were, of course, poachers there. I studied the maps I had, looking avidly for rivers that could contain water – always a good way to find animals and an easy route to walk.

The Mulondoshi river had water most of the year, and there were lagoons a few kilometres upstream with permanent water. The Lukokwa river also had rock pools upstream and one had a big crocodile in it. The Mwaleshi river had all the game, but we were a long way away from it. I decided to walk along the Luangwa as far as a lagoon, and from there head inland following a hippo path until we reached another lagoon. Then I would cut across country to the Mwaleshi river, spending two nights there and walking down the Mwaleshi to the Luangwa, where we had a boat to cross the Luangwa and a vehicle to drive back to camp.

The Harveys from Shiwa Ng'andu were using the top part of the Mwaleshi for their safari operation. John Coppinger from Chibembe had built a camp at the bottom end of the Mwaleshi river.

I did an exploratory walk up the Mulondoshi river with Peter Carlson, a young Australian volunteer and friend, intending to meet up with the Lufwashi river and reach the Mwaleshi. This was the route for the long walk advertised in my brochure, which took in the usual riverine environment with more diverse upland areas and some escarpment forest.

We found a series of lagoons nestled in good woodland. Buffalo used the lagoons and we found one stuck in the mud. I asked one of the porters to give it a crack on the head with his axe to put it out of its misery.

We stopped for lunch on a high bank where there was plentiful water in the sand below. We heard voices. These were poachers who had spotted us and were interested in talking to us. Two actually strolled into camp while were resting. We caught one of them and Phineas handcuffed him.

As we got higher up, the terrain became more interesting; there were tall palm trees. We saw a small herd of hartebeest and an oribi, which you never see in the South Luangwa park. The tsetse fly were very bad.

We reached the junction with the Kabale river, and the terrain changed. We slept that night by a pool. In the morning the poacher had vanished. I was sure that Phineas had released him after having cut a deal with him.

We reached the Lufwashi below the prominent mountain that one sees at the top end of the Mwaleshi and camped there for the night. The next day we climbed the mountain.

After that, Peter and I walked up to the Owens's camp with Phineas, leaving the porters with Alec Zimba. We radioed our camp and got Lameck to come up and meet us in the Land-Rover.

My new shareholder wanted to get Mark Owens to take us on a flip around the area so that we could spot concentrations of game. We slept in the dining room in sleeping bags as we were due to take off at 7.00 a.m. before it got too hot. I climbed on to the back of their smart orange Unimog truck and was standing behind the cab; Phineas was beside me.

As we were due to leave, an assistant appeared

A view of Kamemena Island camp from across the lagoon showing the dining room and bar.

My friend Ki'i Idenburg, who helped with catering at Kamemena Island

Ki'i Idenburg and Peter Carlson in the dining-room under the *Faidherbia albida* tree on the edge of the lagoon at Kamemena Island. A cobra lived in the pole behind Peter.

Tax Ngoma, our cook at Kamemena camp, demonstrates the clay oven he used to cook bread and fancy dishes.

The interior of a hut made from grass, mopane poles and millet stalks.

The front of my hut in Kamemena camp, North Luangwa, incorporating ideas from Wilfred Thesiger's book, *The Marsh Arabs*.

and asked Mark if he could attach a Land-Cruiser to the truck to get a pull start. Mark half heard and nodded. Someone else appeared and got into conversation with Mark. By this time Mark had completely forgotten about the Land-Cruiser, which was now attached by a chain to the tow-hitch of the Unimog. He finished his conversation, put the Unimog into gear and accelerated. The chain attached to the Land-Cruiser snapped and whipped over the back of the Unimog. The tip clipped me behind the head and buried itself in my forehead. I fell unconscious.

Delia appeared with the first-aid kit, and instead of it being a pleasant game-viewing flight, it became an emergency run to Chilonga mission hospital near Mpika. As we landed, Mark was unwilling to spend time on the airstrip as he had had an argument with an anti-poaching unit the day before who had refused to go out on patrol. In his exasperation he had drawn his revolver and fired into the ground at their feet. As we were landing, a military vehicle was seen approaching the plane, so Mark dropped me and Phineas with the engine running, turned, and flew straight back to Marula-Puku.

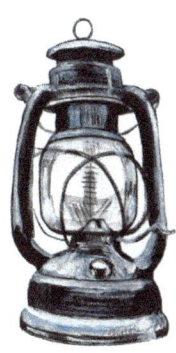

I was picked up by a driver from Luangwa Research and Development Project and taken to the hospital, where I received a few stitches and a big bandage. Later in the afternoon, Delia drove all the way up and took me down again to their camp. Mark was convinced that he was about to be arrested and was nowhere to be seen. He had packed a back-pack with food and a radio and gone out into the bush with his rifle.

On another occasion, I decided to take the same shareholder on a safari to some local lagoons – those that I had found earlier with Peter Carlson. We sent

the porters up ahead with Alec Zimba to build the camp. We set off a little later, and in the distance we saw a line of a hundred poachers walking in single file; they had five guns in the party. We turned back.

That evening our porters reappeared and told us that they were about to set up camp when they had met this group. They managed to talk their way out of it by pretending to be poachers themselves and sneaked back, carrying all the equipment with them. Alec had hidden himself in a bush so as not to be recognised.

I made contact with a South African agent who wanted to visit us and see what our operation consisted of. I warned her that it was very early days and that we had not yet worked out where to take our clients. I told her that she could walk with us but that it would cover new ground for me, so she would have to be prepared for some tough walking, some of it in very boring woodland. She arrived with a photographer and a travel writer from the magazine Man Magnum. Amber came along, too.

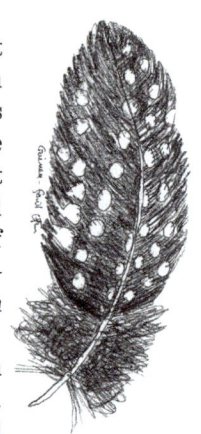

On the first evening, I noticed the two South Africans huddled together, studying their blisters. The next day we set off and were watching a small group of male buffaloes coming down to drink. I had positioned us so that we could watch them but, much to my surprise, we noticed two lionesses waiting in ambush for them. The buffalo picked up their scent, and instead of retreating they came forward and attacked the lions – who had to retreat instead.

After that, the walk went through very boring countryside, with little to see. By the time we stopped for the night we were all very tired. The two were very silent and angry. To break the tension, Amber and I had a mud fight. When we reached the

Luangwa river and the vehicle, I knew we had not scored. The agent threatened to sue me later on and made all sorts of threats about arresting me if I ever landed in Johannesburg.

My safari strategy

I arranged for my clients to fly into Mfuwe from Lusaka on the regular daily Zambian Airways flight and booked them into Chibembe lodge for their first night. I spent the night there too, and drove them to my camp the following morning. We spent two nights in Kamemena Island camp before setting out on our long walk. There was a hot spring nearby and we would have a swim in the hot water and take sundowners with us.

At the start of the walk to the Mwaleshi river, we crossed the Luangwa north of camp by banana boat. We walked until midday, then stopped at a temporary camp that we had set up on the riverbank. From there we walked inland towards the Mwaleshi, stopping at midday for lunch and a rest. Wildebeest came galloping past us while we were resting on one occasion.

The porters went ahead of us and set up the camp on the Mwaleshi in a beautiful grove of trees. We spent two nights there and did local walks. On the last day, we walked down the Mwaleshi to where it met the Luangwa, where we were met by the vehicle that took us back to camp.

At least this provided me with a safari scheme that worked logistically while I had time to explore other routes and find other interesting places to visit that had game and pleasant scenery. I very much wanted to explore the Mulondoshi and try to build it into my walk repertoire, but that would take more time.

Finding lion and leopard
I had been operating in the North Luangwa National Park only for a very short time when I got my first international booking. This group had come through an agent that I had had dealings with from my Chibembe lodge days. She operated out of Tucson, Arizona, and her sister was in the group with her husband, a big confidant man and a captain with one of the big American airlines. There was another couple who were their friends.

It was an afternoon walk and not supposed to provide much in excitement or variety. We had done our long walk in the morning. I decided to walk along our airstrip because at one end it came close to the riverbank and there were sometimes crocodiles to be seen and possibly a hippo out of the water. We were totally exposed. There was not a scrap of cover, as it had all been cleared to make the airstrip. I was not even looking for anything in particular, just aiming to reach the river and then see what we could see.

We sauntered along, the riverbank about fifty meters away. I looked ahead and got the shock of my life: there, facing away from us, lying side by side, was a pair of lions. This was a courting couple, the female in season and the male her escort.

The scout had not seen them, nor had my clients. I whispered to Phineas and pointed, without drawing attention to ourselves. The only thing we could do was retreat quietly and try to put as much distance between ourselves and the lion before they noticed us.

To watch mating lion from a raised seat in a safari vehicle with the engine running is one thing. To do it when you are on the same level as the lion, close enough that you can see the fly perched on the

end of its nose, without a tree or scrap of cover to hide behind, is quite another thing.

Not only that, we were now within what I would call the lion's red zone – the invisible ring that a lion will not allow another predator to enter without permission, because that would imply a threat. We had just done that, and we had not asked permission. We were now a threat. When you feel threatened, you attack – it is a basic instinct. I knew very well where we stood as far as that was concerned.

The male was so infatuated with his partner that he proceeded to mount her. As we watched, with emotions ranging from amazement to absolute terror, the male climbed off and lay down again. The female nonchalantly turned her head to lick her tail. And then the penny dropped. She saw us. The idyll was shattered for the honeymooners. She spun round, faced us with a look of pure hate, and charged. Her lover, caught in post-coital bliss, took a second or two to come to his senses but also charged, growling and expressing emotions that had a lot to do with heightened testosterone, outrage at being caught off guard, and resentment at having been made to look a fool on camera.

'Don't move,' I shouted. My shout gave me courage, and this emboldened Phineas, who brandished his rifle defiantly, holding it at arm's length and shaking it. I think I shouted again and waved my arms and the poor lioness took fright. She swerved past us and ran off at a gallop towards the river. Her beau came on for a bit longer but then he, too, thought better of it – he didn't want to let his lady out of his sight for one second. He followed her in a series of extended bounds that took him over the bank in a cloud of dust and out of sight.

There was nothing much more we could do then, other than walk slowly back to camp. You can't top the sighting of lion on a walk. You certainly can't top the sighting, on foot, of mating lion, followed by a charge, and without the need for a warning shot. We were all perfectly intact. None of us had suffered any form of hurt. All that had changed was our blood pressure and heart rates. Both had risen dramatically!

On the walk back to camp we all tried to gather our wits. I think I tried to be chatty and play the event off as just another exciting moment to be enjoyed to the full while walking through the African jungle. The American airline captain never said a word. I learnt from his sister-in-law – much, much later – that the experience had totally traumatised him. Never had he ever felt so exposed and so helpless in all his life. Flying jumbo jets, he always knew what to do in a crisis, but when those lion appeared, he had to rely on someone else. He had expected Phineas to blow the lion to bits with his rifle. All Phineas had done was wave his arms and shout. It had made no sense at all. He put Africa out of his mind and never wanted to hear the word ever again.

This had been the start of a long walk that would culminate in several nights on the Mwaleshi river, which was a long way from us at that point. We were following the Luangwa river itself and our destination that day was a temporary camp upstream on the Luangwa, close to a lagoon. It would take us five hours of walking to reach the camp with a stop for tea mid-way.

We had been walking for only an hour when I

heard the alarm call of a puku. This is a harsh whistle, repeated every few seconds. The secret is always to find the animal that is doing the whistling and then gauge from the direction in which it is pointing what it was that had alarmed it. This is a tricky business, because you don't want to frighten the puku before you have spotted the predator.

At the beginning of a walk, the clients have not settled into any sort of rhythm. They are not bush wise: they make a lot of noise, they talk at the wrong moment, they are not aware that sudden movements signal aggression and will frighten off any animal you are trying to get close to. They haven't learnt to use their instincts or their senses properly.

We stopped in good cover. I raised one finger to my lips and began a very thorough scanning of the bush with my binoculars. There was only one lion calling and the grass was very tall, which made this difficult. If it stopped calling before we spotted it, we would lose a great opportunity of seeing something exciting. This is always a good time on a safari to reach a climax. It puts everybody on their mettle. It reaffirms all the things you mentioned in your briefing the night before.

The puku was very upset. She kept up her alarm whistles for some time. She was so engrossed in telling the world about her problem that she was not concentrating on other predators – like us, for instance.

At long last I spotted her. She was alone. Her head was raised and pointing up into a tall *albida* tree that had died owing to ring-barking by elephant. I studied the tree very carefully, looking for something in a fork or on a horizontal branch. At this point, my mind had 'leopard' very strongly underlined. It took a very short time for me to spot the offending party. I was right – it was a leopard, and it was still there, crouched over the limp form of a baby puku as it licked the fur away from the belly. The long graceful neck hung down from the fork. The neat little hooves glinted in the early-morning sun.

The tree was too far away to provide a photograph for my clients, so we had to get closer without spooking the puku, which would then also spook the leopard. We crept closer, hugging the ground. The leopard was engrossed in what it was doing and not paying attention to anything else. When we had closed the distance sufficiently, I indicated to my clients that they should sit down. Then I pointed to the leopard. As the group saw what I had seen, their look of amazement was very clear to see. Cameras started clicking away. The leopard worked away at its meal, unaware of us.

Once everybody had had a chance to take one good photo, it was time to get a little closer. Seeing a leopard descending to the ground at full speed and in full view is a thrilling experience. They usually grunt or growl when they hit the ground, and that adds another element of excitement to the experience. On this occasion, we managed to close the gap just a little bit before the leopard spotted us and made its exit. It bounded into the grass at the base of the tree and vanished from sight. We moved right up then, and I was able to find clumps of bloody fur on the ground around the tree trunk. You could also see the claw marks on the tree trunk and the blood as it had hauled its prize up the sheer trunk.

After a year, my expat accountant decided that he was not going to make any quick money from my safari operation so he pulled out.

We had a big booking from the Mark Carwardine Trust, and I was asked by the remaining shareholder to come back and set up the camp for this group alone. To have to rebuild the whole camp just for a single group, and then take the whole thing down again, was too daunting. I just couldn't face it. I declined.

My relationship with the remaining shareholder was not good at the best of times; had it been better, I might have reconsidered. All the equipment was stored away miles from Lusaka, some in the village, some in Lundazi with our Indian friend, some with Father Van der Pol. Bringing it all together had taken a lot of work and money – my money and my friend's. What would happen to it? The banana boat was sitting in a game-scout camp with Patrick. I decided to put the whole experience behind me, for better or worse, and start a new life.

I felt much like T.E. Lawrence must have felt returning to England having defeated the Turks in Palestine without any recognition or thanks from anyone for his achievements.

I had no money of my own and couldn't continue any longer. I had not a penny to bless myself and needed money to buy an air ticket back to Harare. I did have a new industrial mincer that I had just bought in South Africa. I managed to sell it to Jo Pope for their safari operation and this was enough for an air ticket.

The wreck of the cruiser Königsberg that was sunk in the Rufiji delta in 1915 during the First World War.
Süddeutsche Zeitung Photo / Alamy Stock Photo

General Paul von Lettow-Vorbeck, the charismatic and highly versatile leader of the German forces fighting the British in what was then Tanganyika.
Süddeutsche Zeitung Photo / Alamy Stock Photo

F. C. Selous seated beside his wagon while writing up his diary. Two Kori Bustards hang beside him.

The last resting place of the celebrated hunter and naturalist, after whom the Selous Game Reserve was named. He was shot by a German sniper during the First World War.
Nick Greaves / Alamy Stock Photo

The Selous Game Reserve, Tanzania

I had always wanted to work in the Selous Game Reserve, named after Frederick Courteney Selous, the hunter who had guided the Pioneer Column into Rhodesia for the British South Africa Company under the instructions of Cecil Rhodes.

The Reserve was named after him because he died there, shot by a German sniper during the last months of the First World War. He had retired from hunting and was living quietly in England. The Germans had a very charismatic general in charge of their troops in Tanganyika, as it was called then. Von Lettow-Vorbeck was making a fool of the British forces as he was conducting a very successful guerrilla campaign, much like the Afrikaners had done fifteen years earlier during the Anglo-Boer war. His army was highly mobile, capable of living off the land and using local askaris.

Selous's grave is not far from the Rufiji river, close to Sand Rivers safari lodge. It is a sad reflection of a very courageous life, and consists of a plinth made from stones, which requires maintenance, and a brass plate bearing his name and dates.

The Rufiji river was the scene of another exciting episode during the First World War. The Germans had a large cruiser named the *Königsberg* operating off the east coast of Africa. It had ten large guns and was a menace to allied shipping along the East African coast. The British navy was determined to destroy it after it had successfully sunk a British ship in the harbour at Zanzibar. The *Königsberg* was forced to retire to a prepared base in the Rufiji delta for an engine refit. While there, the British discovered its whereabouts and blockaded the Rufiji

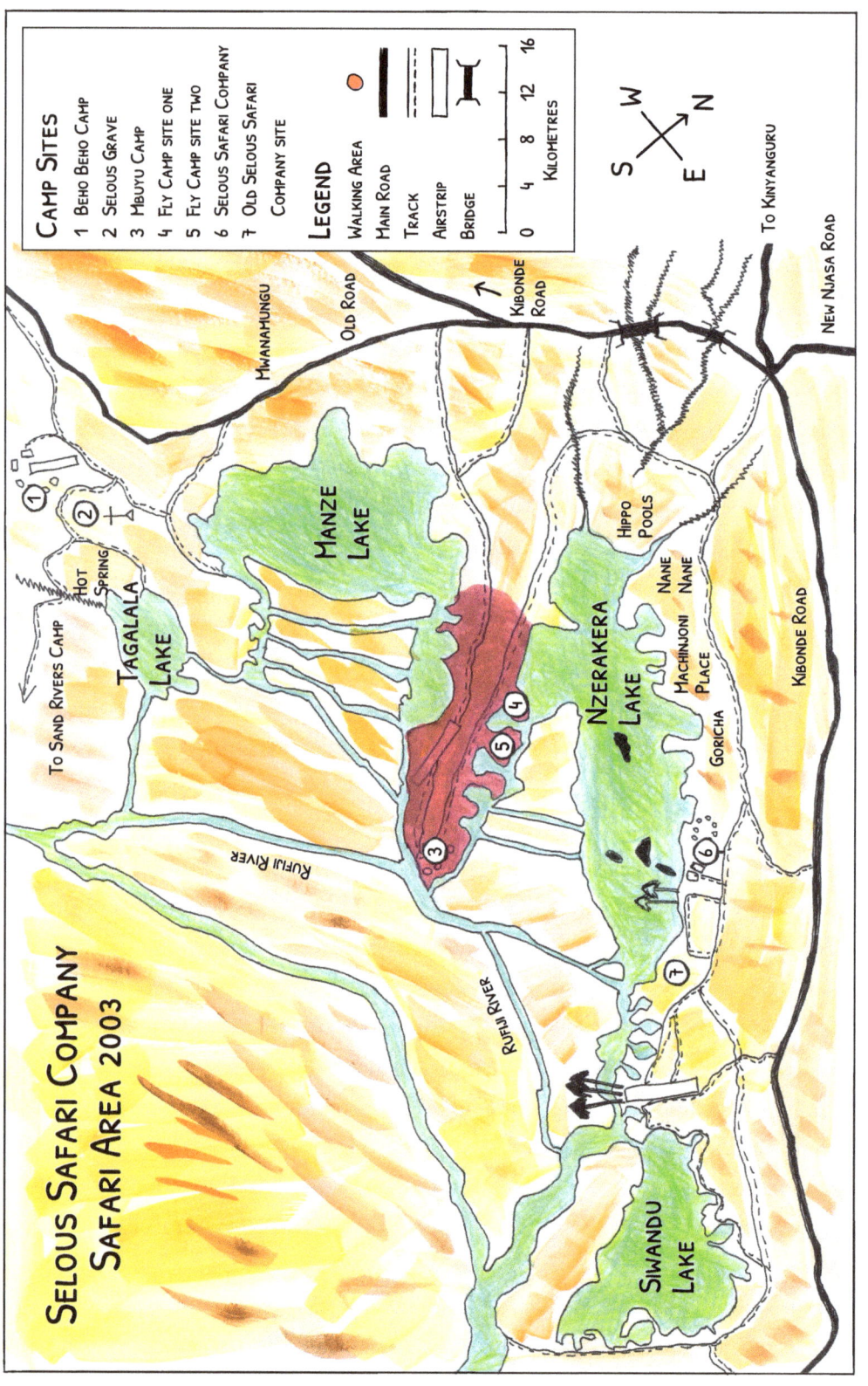

delta. The *Königsberg* was finally disabled after a prolonged battle involving flying boats, shallow-draft lighters armed with heavy cannon, and cruisers. Before the ship was abandoned, the ten guns were removed from the boat and put to other uses. The crew joined Von Lettow-Vorbeck in his East African campaign.

Most of the Selous Game Park is devoted to commercial hunting. What remains is reserved for photographic safaris, which is the area to the east of the Rufiji river. The elephants that one encounters may well have been shot at, so they bear a resentment towards human beings that makes them more difficult to deal with when on foot.

When I joined the Selous Safari Camp as Activities Manager, there had been a crisis among the senior guides. Apollo had been leading a group out of camp on a morning walk and had come on a cow herd of elephant. The matriarch had charged and knocked him down, putting her tusk through his scrotum. He was lucky to survive with only dented pride and superficial damage to his genitals. The guides refused to walk after that.

I introduced the Zambian approach to walking, with an armed guide to deal with aggressive animals, followed by a second guide to deal with the clients. This worked well, and soon the guides were happy to walk. I preferred walking and they were more than happy to take the drives, so it was a successful compromise.

I did most of the walks out of the main camp and also from the fly-camps. These fly-camps were special for me; they reminded me of my Chibembe

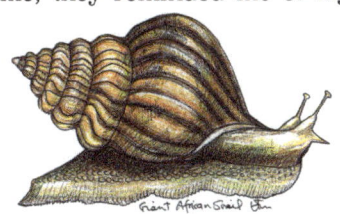

walks. They enabled me to get out of the main camp and the never-ending cycle of tourists and to give a very special personal experience to a couple on honeymoon or to a small family.

When these fly-camps became my responsibility, I moved the camp site from where it had been to a new site that offered much greater opportunities. The old site was in a grove of trees, miles from water with little game to be seen. And there was a beehive in the trees. My first safari was with a young American honeymoon couple. The wife had a terror of insects and her husband a terror of spiders. At breakfast on the first morning, the bees descended on the marmalade en masse, so I had to put her in her tent and hand the fried eggs to her through the fly screen.

My camp was on a hill overlooking the lake, about a hundred meters from the water. Dense bush fringed the lake shore, and this consisted mainly of doum palms at all stages of development. Doum palms, *Hyphaene thebaica*, look a little like candelabra because their stems branch out in different directions. Mixed in with the doum palms were *Borassus* palms that I was familiar with from my Zambia days. They have a swelling half way up the trunk. The fruit looks a lot like a coconut, but the flesh is yellow and juicy; elephant and baboons love it.

The site I chose was easily reached by boat from the lodge. It was on high ground, with good views all around; it attracted a breeze and had good shade provided by four enormous pod mahogany trees, *Afzelia quanzensis*, and was surrounded by water on three sides. Two huge baobabs grew to one side of the camp. One of the cooks from the lodge did the

cooking, and he was helped by a waiter and one other chap who collected firewood for the showers.

One honeymoon couple had booked a fly-camp; I had a feeling that it was an arranged marriage. They came from New York. The wife was beautiful and very much in control. The movie *Out of Africa*, with Robert Redford and Meryl Streep, had made a deep impression on her; she must have dreamed of meeting her Robert Redford. Her husband was pale and skinny and hardly spoke.

On our morning walk I spotted vultures. They were flying low over our heads with a sense of great urgency. We found the remains of an impala. The skin had been turned inside out and all that remained was the head and the hoofs. I felt sure that wild dog had done it.

Later, we found a shady tree to have our tea break and the husband went off to have a pee, but instead of going behind the tree he faced us. As he returned, I said to his wife, 'There is your Robert Redford.' It was unkind and I felt bad about it later.

That evening, they asked for a candle-lit dinner by themselves. This was prepared and, just before I called them, I lit the candles. They sat down and I went off into the kitchen to have my own supper. A little later she called me to join them. Being all alone in the African bush was too much like the real thing.

From the fly-camp I would walk my clients across to Lake Manze. A pride of lions moved around within our walking area and we often came upon them. They had killed an eland that we found one morning, though it was in thick bush so we were not able to get

a good sighting of the lion feeding. Lion have developed a strategy of chasing giraffe into thick bush where the overhanging branches restricted their movement. They may have used this strategy with the eland.

Tanzania had a very healthy elephant population, and one of the spectacles was seeing a herd setting out to swim across Lake Nzerakera to the outer islands. You could watch them from the dining room, which was raised high above the trees on stilts. The lake is very deep in places, and when the elephant reached the middle they were not swimming but actually walking on the bottom. All that could be seen then was the occasional curled trunk, though they often raised their tails to keep them dry.

With elephant around, walks were always challenging and exciting. The thick undergrowth along the shoreline also gave leopard good cover, and there was an abundance of impala. Together with the pride of lions that moved about from one area to another, visitors had everything one could possibly desire.

Along the Rufiji river are groves of tall *Borassus* palms that must be extremely old. Here and there one sees only the trunk, rising from the ground without the crown; they lose them in strong winds. These tall crown-less tree trunks are popular perches for Fish Eagles and Palm-nut Vultures. Egyptian Geese nest in their hollow trunks. Red-necked Falcons are fast enough to catch swifts, and even bats on the wing, and they also nest in the trunks.

We often saw cobras around the lodge – forest cobras, *Naja melanoleuca*, which can grow up to 270cm in

length, the longest cobras in Africa and highly poisonous. Their venom is neurotoxic as well as being an anticoagulant, like the boomslang's.

I had some interesting experiences on these walks. Coming back from a walk with a British honeymoon couple, we were nearing the camp. The husband had been an officer in the British army and an equerry to the Queen Mother. His young wife was a kindergarten teacher from London. We came through a grove of trees close to the water and, from nowhere, an old buffalo bull appeared. He snorted, which was what made me turn. There he was – huge, dark and menacing. He pawed the ground with his front hoof while he made up his mind what to do next. I realised that, one way or another, he was going to charge.

Abdullah, my assistant on these walks, had worked for National Parks so had an understanding of animals. I had trained him to follow behind me on these walks and, if we were to be charged, his role was to lead the clients to safety behind a tree or an anthill, performing much the same duty as the trail-leader in the Luangwa Valley walks.

Abdullah had quickly taken the couple behind a tree, as he had been trained to do, and before the buffalo could change his mind, I aimed and fired. The .458 Solid struck him under the left eye and travelled all the way down his spine to exit above the right hip. He dropped, got up and walked away, then dropped again.

I decided to leave him and we walked briskly back to camp. I stayed at the back to ensure that he was not following us. Back at camp I radioed the lodge and

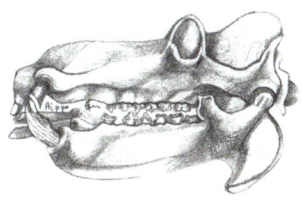

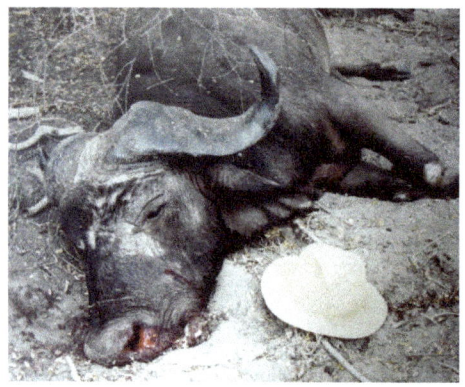

A solitary buffalo bull that I had to shoot when he charged a honeymoon couple on a walk in the Selous Game Reserve.

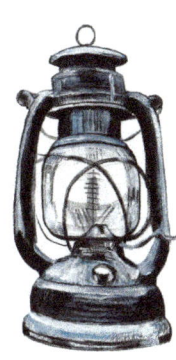

got the manager to call National Parks. When they arrived in their own vehicle, I went back with them to where I had shot the buffalo. He was nowhere to be seen. They had a defective rifle so had wanted me to finish him off. After some urgent searching we found him lying in the place he must have been in at the very beginning, in a narrow crevasse. I fired two more shots into him, which finished him off. I felt sorry for him. He had lost all the hair on his knees. The National Parks staff took the whole carcass away without leaving a single scrap of meat for our own staff.

From the fly-camp one afternoon I spotted a very big elephant bull in the distance. He was striding leisurely across the swamp in our direction, the water up to his chest, and was likely to make landfall where we were standing. His mind was preoccupied with thoughts of his own agenda. I warned my clients to have their cameras ready for a good close-up.

I intended waiting until the very last moment before retreating. The bull came on, getting bigger and bigger. He came to a shallow stream and waded it effortlessly, the water reaching to his shoulder blades. After that he rose up, the water streaming off his body, and was on dry land – the same dry land that we were standing on – his wet and dry skin in sharp contrast. As he turned to follow the contour of the hill, I whispered to the clients to keep very still because this was the magical moment I had been waiting for to give them a perfect opportunity to photograph a big elephant that was oblivious of our presence and very, very close. It was so quiet. I looked back to see if all was well. There was nobody there. I was entirely alone! Abdullah had lost his nerve and taken the clients to a tree.

On one morning walk we entered a small promontory that jutted out into the lake. The ground sloped up on all sides from the water, forming a ridge. There was not much vegetation on the ridge but the bush got thicker as it reached the water.

We were walking along the exposed spine of the ridge. I knew that there was a very long python in the vicinity and had seen its track on several occasions – it must have been about four metres long. Pythons don't wriggle in the same way as smaller snakes but inch their way forwards using their belly muscles. I stopped. In the dry earth, clear to see, was a long drag mark that cut deep into the hard ground and snaked away down a game trail; it seemed to be going in the direction of an African mangosteen tree, *Garcinia livingstonei*, in the heavy undergrowth that fringed the banks of the lake, in this case Lake Nzerakera.

I had a strong suspicion, however, that this was the work of a leopard, that it had killed an impala and dragged it away to this tree. The only way in was down the narrow game trail that the leopard had used with thick bush on either side. Elephant were particularly fond of feeding in these thickets, and one could guess that lion would also find them good places to spend the hot hours of the day – not a good place to be with overseas clients, and yet here was a chance to see a leopard out in the open, even if it was for just a second or two.

I decided to leave the two clients with Abdullah in a safe place and go on alone in the hope that the leopard would show itself for long enough for the clients to get a glimpse of it. Leopard are very

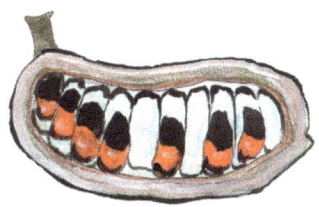

shy during the day and will always run if they see human beings.

I cocked the .458 rifle, held it at the 'ready' position and started walking down the path very slowly, keeping a very good look out on either side and with my ears tuned for the slightest sound. I was sure the leopard was in the African mangosteen tree, which I had told my clients to keep a close watch on. Its trunk was exposed for two or three metres before it reached the bushes around its base. If the leopard jumped down the tree they would at least catch a fleeting glimpse of it.

I was halfway down the path when something moved in the tree. There was a golden flash of tawny hide and spots, and a leopard bounded down the tree and disappeared into the thick undergrowth. My clients got a good view of it for a few seconds as it came down the tree. They were enthralled.

On another early morning walk, we were in very much the same area as this incident, but this time there was no indication of a leopard to guide us. In a small *Manilkara mochisia* tree, also known as Lowveld milkberry, I saw a leopard fast asleep on a horizontal branch. It was in full sunlight and about five metres from the ground. Its coat shone and it was a wonderful sight. As we edged closer for a good photo it heard us and woke up. It let out a growl of annoyance, bolted down the tree and disappeared.

In a different direction this time, we were walking through *Terminalia* woodland that was open and flat, with low bushes here and there and good visibility. There were many clumps of whistling thorn, *Vachellia drepanolobium*, in the area.

Impala were usually around and sometimes giraffe that liked feeding on the *Terminalia* leaves.

It was early in the walk and we hadn't had our stop for tea. As we were going along slowly and quietly we could hear impala making their alarm calls – their call has been likened to someone tearing up a telephone directory. I changed direction immediately and went in the direction of the calls. Seconds later we came on very fresh leopard spoor. I was convinced that the leopard must have been just ahead of us and making for a very big *Manilkara mochisia* tree about half a kilometre away. When you are convinced well in advance of a leopard's whereabouts, it is just a matter of walking quietly and seeing if you can spot the cat before it spots you.

I told my clients not to make a sound and to walk very quietly. We crept forward, eyes peeled. Then I saw it. It was obviously watching us: it lay stretched out facing us in a fork in the tree. I pointed it out to the husband, who couldn't see it at first. Directing a person's gaze to an animal in a tree is a practised art, and I owe a lot to my army training for this. Visualising a clock face is always helpful. Once he had spotted it, he was able to show his wife. They took a few shots and then the leopard had had enough. It came down the tree in one or two bounds and was gone. We had our tea under the tree and then made our way back to camp. Forever after this incident, whenever I saw this tree I gave it a very good checking out in case the leopard was back in it, but we never saw it again.

This time it was a walk from the main camp. We would reach the area by boat and the boatman would wait for us. There were three or four people in the party, and not long after coming ashore I heard a baboon making its alarm call – a bark, repeated over and over again. It is usually a dominant male that does it and, for safety reasons, he does it from a high vantage point, often in a tall tree.

I started walking in the direction of the sound and very soon came upon the prints of lion in the soft sand of a small river: there must have been three or four of them. It was the prints that created my mindset and I started looking in all the obvious places for lion – anywhere with deep shade. We looked and looked but I couldn't see anything. The baboon making the call was still at it, but there seemed to be no sign of lion anywhere.

By now, the baboon making all the noise was close and I was able to pick him out. He was standing in a very tall *Cordyla africana* tree, barking for all he was worth. I needed to find out which way he was looking, because that would give away the source of his anger. He was looking down and to our left. Again I looked for the tufted ears of lion under bushes and in shade, but still I couldn't see anything.

Suddenly we all heard very clearly an unusual sound. It sounded like brittle twigs snapping. About forty meters away, there was a dense *Terminalia* tree. The cracking sound seemed to be coming from this tree. As I concentrated on the sound, I realised that it was the sound of bones being cracked. I brought my clients around me and pointed to where the sound was coming from.

There, in the tree, was a very big male leopard, and he had a baboon that he was eating in a very great hurry. He could see us and realised that he did not have much time left to complete the job. He

wanted to swallow as much of the baboon as possible before he had to leave it.

We watched him for some time. When he had had enough, he jumped down, gave a loud growl of protest and bounded away. The baboon in the tree barked even more ferociously while the leopard was still visible, but it stopped once the source of its anger had disappeared.

Conservation Corporation Africa was a big South African safari company, founded by the Varty brothers, with lodges in several African countries. They were interested in merging with the Selous Safari Company. While I was there, they brought in all their experts, and I went walking with one of their safari managers. He was highly self-opinionated. He asked me if I knew the difference between the call of the male and female Black Cuckoo. I said that I didn't. If the merger took place, many of our senior staff would be replaced, me included, so I resigned from the Selous Safari Company and went back to Zimbabwe.

Before I left, we had a staff Christmas party. The senior guide thanked me in a speech for my work with the guides at the lodge. I was very touched by his words.

The big rains had started and already the roads into the camp from Dar es Salaam were becoming very muddy and difficult to negotiate. I decided to take my chances with one of the numerous charter flights that came in and out of the game reserve.

We heard that one was coming in to an airstrip close to us and returning to Dar es Salaam, so I made my farewells and was driven to the

 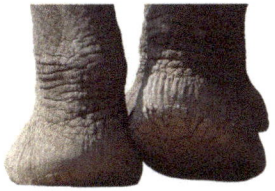

airstrip. A small plane arrived and dropped off two passengers. I asked the pilot if he could give me a ride to Dar es Salaam. He said he was going to Zanzibar, not Dar es Salaam, which would have meant waiting for another plane to Dar es Salaam later in the day, which was unlikely as the safari season was coming to a close. I climbed aboard and was in Zanzibar before I knew it – not where I wanted to be. However, as Safari Manager for the Selous Safari Company I could obtain a free seat on any Coastal Airways flight as long as there was space. It was a wait of several hours before I could get a seat on a Coastal flight going to Dar es Salaam.

This was to signal the end of my walking safari experiences, though I continued to seek personal walking challenges in exciting places whenever I could.

Part Three

What a Walking Guide Should Know

What makes a good safari guide?

*They grunted and blew, and their flanks
heaved with heat and exasperation. ...
It was exciting to be close enough to smell
[the wildebeest], to hear them breathe,
to see them blink their dark and bluish eyes
or lick their wet nostrils.*
Vivienne de Watteville, Speak to the Earth
(London: Methuen, 2nd edn, 1936), 43.

I have used the term 'safari guide' to describe the individuals who have the responsibility of leading tourists in pursuit of wild animals for photographic purposes. This is the name given to them in Zimbabwe, though they go by other names in other countries.

In Zambia they are called 'trail leaders', the term being derived from 'wilderness trail', a trail being a route chosen by hikers to take them from one part of a wilderness area to another. We also speak of 'game trails' – the routes chosen by animals for the same purpose.

Some know them by the name of 'ranger' or 'warden', though these terms generally denote ranks within a government department that oversees a national park: they are civil servants. As most individuals who take tourists on safari are in the private sector, neither of these terms is suitable.

Though many safari guides are male, it would be a mistake to speak of safari guiding as a male domain: I have known several highly competent female guides. It is true, however, that females have **a harder time fitting the image than their male counterparts**, which is probably due to the fact that

safari guiding has a great deal of machismo attached to it, something I think it borrows from hunting.

Knowledge, of course, is of great importance, but knowledge by itself does not make a good guide. During one full safari season, a trainee guide can learn enough to provide satisfactory answers to most of the questions posed by the average first-time tourist to Africa – presuming, of course, that this individual is well motivated and has a good general knowledge of natural history.

Expanding this basic knowledge comes from listening to more-experienced guides, through reading, and even through watching wildlife videos. The off season is the best time to get up to date with new publications and developments. As in any profession, you must keep up to date with new research in your field. A guide, if he or she is serious about the job, should begin to build up a good library of reference books as soon as possible. When I started guiding, books were not as plentiful as they are today. On the other hand, when a book was available, it was a lot cheaper than the average reference book is now. A knowledge of current affairs is also invaluable. Many of your clients will enjoy the opportunity to talk about their own country and their work.

A mistake that many aspiring guides make when they lack information is to try and bluff, or, as it is known in many professions, 'bullshit'! There will always be one well-travelled and knowledgeable client who knows more than you do. It is wiser to admit that you don't know something than to try and bluff your way out of it. You will soon be found out and made to look a fool in front of everybody else. There is nothing worse, to my mind, than a cocksure

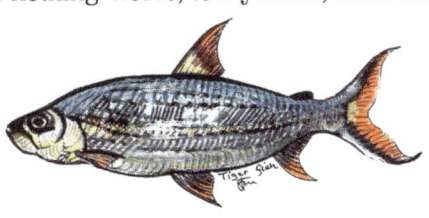

guide. No matter how knowledgeable you may be, you should never be so self-assured that you are unable to acknowledge when you are wrong. A little humility is a good quality to keep in reserve. Never be so proud that you can't say, 'I have no idea what that is.'

Good guides should make full use of all their senses all the time. How often has a whiff of rotting meat lead you to a kill? Are you able to smell where a lion or leopard has scent-marked? Alarm calls are one of the most valuable clues to the presence of predators. A good guide should be able to identify the alarm calls of impala, bushbuck, kudu, puku, baboons, hyraxes, vervet monkeys, squirrels, ox-peckers and bulbuls.

After you have been a guide for some time, seeing becomes second nature, so much so that your eyes often see things before your brain has had time to process it. You know that something has moved in a thicket ahead of you, but you have no recollection of actually seeing anything. However, something tells you that you should take another look – and when you get closer, three lions suddenly leap up and run away. What had caught your eye was the movement of one of them as it walked across a patch of sunlight – too brief to be recognised as an animal, so your brain ignored it. Once you can trust your senses, you know that you are really using them to best advantage and beginning to behave like an animal yourself. Once this happens, you will become conscious of all sorts of things that other humans are not aware of. Never ignore your instincts.

On one occasion I spotted a zebra that was standing very still by itself. Zebra are normally social animals; finding one by itself is unusual. The fact that it was frantically swishing its tail from side to side was also abnormal behaviour. On closer scrutiny, I could see that it had very deep wounds down both flanks, suggesting an attack from a lion. Flies were swarming around the wounds, and it was this that was causing the irritation. Had I not been observant, realising that the zebra was behaving abnormally, I would not have been aware of its predicament and my group would have missed the opportunity of observing an animal that had miraculously escaped death from a predator.

I once had a very good season of pythons: I must have seen eight or nine. One would normally be lucky to see one or perhaps two. Meves's Starlings spend a lot of time looking for food on the ground, and a trick I learned was to recognise the call they make when they spot a snake. Once I'd heard it, I could surprise my clients by rushing up to a patch of grass where a python would be lying. It worked nearly every time and my clients thought I was very clever!

On another occasion I heard the starlings chattering, and when I checked it out I saw them on the ground at the end of a long lagoon. I couldn't see anything unusual but, as I watched, a Yellow-billed Stork alighted close to them, followed by a Sacred Ibis. I decided to get closer, and when we could get an uninterrupted view of what had attracted the birds I realised that they had found a very long python sunning itself on the sun-baked earth next to the water.

The stork was standing beside the snake, gazing at it with a puzzled look on its face. The ibis was walking up and down the length of the snake, trying to make out the head from the tail and not

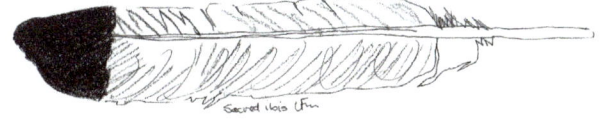
Sacred Ibis Feather

succeeding. The starlings kept up an agitated chatter, telling everybody to beware and not to get too close.

When we walked up to the snake, the birds flew off but the snake remained motionless – something I have seen pythons and puff adders do before. They believe they are invisible. I lined up the whole group behind the snake with the scout and tea-bearer and took everyone's photo. The python never moved. It must have been about four metres (thirteen feet) long. Another python I spotted – a small one this time – was thanks to a bush squirrel; it was in a mopane tree. Squirrels will often alert you to the presence of slender mongooses in trees.

Often there may be nothing to see on a game drive. You have not seen any lion, your clients are getting bored, so it is time to divert their attention to something totally different. Often it can be small, insignificant things that provide as much value as a lion kill or the sight of a fleeing leopard.

I remember when I was a trainee on one of my very first game drives in the company of Norman Carr, one of the most experienced of safari instructors. A few hundred metres out of camp, he stopped the Land-Rover and pointed to a tiny little plant by the roadside. It was so small that it was practically invisible, but he had noticed it. It was a sensitive plant, *Mimosa pigra* – the leaves crumple up when touched. I have never forgotten that.

The buck stops at your door when you are responsible for everything for a whole group. If the chef misreads his instructions on the menu sheet and makes bar snacks out of the bacon for the entire

safari, it is your fault because you should have checked that he had understood what he had to cook that day. If the refrigerator was not stocked up with beer the night before and you have a group in camp who think nothing of having a beer with breakfast, don't go blaming the barman. If someone in your party fails to get a seat on the plane because it was not reconfirmed in time, don't go blaming the airline.

Buckets of enthusiasm will carry a young guide through situations that would, under normal conditions, cause a group to write letters of complaint to their booking agent. If the vehicle is playing up, the lion you promised has not materialised, one of the party has a tummy bug, and all you can find are impala, you will be forgiven as long as you have tried your hardest, gone that extra mile, and been open and good humoured about the whole experience.

A guide should always look smart. That doesn't mean that you have to look as though you have just stepped out of a TV commercial, but if you look as though you have not taken care of yourself, your clients will begin to wonder if you have also neglected to maintain the vehicle, or forgotten to clean your weapon.

Being a safari guide might appear glamorous and a great way to earn a living, but in essence it is as hard to do well as any job you can mention. Come the end of the season, you will be suffering from 'client burn-out', and the energy required to retain your enthusiasm has to be drawn from resources you never knew you had.

After one season as a guide, you will have driven a particular route so many times that you can recognise every single impala you pass and remember how many eyelashes each has, and will be able to predict that a **Lilac-breasted Roller** will be sitting round a certain corner on the dead stump by the anthill. Despite this, when your new group clambers aboard your vehicle, you have to make them believe that they are extremely special and that you are as excited as they are about the safari. You may feel that you have rattled off your set speech so many times that the words have no meaning any more. Even so, you have to make a superhuman effort to inject a tone of enthusiasm into your voice so that what you are saying sounds interesting and relevant.

Some clients are very demanding, and the guide must have the self-confidence to know how far to allow a situation to go before calling a halt. The most common scenario is when a client pleads with the guide to get closer so that she can get a better photo of a herd of elephant. The guide knows that to approach will be dangerous because it is a cow herd – and therefore knows how close will be acceptable and how close could put the lives of the group, as well as those of the animals, at risk. This is where experience comes in. Clients will often take advantage of a young and inexperienced guide. They will use excuses such as, 'In Kenya, the guides let us get much closer.' I have seen visitors from Europe standing on a riverbank throwing clods at hippos to make them charge in order to get a good photo.

A good guide should be well organised and self-disciplined. If you are going on a drive, make certain that you have checked the vehicle beforehand. Is it clean? Does it have a jack and wheel spanner? Is the spare tyre pumped up? Is there enough fuel, oil and water? And so on. If you are going on a walk, have you decided where you are going to go? Have you taken into account a comment one of your clients has made about wanting to see a termite mound?

The night before a long walk, you should realise that you need a full night's sleep as much as your clients do. Don't spend all night drinking at the bar and then battle to wake up in the morning. You don't want appear at breakfast, find all your troops standing ready to leave, but you have yet to swallow your first cup of tea. Punctuality is critical in a guide. Those vital few minutes wasted in the morning can mean the difference between catching lion on a kill and missing the whole thing altogether. If the guide is punctual, his troops will also be.

A small backpack is a useful item in which you can keep essential equipment for walking and driving. You should carry a small first-aid kit that contains the basic remedies for bites and stings, antiseptic, sticking plaster, and a few large bandages. Sunscreen is also vital, as skin cancer is a very real danger for fair-skinned people who are exposed to the burning sun, day in and day out. I always had shirts with long sleeves to protect my arms. On a walk you should also have a roll of toilet paper in your pack, too, and if you are going out for the whole morning, be sure to take something to drink.

You should have your own pair of good binoculars: they will endure a lot of hard knocks, so quality pays off in the long run. For driving safaris and trips to the airport, a good pair of sunglasses is essential. A guide's eyes are his most valued possession and need to be taken good care of. In your backpack should also be a small bird-guide book. It is always handy to be able to refer to a book if there is a dispute about

the identification of a particular species – which often happens. You might immediately recognise a bird without having to think about it, but try and explain how you recognised it to someone who has seen it for the first time and you will find yourself talking all day.

While we're on the subject of spotting birds, don't simply pass them by because you think that nobody will be interested. Often your clients will be fascinated when you identify the answering calls of a pair of Tropical Boubou. I learned how to call up African Wood Owls at night, and my clients would be enthralled. An American tourist was fascinated by my description of a male Hornbill sealing his mate in a hollow tree prior to breeding. A friend of mine could call up lions; another used an enamel jug to make the sound of a lion roaring. All these make for a memorable safari.

Some sort of briefing is essential when you encounter your clients for the first time. For a drive, you should always introduce yourself first, and then you can find out the names of your clients at the same time. This always opens the door to a more friendly atmosphere. You can mention where you intend going. You can ask if anybody has special requirements. Where have they been already? Have they seen the Carmine Bee-eaters yet?

In your pre-walking safari briefings, you should be most emphatic about what people should wear. When you are on foot, you do not want anyone in the group to appear too conspicuous – which makes it difficult to get close to animals and also limits your chances of getting away safely if an animal

is pounding along behind you. White clothing should be forbidden. Appropriate clothing is usually mentioned in the literature that clients receive from their travel agent, but there is usually someone who comes ill-prepared and you will have to help them out by lending them a hat or daubing their white sun hat with mud.

A good master plan for the whole safari is also an essential item. This will naturally change as the days go by, but it is important to decide what you intend to do with your group right at the beginning of the safari so that they get the greatest satisfaction from their stay with you. You should structure the master plan so as to provide as much variety as possible. Talk to your clients at the beginning. Involve them in the decision-making. Find out what their preferences are. Many who come out on safari have saved up for it for years. It means a lot to them, so give them the very best. This is why a pre-safari chat is so important – you can find out who are the bird specialists, who likes walking, who is allergic to bees, who smokes, and so on.

You can offer your clients a choice of activities and get from them what they would like to do on the next day. But be careful – don't spend a whole evening going on about how great a particular area is, only to find when you get there that what you had guaranteed can't be found. And don't bamboozle your clients into doing something that they secretly would not have wanted to do had you not been so persuasive in your arguments.

It is important to listen carefully to what your clients are saying. Some safari guides make up their minds what they are going to do long in advance and, even if their clients want to do something totally

different, they will always bring them round to their way of thinking in the end. What is vital is that you have a very clear idea in your mind the night before what you plan to do the next day so that everything can be prepared in advance. If you are taking sandwiches with you, this will allow the kitchen staff sufficient time. If you are driving to where you start your walk, the vehicle can be cleaned, fuelled, and the spare tyre pumped up.

Safaris should be fun. Being responsible for a group of clients for four days at a time is very hard work – make no mistake about that. At the end of the day, safari work is more to do with being good with people than with animal knowledge. To be good, you have to be concerned about all your clients – and not just the pretty ones, or the ones who enjoy their beer in the evenings, or the ones who are immediately easy to get on with. You have to make an effort to like all your clients, no matter who they are.

As I have said, getting to know their names is a first major step. I have known guides who still did not know their clients' names when they were saying goodbye to them at the airport after a five-day safari. If you aren't very good at remembering people's names, take along a notepad and write them down – perhaps with some clues: 'the tall one', 'the redhead' – and study the list before you meet with them the next morning so that you already have their names sorted out in your mind.

It can also be a good idea to make a note of their addresses so that follow-up work, such as a newsletter or Christmas card, can be done once the season is over. This information may be contained in your visitors' book but, if it isn't, you should keep your own record. If you want to be a guide because you want to get away from people and develop a one-on-one relationship with nature, forget it! You will never make a good guide. A good guide is someone who likes people.

On a great many occasions you can feel like a nursemaid. When you get back to camp after a long tiring walk, all you feel like doing is slipping away to your bed and having a snooze. Oh, no. You might have to deal with a host of problems that suddenly surface – all the milk for the entire safari has gone sour, or the gas for the refrigerator has run out. Suddenly the sweet little lady in the group is spitting mad because she has found a spider in her tooth mug, or somebody announces out of the blue that they are vegetarian as the chef triumphantly wheels in the T-bone steaks at dinner time.

An ability to tell a convincing story is a useful attribute and requires good communication skills. To create a plausible story to explain a lot of bewildering signs and sounds is a useful gift. Even if a guide becomes over fanciful about his reading of events, his clients will be far more likely to excuse him than if he just shrugs his shoulders and says he doesn't know what is going on. Even if you know for a fact that a few vultures circling ahead do not indicate a kill, it will be necessary to demonstrate this by walking up and proving it.

Some guides I have known are so full of 'book learning' that they are unable to relate what they know to what is taking place in front of them at that moment. Being in tune with the needs of your clients will often direct you to an area of interest that you might have totally overlooked. The only way

you will learn what these are is by talking to them and by being in tune with their needs. This might mean leaving your mates at the bar in the evening and spending time with your clients, perhaps even inviting yourself to eat with them at dinner. They will appreciate this. Many relationships established on safaris stand the test of time.

There will be times on a safari when you have not seen much and you feel it is necessary to raise the spirits of the group in some way; it may be time to play a little game. One good one is this: during the safari, each person has to choose a bird call and become proficient in making the call. On the last night, after a few drinks around the fire, you announce that the game will begin. Point to one of them, who has to make their call. While the first person is cooing, point to another person, who has to start clucking, and so on until the whole group is hard at it, sounding like feeding time in the birdhouse at the zoo!

Another game, which can also be a good icebreaker, can be played only if a mole cricket is available. Mole crickets are harmless little insects about the size of a pen top. What is distinctive about them is that they burrow when alarmed. They often appear in the evenings under lights. Hold the mole cricket in your hand and ask the team to form a circle, holding hands. The rule is that on receiving the object from you the first person has to pass it on without dropping it. The first person to do so has to pay a forfeit. I don't remember the mole cricket ever going further than the first individual in line!

Another way of making the safari memorable is having each member compose a limerick about a member of the group. These can be read out on

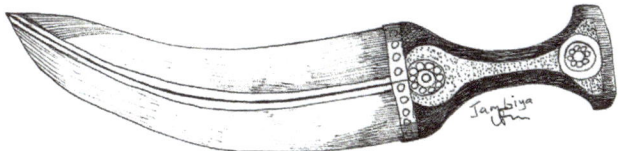

the last night. They can be written down and copied later so that each member has one for their album.

As I have outlined already, safari guides are responsible for the safety of their clients, which should go without saying. They are also there to inform and educate their clients about all aspects of the bush. In addition, they also have a responsibility to protect the biodiversity of species in the region in which they operate their safaris.

In Africa today, as the resources available to manage national parks become more and more scarce, safari guides often find themselves burdened with concerns that should not be their responsibility. When I was conducting safaris in a very remote and often dangerous national park, I had to chase and arrest subsistence poachers who were operating inside the park. National parks employees generally are poorly paid, poorly trained and poorly motivated. They lack the will, understandably, to put their own lives at risk for the sake of animals from which they do not receive any tangible benefit. In many cases, the only incentive for them to join the parks service is for an entitlement of free game meat. Ironically, instead of working to protect wildlife, they serve purely to eat it. The revenue from national parks finds its way into the coffers of the central bank, so, no matter how well the staff perform their duties, their wages remain the same.

With the population rising dramatically, the pressure on land will continue to outstrip supply – and with it, land set aside as national parks. Tied to the problem of population growth is the scarcity of food, and in particular protein. This produces an

increase in subsistence poaching for game and fish. Along with this is the never-ending need for firewood for cooking and heating purposes. The need for bush meat is becoming an ever-increasing demand in large urban centres of Africa. One can overlook the efforts of small subsistence poachers, but when meat poaching is conducted along commercial lines, it is very destructive.

As it becomes apparent to governments that wildlife tourism is an important resource, with a big US dollar tag attached to it, politics very quickly becomes a factor in issuing licences for hunting and photographic safaris.

It is not the law that lacks the teeth to stop illegal traffic in protected species but the civil servants who are empowered to enforce its measures. Concern for the environment is a low priority for emerging African nations. But we are told that a nation that takes good care of its environment will also take good care of its people.

Blame can also be attributed to well-intentioned non-governmental organisations (NGOs) who appear in an area that they have very little knowledge about and proceed, without taking into account community needs or sensitivities, to implement a scheme to improve the lives of its people. Five years later, when the timescale for their project has elapsed, they leave – and another NGO appears on the scene with a new scheme and new priorities that often contradict the previous one. It is in this challenging environment that a safari guide must operate today.

Walking safaris

But if I could smell danger I was equally conscious of its absence; and although to have walked up to the elephants would have seemed outwardly a crazy risk, I believe that at that chosen moment there was no risk at all.
Vivienne de Watteville, *Speak to the Earth*
(London: Methuen, 2nd edn, 1936), 127.

I wake during the night. I am at Chikoko camp, in a small thatched hut assigned to the Trail Leader, deep in the South Luangwa National Park. The camp is built on the bank of a small tributary of the Luangwa. I have a group with me on this walk, which will take in two other camps before we walk back to Chibembe Lodge, five kilometres away.

I listen for any sound that might have woken me. If I hear lion roaring in the night this would indicate that they have killed, in which case I draw an arrow in the dust beside my bed with my finger so that in the morning I have some idea where they might be. I hear the call of the African Scops Owl, one of the most distinctive calls of the African bush. A high-pitched *kruup* uttered on one note every four seconds with the precision of a metronome. The camp is silent. I turn over and go back to sleep.

I wake again in the pre-dawn darkness to the sound of my alarm clock. I lunge to silence it. I am foiled by the mosquito net. Working my hand down the side of the mattress, I free my arm from the net and silence the alarm. By this time I am half out of bed. I fall back on to the bed and lie still for a few seconds, taking in my surroundings and searching for some clue that will convince me that the night is over – the bark of a baboon or the cooing of a dove.

All I can hear is a loud buzzing sound. My hut is nestled under several huge evergreen trees that were a mass of white blossoms. What I could hear was thousands of industrious little bees who had started their day well in advance of other animals to a call far more compelling than mine.

Getting ready in the dark without the assistance of electricity is a challenge. To will yourself out of bed requires courage, because there are always several better reasons to remain under the blankets a little longer. The enveloping roofs of the small huts with their small windows were designed to keep the interior cool during the hot months and not to provide light. Light enters the hut only through a narrow space along the top of the walls.

Escaping from the folds of the mosquito net is one thing, finding the torch after it has rolled on to the floor the night before is another matter. Finding my clothes takes a few seconds and putting them on no time at all. The night before, I had laid out my clothes for the day on a chair, a habit I had learned from my army days.

Once I am dressed, I usually take my shoes and socks outside the hut and complete my dressing beside the fire, which is easily coaxed into life with a few steady, well-directed puffs, assisted by three or four splinters of mopane wood that I peel off a log lying nearby. Once outside, the thrill of a new day takes hold of me. With my shoes and socks on, I shave standing outside my hut. Once, during the night, a hyena had bitten a chunk out of my shaving brush and eaten the soap.

Standing there now, I listen to the sounds of

the morning, paying particular attention to any alarm calls. Baboon barking because they had spotted lion moving. Puku whistling for the same reason. Impala making their alarm calls, indicating lion or leopard on the move. Lion roaring nearby, following a kill and announcing the fact to others in the pride. Hippo grunting as they return to the river after grazing all night. The raucous screams of starlings as they begin feeding on the sweet, sticky fruit of the ebony tree. Occasionally, the deep booming call of Ground Hornbill as they float to the ground from their roosting tree. It is too early to spot vultures, but once the sun was up I would be looking for them, too. Often my game plan for the morning walk would be based on what I could hear while I was still in camp.

The bedroom attendant is now making his rounds with a bucket of boiling water and a jug, providing hot water for shaving, pouring the water into metal basins on tables outside each hut. He takes the water from a 44-gallon drum that has a small fire lit under it – just enough to keep the water warm during the night. The clatter of aluminium jug against enamel basin, and the sound of the water from the basins splashing on to the ground as they are filled, is the warning most guests get that the new day has arrived.

I usually wait a few minutes after he has finished before I go from hut to hut, banging loudly on the wooden door and wishing the occupants a hearty good morning. I remain outside the door until I get a satisfactory response. This can be a muffled reply, a grunt, a muffled oath, or even the creaking of bed springs. Any of these is sufficient evidence that the occupant is sufficiently awake. Often I am beaten to it. The occupant is already up, sipping coffee and

enjoying the dawn. I then make a call on the game scout and discuss where we should go that morning.

With everybody dressed, there would then be a simple breakfast of cereal, toast and marmalade with a cup of coffee, then off. It was critical to be up and moving before the sun was up so that any predators still active would still be visible.

After an hour of two of walking it would be time for a break by a lagoon, and the tea-boy would get his fire going, using dry elephant dung for kindling, and quickly put the aluminium kettle on. The box would serve as a table and he would lay out a tablecloth on it. There would be cake or biscuits, or the remains of the dessert from the night before.

While this was going on, there was always a lot to see. A great variety of thirsty game would appear from the woodland and make their way to the water to drink. I chose our tea spots so that we had good visibility in all directions. On one occasion, a herd of buffalo appeared and waded out into the water – so close to us that even without the use of binoculars one could tell which species of oxpecker was feeding off them.

After morning tea, it would be a leisurely walk back to camp, arriving just before lunch. While we were out, any resupplies would have arrived, the beds would have been made and fresh bread baked. Cold drinks were in the freezer. After lunch, a snooze, or sit and observe. At 3.30, tea, and then a walk in the vicinity of the camp when you could be really lucky and spot a leopard going down to drink, or sit on the bank and watch a large pod of hippo spluttering and guffawing.

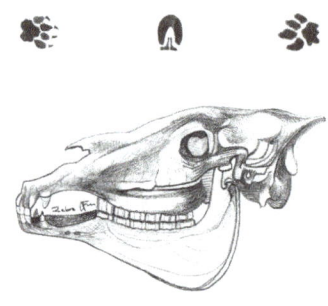

At the start of the safari season there would be water in the Chikoko river. It looks out on to Acacia Park with a beautiful grove of *Faidherbia albida* trees, popular with elephant when the pods were ripe. Zebra would crop the short grass during the day with the waterbuck, but at night they would go out into the woodland for safety. Giraffe would reach up and eat the leaves and the pods.

When it was my responsibility to build the camps I would construct the Trail Leader's hut so that it was near the toilet and so provide some degree of reassurance for clients having to use it during the night.

I knew of an elephant crossing point that could be reached from Chikoko camp. If you were lucky, you could admire the spectacle. Close to it was a Carmine Bee-eater colony that was also worth watching. This is an extract from my novel, *Cleopatra's Journey*:

Without any prompting, one of the old cows heads for the water. She is Mary. I know her by her single tusk, which is perfectly straight and very long. This is the cue the others have been waiting for. They emerge one by one from the grass, and descend the steep bank to the water's edge in quick, jerky strides, hind legs dragging behind like sea anchors, trunks flopping loosely from side to side. At the water's edge where there is a narrow sandy beach, Mary stops, extends her trunk to the muddy water, draws water up her trunk, curls the trunk under her chin, then pours the water into her mouth. Some spills down her shrunken cheeks.

Cleopatra appears at the top of the bank. Her breasts are swollen. Her new twins, Cordelia and Conrad, appear on either side of her. Conrad is slightly taller than his sister. They

easily walk under Cleopatra's belly. The smell of the water has a galvanising effect on them both. They manifest this by wrestling with one another, entwining trunks, pushing and pulling and having a marvellous time like any small children catching their first glimpse of the sea.

Cleopatra decides to join Mary. Slipping and sliding down the steep bank in a series of loose-legged strides, her ears flapping forward over her eyes, trunk flopping about, tail up, she comes to an untidy halt beside Mary, a fine cloud of reddish dust clinging to her ankles. Cordelia and Conrad, realising they have been left behind, stop their cavorting and rush down the bank after their mother. On the way down Conrad gives a shrill trumpet.

Cleopatra throws water over her body, first over her back, then under her belly. The twins stand under her chest so that the water sploshes over their rotund bodies until their dusty skins are black and shiny. When they are both sopping wet, Conrad tries to climb on Cordelia's back. She deftly swivels her shoulders and Conrad falls off into the water. Infuriated, he is back on his feet in a flash, and rushes after his sister, ears outspread, trunk raised. Cordelia, reading his mood, has taken refuge under her mother's chest. Other members of the group come alongside and also drink.

One elephant begins to defecate, then urinate, and as if on cue, all the others follow suit. The boluses, shaped like huge balls of thatching twine, tumble onto the hard sand, or splash into the water. Some float away on the current, others form small piles behind each elephant

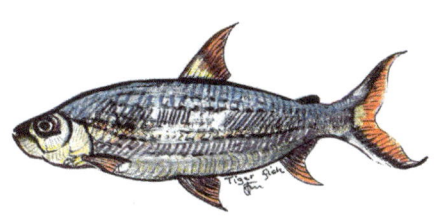

– clear reminders of where each elephant has been standing, already swarming with small flies. When she is satisfied that the time is right, Mary begins to wade sedately out into the river, drinking as she goes. Cleopatra falls into line behind, her twins at her ankles. To begin with they are able to walk on the bottom; however, very soon they are out of their depth and swimming, bobbing about in the water like corks. If they are lucky, they receive the odd helping shove with a trunk from their mother or auntie, but that is all.

This is the Luangwa River. It is also the South Luangwa National Park boundary. Over the river is the hunting area. Elephant know they can be shot if they cross into the hunting area, so they wisely wade the river just before nightfall and spend the whole night feeding, returning to the safety of the National Park in the early hours of the morning. My camp is in the National Park. Johnnie Pascoe, my professional hunter friend, has his hunting camp in the Game Management Area where licensed hunting is permitted.

On reaching the hunting area the long line of elephant snakes out of the water, the wet area on each animal as distinctive as a Plimsoll line on a ship. The next ritual is a dust bath, which coats the skin in a protective layer against biting insects. After that, with Mary still leading, they enter the forest in single file and disappear from my sight as the shadows are long on the coppery-coloured grass: a reminder that I must get back to my camp before the African night envelops me in her dark folds.

The sound of ten or twelve six-ton elephant bodies wading the river at night is an unforgettable sound. In the stillness, the sound is amplified dramatically. It goes on and on. Splash, splash, splash. Once across, you can hear the waves caused by their large bodies rushing up the banks and then receding. You could be on a beach by the sea. The quiet that follows is palpable.

An American client who came on a walking safari with me said, at the end of his five days walking in the wilderness with his return to civilisation imminent in a few days, that while he had been out in the bush living simply, he had never once missed the television, or the weather report, or the world news, or the newspaper. The main lesson that one learns from a walking safari is that one can have deep and wonderful experiences as long as one travels light. It means casting aside preconceived ideas, fixed ways of behaving, living life at the point where it counts most.

In a national park, animals have right of way and we are the intruders. Walking safaris fall under the heading of adventure holidays, along with canoeing, white-water rafting and rock-climbing. No doubt there is an element of risk involved, and it is this risk which gives them that added thrill. But there is a fine line between pushing the risk element too far and courting disaster. At the same time as seeking to maximise risk, you are actually exploiting the animal: that is something we must never do. You will see individuals who provoke elephant to charge by banging on the door of the vehicle. In dealing with the public, you obviously have to take every precaution to avoid unnecessary risk, because ultimately the finger of blame will be pointed fairly and squarely at you. The cost of litigation these days is too horrendous to consider.

The relationship between man and beast on a walking safari is unique. Every country has its own rules that govern walking in a national park. You must know what these are before setting out. For instance, in the Mana Pools National Park in Zimbabwe, the public are allowed to walk without a guide or National Parks scout. In Zambia, you have to have a National Parks scout with you if you walk in any national park.

All wild animals establish in their minds a safe zone around them, within which they will react aggressively to any intruder. With human beings it is not so much to do with safety as an invisible buffer that we like to have between us and any stranger. This differs from nationality to nationality. The British like lots of space around them. Africans will tolerate others in close proximity without feeling pressured.

When walking up to wild animals, one should never enter their safety zone without giving them adequate warning. This can be conveyed by sound or with smell. If you approach a thicket that you suspect might contain a dangerous animal, approach it so that your scent is blown towards the thicket by the prevailing wind. If you are not able to do this, then talk or cough loudly. On occasions, you may have to cut through a narrow patch of thick grass to reach easy walking country on the other side. Before you do this, start talking, or make a noise that will be interpreted by any animal in the vicinity as a human sound. Sleeping animals are what you must really watch out for. If you stumble on a sleeping buffalo, he is almost certain to charge. However, if you wake him up in good time, he can assemble his thoughts and move off without having to confront you, retaining his dignity.

One of the first rules when confronted by a dangerous animal is to dispel any thoughts it might have that you are acting aggressively. Retreating immediately conveys that message. However, the retreat must be a tactical retreat, and not a rout, with everybody running in different directions and tripping over their own feet. If it is the latter, lion, particularly, will turn the confusion to their advantage, which is in their nature, and catch somebody. Your pet dog will immediately chase your cat if it runs. At other times they are the best of chums; it is the running that does it.

Another cardinal rule about walking up to animals is always to give them an escape route. Animals do not want to attack you. They are putting themselves at great risk by doing this. Let them run away, and you do yourself a favour at the same time. The dumber the animal, the more it needs your help.

I immediately think of hippo when I say this. It is not a myth that hippo feel safest when they are in deep water. If you come upon them on dry land, they will instinctively try to get to the main river. Do not halt your party in a long line along the top of a riverbank with a hippo inland of you looking for an entry point to the water. He will take the shortest route to water, and this may well be straight through your group. As he passes he will give the nearest person a good nip: something to be avoided if you have ever studied a hippo's teeth!

In a canoe, the same thinking applies if you encounter a lone bull in shallow water. He will want to reach deep water. You are tempting fate if you allow your canoe to drift down so that you are blocking his route. For instance, you might be out early one morning and encounter a lone bull hippo out of water walking slowly along in the direction of the main river. You may presume he is aware of your presence, because he raises his head and looks in your direction, but it is wise to make certain before you continue on your way. To do this, all it takes is for you to speak loudly. If this does not get him going, then you might have to throw a clod of mud in his direction to make him speed up and go on his way. Once you have done this, he will move into top gear and be gone in seconds.

Watch to see where he has gone, and do not proceed until you actually see him plunge into the water – he could be hiding behind a bush. If you do not take the trouble to flush him out then, there is always a likelihood of him doubling back in confusion when he does smell you, and threatening you when you least expect it. A bull entering water has to contend with the dominant male for that stretch of water. He will only take the plunge if he is really provoked.

Most animals, even those with good eyesight, will wait until they obtain a 'scent fix' before they are convinced of the identity of an intruder. This means that, if you are on foot and you get the wind right, you can get very close to an animal before it realises who you are and takes off.

Often the secret is to try to anticipate the movements of an animal. This is most easily done if the animal is moving in a clearly defined manner –

towards water, to a particular food source, or simply strolling down a road or game trail. Once you know the intentions of an animal, it is easy to position yourself and your party so that it passes you. I have found that if an animal walks into your safe area he is less likely to act aggressively than if you walk into his safe area. I have found that this works very well with elephant, warthog and buffalo, and there is no reason why it should not work with other animals, too.

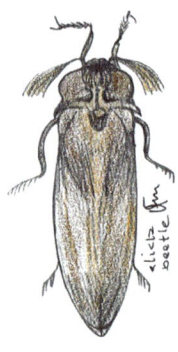

Warthog have eyes facing outwards, which gives them good all-round vision but poor frontal vision. If you are on the same game trail as a warthog and he is coming towards you, stand still, and wait for him. He will approach within a few feet of you before he realises who you are and trots off.

On another occasion I spotted a large breeding herd of buffalo feeding slowly towards us through an area of short grass with the odd tree here and there. We chose our spot carefully and waited. It was a magical experience. Just listening to the sounds they made as they came closer and closer was exciting enough: the moos, the grunts, the occasional clack of hoof against rock, the mumbling and grumbling, and, more especially, the sound of many bodies moving slowly through the grass, the swish of their tails, the ripping noise as the grass was tugged by their sharp teeth, the chomp-chomp of their jaws. All these sounds were thrilling and created a picture of a vast herd of wild animals behaving in a totally natural manner.

When we could feel them all around us we raised our heads, ever so slowly, and there they were, some within ten metres of where we were sitting. The animal closest to us was a cow, a strand of

grass hanging from her mouth and a small russet calf beside her with horns that were mere bumps on its hairy forehead. A little further off, three females were grazing contentedly, heads down, their rounded bodies supported by stocky little legs and neat black hooves. Because the wind was right, they just stared at us in disbelief, then others wondered what the first lot had seen and came forward for a better look, then others followed suit until we had about sixty buffalo gazing at us as though we were some sort of freak show. Then the wind changed and without another thought they were off at a gallop, tails twisted up over their rumps, heads held high, and in seconds all that remained was a cloud of dust and an irate flock of oxpeckers fluttering above.

To be intimidating to a dangerous animal, you should always appear as big and threatening as possible. To do this you must wave your arms and make a lot of noise, which will work with most animals. The only exception are elephant, but if you have nothing else, give it a try.

It always amazed me that the individuals we employed from the villages to build our camps and to porter for us would happily walk through the bush, day after day, without incident, encountering all manner of dangerous game in the process without harm – because they were observant and because they treated all animals with respect.

It is amazing how one's behaviour changes dramatically once you leave the gun behind. I often had to walk back to the lodge alone after supervising the construction of a camp – a distance of five or six kilometres through countryside thick with buffalo,

elephant and lion – without the reassurance of a gun; I never took any chances that might bring about an incident that I was incapable of dealing with. It is with this same attitude that one should carry a rifle on a walking safari. You should take all the precautions that you would normally take if you were walking without a weapon.

When you are out walking, female elephant with calves are very bad news indeed. If they get a whiff of your scent, no matter how far off you are, they may decide to charge, and there is nothing that will stop them except a bullet – a course of action that you should try to avoid at all costs. An animal alive is a valuable asset and a guarantee of your future as a guide. By having to shoot one, you will have precipitated a crisis that could have been avoided.

In most cases, resorting to the use of the gun is an admission of failure. It is essential when encountering elephant to stop and give the group a thorough going over with your binoculars to ascertain whether it is a breeding herd. If you spot a calf, you know it is a breeding herd and your best course of action is retreat – immediately. Bulls sometimes mingle with females so don't assume that because you see one big bull that it is not a breeding herd. The females may be at the back, hidden by thick bushes.

A breeding herd may be a long way off when you first spot them and you may be tempted to delay for a few minutes to give your clients a chance to study them. Don't! Retreat immediately and make as big a detour around them as you can. I remember returning to camp one evening after a nice walk and being confronted by a breeding herd. As soon as the wind changed they started trumpeting, gesturing and advancing. They would not let us get into camp,

and we only made it eventually as darkness was falling, having completed several circuits of the camp.

I have mentioned already that you should be conscious of the mood of animals before you decide to approach. Elephant suffer from stress, like all creatures. This can be attributed to many causes: the recent death of another elephant, a shortage of food or water, the presence of too many uncontrolled tourists, or a combination of any of these. Stress is visible by streaming temporal glands – the glands erupt on either side of the skull, halfway between the eye and the ear.

Elephant will very quickly tell you by their posture whether they are relaxed or agitated, whether they are going to retreat or attack. When in rebellious mood, the females will form a laager, adults facing outwards and babies in the centre. They will have their trunks up and will be searching for you with all their sense organs turned up to maximum. When you recognise these signs you should be miles away already. If you are walking in an area that is close to a hunting area you may well encounter animals that have had a bad experience. This will make them much more likely to behave aggressively than if they have lived all their lives within the boundary of a national park, free from poaching.

Bulls are another matter entirely. A solitary bull elephant can be approached, provided you get the wind right. Make doubly certain that he is alone or, if not alone, that he is with other bulls and not in association with females. If you suddenly come upon a bull elephant and you want him to be aware of

you without startling him, talk softly to him. Once he hears your voice, he knows who you are, and he is not startled into doing something foolish. Again, with the wind right, you can approach quite close. If the wind suddenly changes and you can see that he has got wind of you, don't run or do anything stupid. Talk softly to him and stay put.

I always like to approach bull elephants from the protection of a large tree or a termite mound. It is also convenient to meet a big bull when he is on the other side of a small stream, then you can observe him in safety while he provides you with a tour de force of trumpeting, head-shaking and mock charges. The first sign a bull elephant makes when he is irritated is to shake his head from side to side to rattle his huge ears. If that fails to intimidate, he may then try a mock charge, which more an act of bravado than anything else. Females don't bother with gestures: they just charge and follow through.

Another way to get close to bulls is to intercept them while they are on an errand. If you see a line of bulls walking in your direction, try to guess which game trail they are travelling along, find a suitable vantage point close to it, such as a tall termite mound with a tree growing out of it, position your clients in a tight group on the top, and sit quietly and wait. If you are lucky, the elephant will walk right past, providing a wonderful experience. Your clients can learn to identify the smell of these huge animals, hear the light scuffing sound that their enormous cushioned feet make when coming into contact with the ground, hear the grinding of their teeth and the rumbling of their cavernous bellies.

You can intercept elephant in the same way if you are walking along the bank of a small stream

and you see one coming your way and about to wade across. If you can estimate at which point he is likely to emerge from the water on your side, you can lie in wait. Then, just as he is heaving himself up the bank, you can speak to him, quietly, but firmly: 'Njobvu, how are you do-day? What is on your mind?' Or words to that effect. He will stop and listen to you in amazement, a puzzled look on his wrinkled brow, before turning and retracing his steps in a dignified manner, tail erect.

To get the best experiences out of walking up to wild animals, you really need to know their habits, and to recognise when an animal is behaving abnormally. However, animals do not always behave according to a pattern. Like human beings, animals have their off-days!

One must always observe them closely before deciding to get close: notice any idiosyncrasies, any signs that might indicate that the animal is behaving unusually, that it is ill or has been hurt. If this is so, then totally disregard all your established ideas about it and walk right away. Give it lots of space. If it is badly hurt, don't aggravate the situation by forcing it to run away, thereby causing it more suffering. It might also feel that it has to attack you. Animals will always give some indication of their feelings by adopting a particular gesture or stance. Learn to recognise what these look like and take appropriate action in good time.

There are not many areas that have what I consider to be perfect walking country. What you are looking for is unspoiled wilderness – that is, a large area without any human interference. This means no roads, no vehicles, no domestic animals, no villages, no light aircraft buzzing overhead, and no other human beings. In reality, such a place cannot exist because, as soon as soon as it did, people would flock to it.

If there are no people, there must be another problem – and that is usually access. Without proper access, law enforcement collapses and you have poaching. While you can, with careful planning, overcome the difficulties associated with access, if you have to take on the burden of law enforcement as well, you might as well give up, because walking safaris, which preach the doctrine of acceptance of things as they are, cannot exist in an atmosphere where one has to be policeman and law enforcer as well: the two are incompatible.

Another important factor is the type of vegetation present. You could find an area that is teeming with game but you have to walk around in long grass, well over your head, to find them. The only indication of an animal's presence is the sound it makes as it crashes away through the bushes. I dislike getting torn to pieces by thorns or covered by grass seeds and burrs, and I am sure most other people do, too. Nor do you want to walk through dense thickets with zero visibility so that you are having to crawl about on your hands and knees while getting your clothes snagged on thorns.

Apart from being extremely unpleasant, this type of bush is also extremely dangerous. Leave this terrain to the trophy-hunters because they can afford the expensive accident insurance. To be safe, the countryside must be open so that you can see ahead and spot animals before they spot you, providing your clients with the opportunity of taking a photograph after you have ingeniously stalked right up to the blighters!

I like to walk along game trails and, surprisingly, so do most people, be they hardened hikers or soft, city people accustomed to walking on paved footpaths in public gardens. If I have to walk all the time in the blazing sun, I get hot and uncomfortable. At times I like to be able just to sit down by a lagoon under shady trees and watch game coming down to drink. If the game is not plentiful, the presence of beautiful birds can make up for this. I like to have good visibility in all directions, and I like to believe that, if I am lucky, I could see a leopard in a tree, or a herd of giraffe, or an old bull elephant feeding, or, if I am really lucky, come on the spoor of lion and, after tracking them, find sleeping under a tree.

What is also nice is that the animals are not overwhelmed with a sense of panic as soon as they set eyes on you so that, before you have even had time to register what species they are, they have disappeared over the horizon in a cloud of dust. At the end of the walk I like to feel that I have provided my clients with an unforgettable experience without having put their lives at risk, and that the animals we encountered were not made to feel inconvenienced or frightened.

The individual who likes walking is a different sort of animal from the average townie. He or she is usually someone who has already been on one or more safaris before and is looking for something different, something that brings them closer to the animals in a more intimate manner. They are the sort of people who will not mind if they don't see hordes of game all the time because they have seen that sort of thing before; they will be quite content

to observe aspects of animal behaviour that are not revealed when they are bouncing along in the back of a crowded truck.

There is also the physiological aspect of walking, of course. The heart beats faster, the muscles are toned, you take in more oxygen. There is also the aspect of being more aware of what is going on around you – not only seeing, but hearing and smelling. You become more aware. Your mood changes. You become more alive in every respect. A friend of mine who is a very ardent Christian once told me that he envied me because as a safari guide I was more likely to spot the devil lurking behind a bush.

If I walk with someone in a city, I am always being told to slow down. My stride is the one I use when I'm heading out to some far distant peak. It is difficult to change. You can tell a walker by their calves: they are nicely shaped and muscular.

On one safari, after first scanning the countryside from the top of a high hill, I was able to point out a lioness lying beside a stream in wait for three old buffalo bulls. From the hilltop, we clambered down stealthily and stalked closer, and were able to watch as the buffalo reached the stream to drink – and were ambushed by two other lionesses that we had not seen before. But the buffalo would have none of it: they formed into line and drove the lionesses off with great strength of purpose. This is the sort of spectacle that a vehicle safari will very rarely catch.

Being out on foot, you are relying entirely on your own instincts as well as the instincts and experience of your guide and game scout. Because of this, the experience is enriched a hundredfold – you are right there, your feet resting on the same stretch of sand

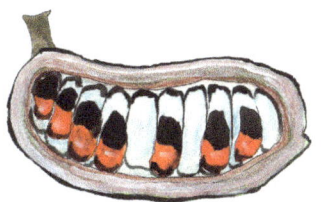

that the lion are standing on; you can almost smell the adrenalin of the buffalo, hear them snorting in indignant rage, sense when it is time to move on lest the lionesses vent their disappointment on you. You realise, with both horror and excitement, that you have become another player in the game, not just a remote observer.

On a walk, you should insist that your group walks in single file. A walking safari is very much like a military operation in enemy-held country. An attack could come at any moment and from any direction, and you have to be able to provide advice and reassurance in seconds, before your clients panic and scatter. To make this possible, it is essential that your walkers can hear you at all times. Good communication is absolutely vital.

When I worked as a guide in the Luangwa Valley, I developed a system of communication that I used with the game scout. If I saw an animal that he had not noticed, I would whistle quietly; hand signals were also important. Seeing animals before they see you is critical. In this, everybody plays a part. The more the group becomes involved, the more they enjoy it. As you move along, each individual receives a different perspective of the bush that you are passing through – which means that an animal hidden from the rest of the party suddenly comes into view for one of them for a fraction of a second. That person can then warn the rest of the group. This is particularly relevant with elephant, which are very difficult to see when they are standing still in thick cover. Often it is only when they make a sound that you become aware of them.

When walking through bush where visibility is restricted, the group needs to keep close together; in the open, the line can spread out more. Allow for a gap between the scout and yourself – a sort of buffer zone – so that, if an animal charges and the scout has to shoot, you would not be flattened by the momentum of the charge.

You should continually check that your group is keeping up, and group members should also inform you if someone falls behind. This is normally the responsibility of the tea-bearer, who walks right at the back of the line. As soon as someone falls too far behind, he will whistle, and the guide can halt the others, giving the person who might have stopped to tie up his shoelace time to catch up. Keeping together as a group is vital for safety. The rule should be that if one person stops, the whole group stops. The speed you walk at should always be that of the slowest member.

If you are walking with a scout and an animal decides to charge, the scout must stand his ground, giving the guide time to lead the clients to safety, which could be behind a large tree or a termite mound. Once the all-clear is sounded and the animal has run off, you can join up again and continue your walk. If you have a third member in your walking team, and in the Luangwa Valley it is common to take a tea-bearer on walks, he then becomes the leader. Without being told what to do, he leads the group in reverse order to safety. The guide will now be in the rear, watching the situation closely and deciding whether a new course of action is necessary.

Sometimes an animal does come on and the guide has to keep walking back and back, and the scout may even have to fire a warning shot or an aimed shot. By the time he does this, the guide and the clients should be a long way away and out of danger. How to react in an emergency must become second nature to those who take groups out walking. The routine should be stressed in the briefing at the beginning of the walk. There should never be a mad stampede. The guide should not panic but keep his voice calm and give clear, precise instructions.

If you are leading a group on your own and do not have any assistance from a tracker or game scout, you are much more exposed and your control over your clients has to be absolute. You will not have much time at your disposal, so what you say and do must be right. Your clients must know exactly what to do the moment the alarm is given, and must carry out your instructions precisely and without panicking, while you watch to see what the animal is up to.

Clients are always keen to take home little souvenirs of their trip. You should make them realise that the bush is like a living museum and that by removing an animal's skull or other interesting items they are actually spoiling the experience for the next individuals who will come along that way. You have to decide where to draw the line. I would allow the odd feather or porcupine quill, but nothing bigger.

When you have a group of people for any length of time, it is a good idea to rotate the order in the line whenever you stop to look at something so that everybody gets a chance to be near the front. The logic behind this is simple: the person in front often gets to see an animal before it is alarmed and runs off. By the time the man at the back fights his way to the front to see what it was that has just run away, camera at the ready, there is nothing to see.

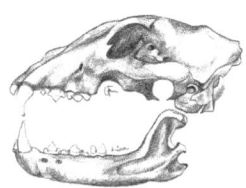

When he asks what the others were looking at and is told that there was a leopard in a tree, he naturally feels disappointed and hard done by. Dominant personalities will expect to be in the front, always.

Many guides make the mistake of presuming that their clients can hear everything they say, even when they are facing away from them. For the person at the end of the line, hearing what the guide is saying is virtually impossible. If you are stalking an animal, the guide is most likely to whisper, and this further reduces the chances of your clients hearing you properly. It is then that mime comes in handy – hand signals to represent a particular animal. As the Bushmen do. If you have an important observation to make, it is better to wait for everybody to catch up and then start talking when the group can form a circle around you. You don't have to raise your voice and you can be sure that everybody will have heard what you have been saying. So many pearls of wisdom are wasted on the African air because the guide is talking while he is facing away from his clients.

At some stage during a walk, somebody will want to attract the attention of the guide, which might be during a stalk. If she raises her voice and says, 'I say, young man, there's a very big lion asleep under the tree ahead of us,' the lion will wake up with a start and be very unhappy about having his dreams disturbed so suddenly. If the lady were to whistle gently – presuming, of course, that she can whistle – the guide can turn around, find out what the problem is, the lion will dream on, the whole group gets the photo of a lifetime, and everyone is happy.

I had two incidents that brought out the importance of being able to hear adequately. An

elderly couple from America came on a walk – they were both physically fit but both were hard of hearing. After supper, we sat around the fire and chatted. The husband got up from the fire and walked off in the direction of the dining room. He was gone for some time. I looked at his wife to see if she was concerned, but she was chatting away happily as though nothing was amiss. Her husband appeared a little later and I relaxed. Before going to bed I gave my usual instructions about keeping hut doors firmly closed during the night.

The following morning, the elderly couple looked tired, so I asked them if they had slept soundly. The wife told me that, following my instructions to keep the hut doors open, they had lain awake, expecting a wild animal to come creeping in. She also said that when her husband got up from the fire to go to the toilet, he had become disorientated and had slipped down the river bank in the dark and had struggled to get back up. The river is fast-flowing and full of crocodiles – if he had fallen in, we would never have known about it.

On another occasion I had a family group with me that included Grandad. Once again, he was someone who was physically fit but very hard of hearing. Coming back from an afternoon walk along a dry river bed I made a comment that leopards favoured these rivers. Not long after, I found leopard tracks. I waited for the whole group to come up and pointed out the three pads at the back of the paw that are characteristic of all cats. Grandad preferred to walk at the back of the group, giving the younger members of the group the best chance of getting good sightings of game. We climbed out of the river bed and, as we did, I saw a medium-sized crocodile

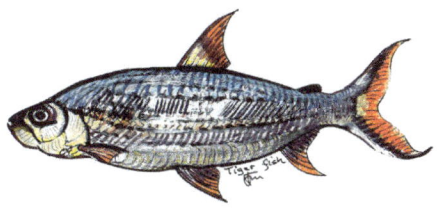

walking ahead of us through the short grass. I pointed and said, 'Look, there's a crocodile out of water.' It was obviously making its way down to the main river as his lagoon had dried up.

The game scout and I sprinted ahead in order to catch the croc before it could hide, but it saw us and hid under a bush. The scout and I reached the bush and waited for the group to arrive. In the meantime I found a long stick. With everybody watching, I prodded the croc, which snapped at the stick, hissing all the time. When I felt that the croc had had enough I said, 'Let's go,' and we walked back to camp. As we reached camp, Grandad came up to me and said: 'Iain, you were very brave back there, poking that leopard with a stick!'

One old game scout that I walked behind through the bush had a way of alerting you if there was a hidden obstacle in the path, such as a hole or a stump, which, if not spotted, could cause someone to sprain an ankle. He would pat either his right or left thigh, depending on which side of the path the obstacle occurred.

A guide should realise the frailty of his clients. You should make a point of stopping for a rest and a chat every hour. This allows your smokers to have a cigarette, and it makes it possible for someone to nip behind a bush for a pee. During these stops, though, you must maintain discipline: your permission must be sought before anybody is allowed to wander off, and you should check out the lie of the land before you send someone to a particular bush. If you haven't said it already, now is the time to give your chat about litter and burying toilet paper. You should

encourage smokers to keep their cigarette ends in their matchboxes. Nothing annoys me more than coming across a cigarette end on a walk: one is, after all, trying to present an appearance of nature unspoiled by human interference. To find a cigarette butt on the ground shatters any illusion you might have been able to create up to that point.

After two hours of walking, you should have a proper stop for half an hour or so. At Chibembe, this was when the tea-carrier came into his own. He produced a tea pot and cups from the wooden box he had been carrying on his head and would set about making a small fire using dry elephant droppings. Within ten minutes, the water would be boiling and each member of the party would have a steaming cup of tea in their hand and a biscuit to nibble. There is nothing like a cup of tea to rejuvenate a flagging spirit. It can also be amazing what you will see while you are sitting quietly. We often chose a lagoon for our tea stops, and on several occasions a herd of buffalo, and sometimes an elephant, would come up for a drink. We just sat, cup in hand, and watched it all unfold in front of us. When tea was over, it was the guide's duty to check that the fire was out and that the twigs used to make the fire had been scattered.

Towards the end of the dry season, the sun beats down relentlessly; after ten o'clock, it is really fierce. This is why a walking safari should leave camp as early as possible and return before it starts getting really hot. While out, if you have to stop for a while, move your clients into the shade; never allow them to stand around in the blazing sun while you wait

for someone to tie their laces. Have you noticed old safari hands remove their hats as they walk under a tree, like old parishioners entering a church? It is a fact. This is not done for any pious reason but to allow a barely discernible breeze to cool their steaming scalps.

As a guide, your vigilance must never flag. Always choose a resting place that gives you good all-round vision. I would position the scout so that he could watch for any animal approaching from behind us, and I would watch the front. Vigilance is a twenty-four hour business. A guide must be alert to the unexpected all the time. You are always most vulnerable when you are most relaxed. You must make a point of being extra vigilant when the camp is in sight after a long walk. Your clients will always start to relax when they see camp. You must not, and you must see that your clients don't either.

Always check out very thoroughly those places that you feel might be harbouring a lion, a buffalo or a sleeping hippo – before approaching them. Only your experience will tell you what these places are. After all, one of the main objectives of going on a walking safari is to see animals before they see you. You will never achieve this if you cannot predict where they prefer to be at different times of the day.

If you are using a boat for any reason, before any of your clients step out on to the land, make sure that either you, or your scout, have checked to see that it is safe to go ashore. The number of times I have seen a hippo browsing in daytime on the bank, just as my party was about to climb out ...

Lion love lying out on a high bank to watch the world go by. Buffalo will often feed very close to water. What I am saying here also applies to

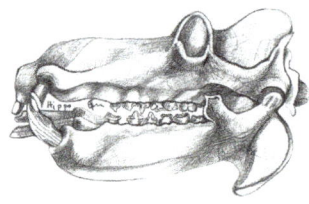

vehicle safaris. The number of times I have seen safari drivers allow their passengers to go off into the bushes without first checking to see that there is anything threatening out there ...

If you are working with a scout, it is imperative that you first work out the ground rules so that there are no misunderstandings when the time comes. On all my safaris working with a scout, I always chose the route. I had a very good knowledge of the area we operated in and knew where most species of game were likely to be found. I also knew the needs of my clients and what they were capable of putting up with. If I had a group of unfit travel agents with me on their first trip to Africa, I would not take them on a six-hour walk across broken country in the blazing sun. If, on the other hand, I had four young men and a girl athlete who wanted a bit of exercise as much as anything else, then I would go for a good hike. The beauty about walking is that, if you are smart and observant, you can spend just one hour of the morning actually walking and the rest of the time observing; because they will have seen so much of interest, they will feel that they have walked miles and miles when in fact they have merely walked in a small circle.

When you decide in your own mind which direction you will take for your walk, be it a morning or afternoon walk, you should take into consideration the direction of the sun. This becomes more important early in the morning and late in the afternoon. If you walk into the sun, your vision is going to be severely impaired because you are going to be squinting half the time. It is preferable to set out with the sun at your back. It will be the animals that are dazzled, not you.

When we were walking in the Luangwa Valley, it was always clearly understood that the scout had the final say when an animal threatened us. It takes time to establish a good working relationship with a scout. Some scouts who came from a part of the country where there were no elephant would at first be nervous about walking up to elephant. Another might be unhappy in the presence of buffalo because of some previous incident. All these things had to be taken into account. If I felt that the scout was acting irresponsibly, I would favour caution and overrule him, tell him to move back. It was this give and take, based on respect for one another, that built a strong team. This was only possible because we had spent so much time on safari together.

One scout played a game when we encountered a large herd of buffalo. His name was Kapususu and he had worked in the Kafue National Park for many years and was familiar with buffalo. They are very inquisitive and behave very like cattle when in a large herd. Kapususu had no fear of them. He would crouch down and creep slowly up to a large herd while rotating his rifle in front of his face like the blade of a windmill. The buffalo just watched him fascinated, like a herd of cows waiting to be milked. As he approached, the herd parted. He would move through them until he was standing right in their midst. Not one of them became alarmed or behaved aggressively. They demonstrated an excessive inquisitiveness, that was all. This was very entertaining for the clients, and it taught them that animals in herds behave differently from individuals. Had the buffalo stampeded, we would have been completely vulnerable. I allowed this game once and no more.

Another scout I worked with had a different trick to distract buffalo. This was to lie down on his back behind a clump of grass and waggle his legs in the air as though he was riding a bicycle upside down. The buffalo would find this fascinating and they became so curious that they would edge closer and closer until they were only a few metres away from us.

Rules relating to the escort of tourists in national parks differ from country to country. In Zambia, all tourists entering a national park on foot must be accompanied by a scout trained by the Department of National Parks and Wildlife Services. In Zimbabwe, tourists entering a national park on foot must be escorted by an individual who has passed the full hunter/guide licence, or a National Parks scout. In the rest of Africa, I am sure the law favours one system or the other.

Whether it is a national parks scout or an armed safari guide is immaterial, as long as the individual responsible has received proper training, is reliable, and has a functional rifle and ammunition. Lives are at risk. The reputation of the country is a stake. Escorting tourists is a task requiring skill and special training. For a start, an ability to communicate is essential, because walking up to animals is a potentially dangerous business, and communication, however rudimentary, must be effective when it is required.

Some knowledge of the habits of the animals one is expected to see is also a requirement, and enthusiasm

about this is vital. Wildlife is an important resource for any country. It is part of its national heritage, and if individuals from the Department of National Parks are not fully involved with the business of guiding tourists in their own parks, they will not appreciate the importance of this vital resource and be motivated to protect it.

In Zambia, the role of guide and scout are separated. The primary concern of the scout is to deal with aggressive animals; imparting knowledge and dealing with the everyday needs of the clients is left to the guide because that is what he is best equipped to do.

I believe that an individual who grows up surrounded by wild animals is likely to know far more about them than someone who has lived all his life in a big city and whose knowledge is derived from reading. Local knowledge is worth a great deal, and many individuals who have lived all their lives in the bush possess it without being aware of it. This may not be 'scientific' but, if it is based on close observation, it is going to be of value and worth listening to. Such individuals also possesses a sixth sense, in keeping with the animals, that has been evolved out of the man from the big city. The man from the bush is also familiar with African myths and legends, and these make fascinating listening for foreign tourists.

How safaris are conducted has a lot to do with the history of the country, as well as the involvement of certain influential individuals in drawing up the rules. In several countries it is the safari-guide association that is responsible for establishing guidelines for conducting safaris: they are, after all, the ones who are sued if an accident occurs. They

have the best understanding of what standards should apply – something that many government departments have little comprehension of.

A close interplay between the private sector and the relevant departments in national parks is very necessary. If one party assumes complete control without allowing the other any opportunity to voice their feelings, the result will be far from satisfactory. Representatives from the safari companies should meet with the national parks' authorities on a regular basic to hammer out procedures that are beneficial to both parties. If a good working relationship exists between the private and public sector, it will definitely be to the advantage of all parties concerned and to tourism in general.

Guns and gun handling for safari work

The laws relating to carrying a weapon on walking safaris differ from country to country. In Zambia, anyone walking in a national park must be escorted by a trained national parks scout with a rifle. In Zimbabwe, only individuals who have a full guiding licence can escort tourists in national parks.

When out on a walking safari, the guide must make it absolutely clear to his clients that they should never walk in front of the gun. If the group stops to look at something, the gun must be the front marker and the group stands behind it. Often, when drawing the group's attention to spoor, the guide needs to kneel down. At other times, the guide will have to turn and face his group because he has some information to impart. In both instances the barrel of the rifle must never point at anybody. A safari guide with a rifle must always be aware of this.

Carrying a rifle in a vehicle with people is a nuisance at the best of times. The rifle should be protected from dust and shocks in a padded carrying case. In this form it can be hidden out of the way behind a seat. Too many fatal accidents have occurred as a result of loaded weapons not being carried properly in vehicles: the weapon falls over when the vehicle hits a bump and goes off.

Never lean a rifle against the door of a vehicle. What can happen is that someone opens the door and the rifle falls to the ground. Not only can this damage the rifle's sights but, if the weapon is cocked, it may go off and kill or wound somebody. It can also happen that the vehicle departs, leaving the weapon behind on the ground – easy pickings for the first pedestrian who comes by. The onus by law is on the

certificate-holder to take all necessary provisions to ensure that the weapon and ammunition do not fall into the hands of unauthorised persons.

For a guide who is working alongside a national parks scout, it is imperative that he understands how to use a rifle, particularly the rifle that the scout is using, in case a moment arises that the scout is incapacitated for one reason or another. The guide should satisfy himself that the scout's rifle is in good working order and that the ammunition being used is sound.

The average safari guide probably gets to fire his weapon only once or twice in a season, if that. The number of times he has to fire under conditions of extreme pressure is extremely rare.

Under what circumstances might a weapon be used on a walking safari? These will be considerably different from those pertaining to trophy-hunting. The trophy-hunter will select his quarry with great care from the rest of the herd and then follow it until a killing shot is guaranteed. He has at his disposal a telescopic sight, a clear field of vision, time to decide where to place his shot, a tree or anthill to lean on, and the assistance of a professional hunter to provide advice and back-up in case the animal is wounded and charges.

The factors that apply in photographic safaris have more in common with military or police work. Most encounters with dangerous animals on safari take place at very close range, and with very little warning. The animal that erupts out of a bush could be a lion, or a buffalo, or a hippo. There is very little time to aim: often you have time for only one quick shot. In addition, the animal will be coming at you head-on, offering a very small target and with most

of the vital organs tucked away either behind a bony skull or a boss. You might also have to fire through a bush. So that one shot has to be telling. As a guide, you also have to be concerned about your clients behind you and how they are might behave – they could also be in front of you and in the line of fire.

Fortunately, in most cases, a charging animal will give you enough time for a second shot. If the first misses the animal by a whisker, it may well have the effect of turning it, or slowing it down so that a second shot is unnecessary.

On safari, the animals that need to be taken most seriously are those that are deemed to be 'dangerous thick-skinned animals': buffalo, elephant, hippopotamus and rhinoceros. Lion and leopard are included in the 'dangerous' list, but they are soft-skinned. Rhinoceros are so scarce these days that it would be a tragedy if a safari guide took his group so close that it became necessary to shoot one of the few remaining individuals. Leopard, though a very determined adversary for the trophy-hunter, do not pose much of a problem to the photographic hunter. This leaves, elephant, buffalo, hippopotamus and lion. A safari guide is going to carry a weapon that will deal with the thick-skinned dangerous animals, so the lion becomes a category all of its own. Lion can usually be turned by a concerted effort of shouting and arm waving on most occasions. This is the line that should be adopted vigorously at first, and if it fails, shooting is the last option.

A warning shot can be of use with most dangerous animals. However, it should be done as soon as the animal signifies that it is aware of your presence and begins to approach in a threatening manner. It should also be early so that it gives you

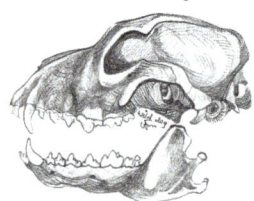

time to reload if necessary – there is no point in firing a warning shot when the animal is almost on top of you. But there is also no point in firing before the animal is even aware of you because you still have enough time to withdraw.

Tracking

> *Always at the beginning of any particular hunt there was one solemn ceremony to perform: an earnest consultation between all hunters as to which spoor was most worthwhile following. The Bushmen would sit on their heels like elder statesmen discussing the size, mood, sex and direction of the animals, study the wind, the sun, the hour and the weather generally. When they had picked out one particular spoor they revealed their decision by flicking their hands over it loosely from their wrists and making a sound like the wind between their teeth.*
>
> Laurens van der Post, *The Lost World of the Kalahari* (London: Hogarth Press, 1958), 231–2.

Tracking is an activity that has a touch of magic about it. To many individuals, tracking has the same aura as water-divining or fortune-telling. Having said this, tracking, like most skills, does have a rational side to it, but it also has an intuitive, subconscious aspect to it that does seem magical: it is this aspect that makes it difficult to describe. I will do my best to reveal the logical side of the art of tracking and leave the other, more intuitive, side for the individual to develop.

Tracking is great fun. It will make even the most unenthusiastic individual an addict. Once learned, tracking has its uses wherever you are and whatever you are doing. What is so marvellous is that there is always spoor about, even when animals are scarce. When you can't find anything to look at, there in the sand is the unmistakable impression of a leopard's footprint. Suddenly you are faced with the reality of an animal that you have only read about but

never seen. The footprints are undeniable proof that this secretive animal actually exists. You become more alert and watchful. The safari suddenly has a dimension to it that hadn't existed before. Other signs become visible. The level of awareness of the group has been raised and, once raised, each individual's level of awareness will remain at that level for ever.

Tracking also gives a safari a touch of authenticity, making it what it really is – a hunt. We use skills passed down to us from our early hunter-gatherer ancestors, skills that have become dormant in all of us as a result of being crushed together in urban centres. We are able to see with more than our eyes; this is the element of magic.

Tracking is much more than the slavish pursuit of marks in the sand. To track anything – whether it is a thief who has made off with your television, or a lion – an intimate knowledge of your prey is essential. The Bushmen believed that to track an animal you had to become the creature being pursued. This empathy with the pursued is essential because much of the time there is nothing to go on; there are no clues. Assumptions have to be made about the animal that are not apparent to the naked eye.

Let us presume that you are trying to find a black rhino. To do this you must have a very detailed knowledge of the animal's habits. For instance, the fact that rhino tend to feed at night and rest up during the day is vital, and that they drink once a day and head back to their sleeping quarters in a thicket in the early hours of the morning. The knowledge that rhino are browsers is important, too, and what they feed on is also relevant. Knowing all this provides us with a picture of the animal that will form the basis of our tracking philosophy.

They could tell very quickly how long it was since the buck, lion, leopard, bird, reptile or insect had signed his time-sheet in the sand. No two hoof-prints were alike to them for all spoor, like finger-prints to a Scotland Yard sleuth, were distinct and individual. They would pick out one from fifty, and deduce accurately the size, sex, build and mood of the great antelope that had just made it.
Laurens van der Post, *The Lost World of the Kalahari* (London: Hogarth Press, 1958), 231.

Having ascertained that a rhino is drinking from a particular waterhole, you should get up very early one morning, visit this waterhole and check for fresh spoor. When you have located it, you can begin tracking in earnest. Another way of finding tracks is to drive slowly along a dirt road early in the morning searching for places where rhino might have crossed during the night. Rhino are creatures of habit, and once you have discovered their preferred routes to and from water, it is relatively easy to follow and make contact with them.

Lion are also worth tracking because they will settle once the sun swings overhead and not move again until it loses some of its heat later in the afternoon. Lion like walking along game trails, dirt tracks, and down river courses with soft sand. Their pads are delicate, so when given the choice of walking down a bush track or across a stubbly field they will choose the easier option. This means that as you drive around on game-viewing exercises you should always keep one eye on the road in case lion have been on the move during the night. This means driving slowly.

The best time to track is early in the morning and late afternoon when the sun is striking the ground at an acute angle. If you have ever tried to photograph a subject with interesting texture, the secret is always to place your light source so that it shines across the surface, bringing out the texture. In the early morning, sunlight slants down, throwing the slightest ripples in the ground surface into sharp relief, which is when the smallest irregularity becomes visible. When following spoor, you should not look at your feet but rather aim your glance to strike the ground about three metres ahead of you.

Using the analogy of photography again, your eyes should be on wide-angle and not on telephoto. By covering a wide area, you will be aware of very small disturbances that you would miss entirely if you were staring at the ground in a fixed manner. Tracking involves all your senses, not just your eyes. You should also be aware of sounds and odours as you move along. Using only your vision restricts sensory input and reduces your success rate. You should be aware of alarm calls from squirrels, starlings and Oxpeckers, and of the movement of large raptors such as eagles and vultures.

All the stimuli you receive should be assimilated as you move along. Leopard and lion will scent-mark on bushes and trees – which is easy to detect if you have ever had a neutered male cat as a pet. To begin with, your pace will be slow as there is a lot of information to take in, but as the picture in your mind becomes clearer your pace can increase. This takes place once you realise what your animal is up to. Is he feeding? Is he heading for water? Is he in pursuit of a female in oestrus? Is he wounded and looking for shade? All these signs will enable you to

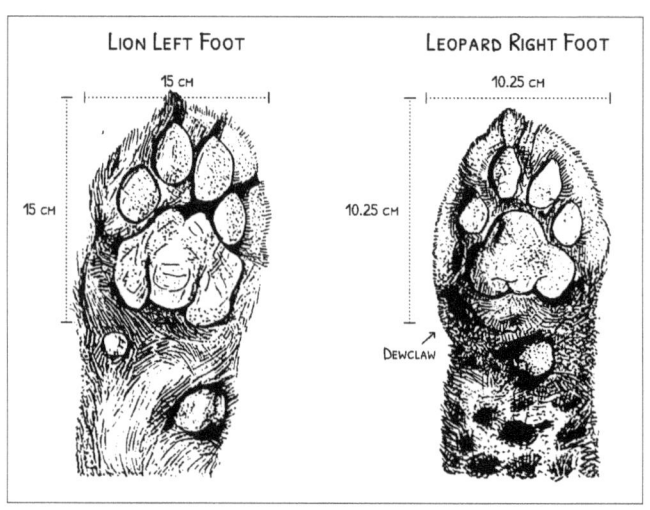

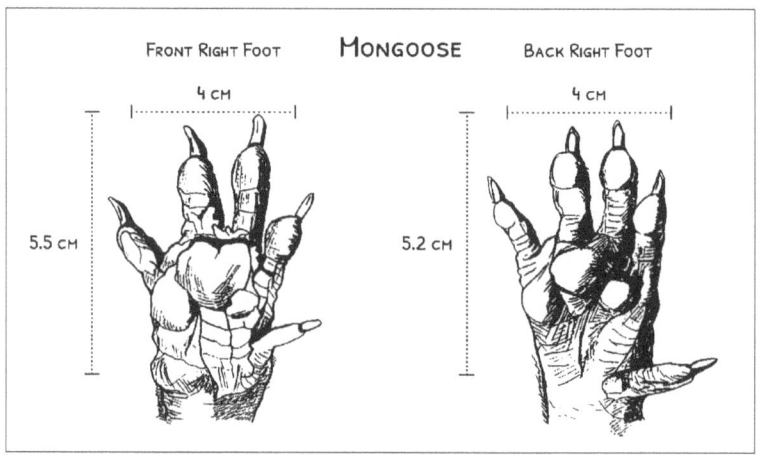

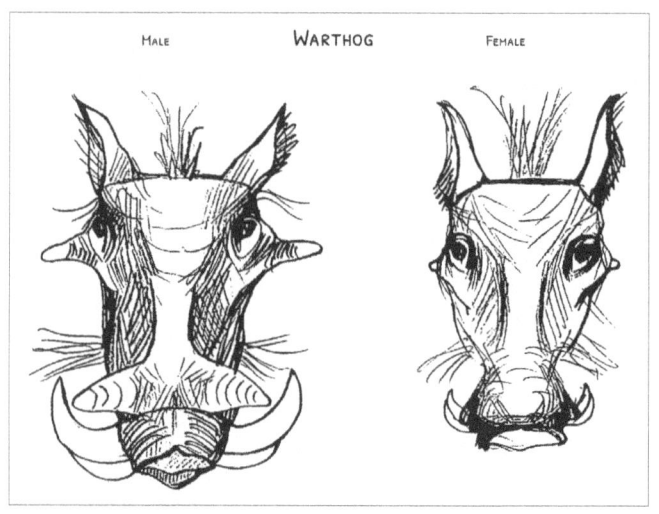

create a thought-picture of his behaviour. You should also be able to separate the animal you are tracking from any others that you might come across in the process.

> *A tracker in action has to think and feel like the animal he tracks. He has to have empathy and a trust in the sort of intuitive feelings that some describe as a 'burning sensation' in the centre of their foreheads, or as a 'tapping at the ribs'.*
> (Lyall Watson, *Elephantoms: Tracking the Elephant* (Johannesburg: Penguin Random House, 2004), 133.

All footprints are unique. If you have read T.E. Lawrence's *Seven Pillars of Wisdom*, or any of Wilfred Thesiger's books about the desert and the Bedouin, you will appreciate how skilled the Bedouin are at identifying the individual peculiarities of each camel. They can spot the footprints of a particular animal and tell you who it belongs to, and they will remember these details long afterwards. Sometimes it is because the animal had an unusual gait, one foot more splayed than the other. Occasionally an old wound will be evident from the skin of the pad. American Indians were also able to identify the peculiarities of their ponies at a glance. Antelope, especially very old ones, have chipped hoofs.

You should also be able to tell whether the animal you are tracking is male or female. Female rhinos will have a youngster with them until it is weaned or until another one is on the way. Male antelope urinate in front of their droppings; females tend to urinate behind theirs.

Elephant that are well into their last set of molars

will not be able to chew their food as efficiently as an animal with a good set of teeth. Their droppings will show this. There will always be something to enable you to set your animal apart from others, which is vital if you are going to be able to identify your animal when it comes into contact with others of the same species.

You should also be able to tell at a glance in which direction your animal is going: often a solitary animal such as a rhino will have both an outgoing track and a returning track, and these can easily become confused.

After a few minutes of detailed study you will suddenly appreciate that your rhino is feeding on the leaves of a particular bush. You can see where he has nibbled the leaves and where he has dropped some of them on the ground as he feeds. The branches on which he has been feeding will have been stripped. In the Matusadona National Park, beside the shores of Lake Kariba in Zimbabwe, rhino love to feed on jackal-berry (*Diospyros quiloensis*) bushes. Your eyes will immediately look for any bushes of this species, in particular those that have nibbled ends. Now you are not even looking at the ground but are scanning far ahead.

The footprint is used only to verify the track when other signs are missing. It is at this moment that you are in possession of information that will enable you to ascertain how far ahead of you the animal you are tracking is. You will also be able to deduce the speed at which it is moving by the number of bushes it is feeding on and by the frequency of its dung.

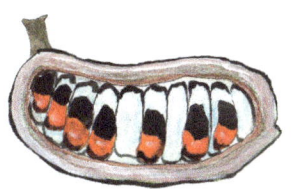

At this point we come on to an interesting aspect of tracking – the ageing of spoor. Many factors enter into this. You should first consider what has happened during the night. If it has rained, things will be a lot easier because new tracks will stand out clearly from those made before or during the rain. If there has been a strong wind during the night, this will also be very important. Fresh dung has mucous visible on it. Fresh elephant dung attracts tiny winged insects that swarm around it. The elephant hunters of old made a habit of pushing a finger into fresh dung to feel it for warmth. Banded mongooses, monkeys and baboons will pull elephant droppings apart for fruit kernels and insect larvae. If this has happened, you know that you are looking at droppings that are already several hours old.

Small insects walking over a track will indicate how old it is. Grass or leaves blown by the wind over tracks also give an indication of age. The edges of a fresh footprint are clearly defined and sharp; as they age, the edges break down and become more rounded. Saliva and mucous on grass stems and twigs also indicate age. Spider webs that are strung across gaps in bushes will be a clear sign that the track was made during the night or earlier. Look for water or mud droplets on the ground where an animal has been drinking.

As you proceed along a trail, be aware of the direction of the wind. Animals prefer to walk into the wind so that the presence of a predator can be detected in good time. If an animal settles down to rest under a tree, it will have its back to the prevailing wind and be watching down its track for a pursuer. As you track, look ahead occasionally in case your animal is sitting down under a tree,

A large lion footprint with Phineas's boot as reference.

A civet midden containing fruit seeds, hair, grass and twists of grass.

resting. As the spoor gets fresher and fresher, listen out for sounds that might indicate how close it is. The rumble of an elephant's insides as he digests his food, the breaking of branches as he feeds on tender shoots. The mooing of buffalo as they feed. The clicking of hooves against rocks. You do not want to stumble over the animal and frighten it off before you get a good look. Listen for the alarm calls of Oxpeckers that feed off the parasites that live on rhino, buffalo, hippo and several species of antelope. They will sense your approach long before their host and give the game away.

If the track enters thick, impenetrable bush or crosses an expanse of hard, dry rock, consider going around the obstacle and picking up the track on the other side rather than wasting a lot of time in futile search. If you lose the track, back-track to the last recognisable track and do a 360-degree reconnoitre until you establish where you went wrong. It is a good idea not to walk all over the spoor as you go along because it will make it very difficult for you if you do lose your way and have to back-track. Get into the habit of walking to one side of the spoor, leaving footprints undisturbed. Grass bends in the direction of the passage of a large animal. If there is dew on the grass, fresh signs of movement can be easily detected.

As you become more experienced, you will be able to recognise spoor even in the most unfavourable conditions. Spoor appears much bigger in soft sand and its appearance also changes because, as the foot sinks in the back of the hoof, the 'false hooves' also make contact with the ground, something that would not happen on hard ground. Learn to recognise when an animal is running in panic, trotting or

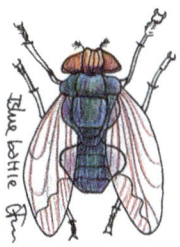

strolling. Stones that have been disturbed may be wet underneath, twigs that have been walked on will create an impression in the sand underneath.

In addition to the obvious signs of an animal's passage, there are many not so obvious ones. Zebra love to roll in loose sand: having a dust bath is an essential ritual in their daily life. Learn to recognise these places and search for hairs from the mane and tail. After wading a river, elephant often have a dust bath and in doing this they draw fine sand into their trunks and blow it over their bodies. The marks their trunks make in soft sand could be mistaken for the impression of a large snake.

Leopard will sharpen their claws on convenient branches beside a path. Warthog, elephant and rhino rub their bodies against tree stumps and rocks. Honey badgers dig up mud-hardened balls containing dung-beetle larvae. Monitor lizards unearth the eggs of crocodiles and leave the empty shells lying scattered about. Many antelope scent-mark on blades of grass and twigs using the exudation of various glands, in most cases the preorbital gland near the eye.

Guineafowl and francolin also enjoy a dust bath from time to time. Their places will be shallow indentations in soft sand with the odd feather scattered about; their droppings have a white tail to them. Eland use their sharp horns to scarify the bark from low bushes. Whether this is for territorial purposes or because they feel frustrated, I don't know. Monitor lizards or leguaans leave a tail drag-mark in soft sand. Dik-dik put a drop of secretion on a twig close to their droppings as a message that they hope reads, 'Keep away – she is mine!'

Most animals lie down and snooze during the day or night. Elephant do this, so do giraffe. Learn

to recognise the indentations made by resting animals as they provide valuable information. Hippo will spend several hours during the night asleep in soft sand on riverbanks. The impressions they leave in the sand, and the heaps of dung they deposit in the process, provide useful information about skin texture and body dimensions. Finding where a crocodile has being sleeping provides similar information. Lion roll in fresh buffalo dung, most likely to disguise their own scent when they are following a herd. Bush pig and warthog love to wallow in mud. Sometimes these wallows are some distance from permanent water, at other times they are close to the edge of a lagoon.

Cat urine is very pungent. If you have ever had a tomcat visit your home and spray your furniture you will know what I mean. Leopard and lion will spray over bushes and trees along a game trail; you can easily identify these places after a while. Leopard also sharpen their claws on tree trunks. Make a note of these because it will indicate that a leopard is in the vicinity – it is an easy connection to make between scratches on a tree and footprints close by in the sand. You should also train yourself to glance up into the canopy of trees from time to time as you walk because often you can spot the bones or skull of an antelope hanging from a tree fork – the remains of a leopard's meal. Often they become firmly wedged in the fork so that vultures cannot dislodge them, and they can remain like this for many months.

An animal's carcass contains information about the animal that killed it. A rodent or small bird with only its head missing is usually the work of a genet. A large predator such as a leopard or lion will peel back the skin of an antelope before feeding. You

often find a carcass of a small antelope with the skin turned inside out; wild dog do this to impala. Leopard lick the fur off the stomach of a baboon before feeding: the fur falls to the ground beneath the tree and provides evidence that a leopard has been at work. The skin of an animal that has died from disease rather than from a predator will still be in place around the skeleton. A buffalo skull sitting in the water of a drying-up lagoon has probably been put there by a hyena. In the horns of large antelope that have been lying in the bush for a long time can be seen the tubes of a particular moth which is able to dissolve the keratin in the horn.

Tourists will often ask which animal is responsible for digging a hole. This is often a difficult question to answer correctly because in most cases more than one animal might have been involved. It is always safe to say that the originator of most large holes is the work of an aardvark or antbear. Aardvark excavate these holes in order to reach termites, which form the bulk of their diet. They have very powerful forelegs armed with long, straight claws, and the holes are usually dug into the base of a termite mound.

Hyena will then arrive and enlarge them to make space for their nursery. Warthog will also make use of an existing burrow, either to sleep in or as a nursery. Porcupine are also capable excavators and will modify an existing burrow for their own needs. Quills scattered around the mouth of a burrow will indicate that a porcupine is in residence; bones, that a hyena is using the place. With a large burrow, it is possible that more than one creature is in residence. I found a complex of burrows occupied by warthog and porcupine at the same time. The warthog exited

Flying termite

from one of these openings at great speed – like a ballistic missile going into orbit! Avoid standing in front of an exit. A porcupine will stay put, indicating his presence by rattling his quills. Smaller burrows usually in soft sand could be the work of spring hares. Wild dog also use burrows as nurseries.

Flea numbers build up dramatically in burrows, forcing the occupants to move to a new site. I sat where a hyena had been sleeping outside his burrow and found myself crawling with fleas.

Ichnyology is the study of fossilised footprints. It is a new science, and in particular it looks for evidence that indicates whether a prehistoric animal was capable of walking fast, whether it belonged to a herd, and how it hunted. By measuring the distances between the footprints, a whole host of conclusions can be drawn about the dinosaurs that made them. Estimations can be made of the width of the pelvis and the distance between the front and hind legs – in fact, what the animal looked like.

Moses peers into a burrow in the roots of a tamarind tree, out of which shot an enraged warthog.

Measuring the distance between dinosaur footprints preserved in rock, Zambezi Valley.

Finding your way back

There is one faculty which the Bushmen possess in an extraordinary degree, and that is the sense which enables them to find their way, by day or by night, through level pathless forests, where there are no landmarks whatever, to any point which they wish to reach, where they have ever been before.
F.C. Selous, *Travel and Adventure in South-East Africa* (London: R. Ward, 1893), 110.

For anyone who has spent a lot of time walking in the bush, finding your way back becomes second nature, particularly if the countryside is familiar to you. However, things change dramatically when you are in strange territory; then you have to bring certain strategies to bear.

When walking somewhere for the first time, it is always a good idea to glance at a map of the area and get the main features clear in your mind first before venturing forth on your own. These features could be fences, rivers, mountain ridges, firebreaks or roads. I always like to have with me a series of maps of the area I am operating in, which can usually be obtained at little expense from the local mapping office. Like lengths of rope and balls of string, maps need to be handled with respect and folded away carefully after use, otherwise they soon become ragged and torn and no good to anyone. I admit that, in my hands, rope automatically winds itself into a tight ball with no ends. Maps have a similar tendency.

To store a map, and to keep it so that you can use it time and time again without damaging it, it is a good idea to buy A4-size plastic sleeves – some come with

little zips these days – and fold the map carefully so that the section you require is uppermost. After the trip, the maps can be filed like any other document. Maps should also be treasured because they are invaluable records of an area. Years later, if you are living in a different country and the mapping office from which you obtained your original map has closed down, you will regret not taking better care of them.

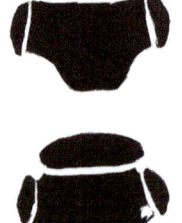

'For a moment things seemed to go round and round. I sat down with my back against the rock and a funny choky feeling in my throat. I knew they were my matches and cigarette, and that we were exactly where we had started from hours before, when we gave up the chase of the koodoo. I began to understand things then: why places and landmarks seemed familiar; why Jock's spoor in the molehill had pointed the wrong way; why my shadow was in front and behind and beside me in turns. We had been going round in a circle. I jumped up and looked about me with a fresh light; and it was all clear as noonday then. Why, this was the fourth time we had been on or close to some part of this same rise that day, each time within fifty yards of the same place; it was the second time I had sat on that very rock. And there was nothing odd or remarkable about that either, for each time I had been looking for the highest point to spy from and had naturally picked the rock-topped rise; and I had not recognised it, only because we came upon it from different sides each time and I was thinking of other things all the while.'
P. Fitzpatrick, *Jock of the Bushveld*
(Longmans, Green, 1922), 148

Orientation is an instinct carried over from our past. Our hunter-gatherer forebears utilised it because they would never have survived without it. It is as fundamental to our nature as the ability of migrating birds to find their way to their breeding grounds. For it to do its work satisfactorily, you must feed significant facts into your brain, much in the same way as a GPS relates to orbiting satellites.

The direction of the sun is very significant. Landmarks such as big trees, riverbeds and rocky outcrops are essential. If I visit London during the winter, when the sun is weak and low on the horizon, I have great difficulty comparing my position with maps of the Underground. Once the correct information is stored in your brain, you can draw upon it for guidance. If you disregard, or dispute, the information it is giving you, then you enter a dangerous phase. By doing so, you reformat your memory's way stations and scramble the original information. This is when you get lost.

When I am in a new area, I always make a few exploratory trips on my own, during which I use as a point of reference a dry riverbed or range of hills that has a direct relationship with the camp. Once you have the broad picture in your mind, then you have something to build on. By establishing a connection between your camp and that feature, you know that you can always find your way back home again.

When making a long route march from one point to another for the first time, it is sensible to use a compass. This is something you should have in your back-pack in case you do get lost, but a compass is not much good if you don't know where your camp is in relation to a definite feature. So, as I have said, you must first establish that relationship early. The

brain is a complex organ and you can very easily upset it by feeding it the wrong information. This is how many people get lost.

I was the driver of a group of tourists on a night drive. We always had a spotter – somebody who stood on the passenger side of the vehicle holding a spotlight. It is the spotter's job to guide the driver. We left the main road after a leopard and were following a small track. After ten minutes, the leopard had disappeared and I decided to make a 180° turn and return to the main road. By mistake, I must have made a 270° turn, but in my mind I believed I was now heading straight back to the main road on a 180° bearing.

After twenty minutes, I asked the spotter if he knew where we were going and he said he did. We continued some more, and then I knew we were lost. When you are lost, there is a critical moment when it is essential to admit to yourself that you are lost. This takes courage. Only then can you take remedial action to resolve the crisis. I had six clients on board; one was a British Airways pilot. When I did admit that I was lost, the clients agreed; they could tell.

At this point it is vital that you stop and let your mind relax for a while so that it can sort itself out. It is a good idea to have a cup of tea – do something to change the subject and allow your brain to disentangle itself. Once you have allowed yourself this downtime, you are better prepared to look at the situation calmly and rationally – something you could not have done before. In the case of the night drive, I remembered that the full moon was above the western horizon: it was actually in the direction

we needed to go. I turned and headed for it. Within fifteen minutes we had crossed our original tracks and returned to the main road.

On another occasion I was on a picnic with friends who had two daughters of about twelve and fourteen years of age. We had all climbed to the top of a nearby hill, and after a while the girls and I decided to return to the car park to collect our lunch. The eldest daughter was in front and out of sight of the two of us who came down more slowly. At one point the path made a sharp turn to the right when it crossed a rock slab before carrying on in the same direction. When I and the youngest daughter reached the cars the elder daughter had not arrived. Half an hour later I decided she must be lost and went looking for her; so did her mother. Mother and I returned to the car park later having searched the whole area with no success. I couldn't understand it. The area was not extensive. You could walk around the whole of it comfortably in twenty minutes. So where was she?

To cut a long story short, I eventually found her about fifty metres from the path sitting silently on a low rock. When she saw me she couldn't speak. I called her name but she still couldn't utter a sound. What had happened was as I had suspected. She had missed the right-hand bend in the path, which had taken her straight down the hill to a fence that was the boundary between the hill we were climbing and a tobacco field. The car park was on this fence, too. When she reached the fence she thought she was too far to the right so she turned left and followed the fence, but the car park did not materialise. She then **turned back and made a circle, but this was not large enough.** Still she could not find the cars.

At this point her brain shut down. The contradiction between the interpretation she gave to the evidence reaching her brain and the visible cues that confronted her became insurmountable. She admitted hearing me call. She had actually allowed me to walk past her but was unable to speak, such was her state of despair. When I saw her she was in such a state of shock that I had to take her by the arm and shake her a little before she was able to comprehend what had happened. All the time that she was lost she was not 250 metres from where the rest of us all were.

This incident encapsulates what takes place when we get lost. There is conflict between the evidence out there and what sense we make of it. It is this adjustment that we make as we progress that clouds the issue. This is why the first thing to do when you are lost is to admit that you are lost. The second most important thing to do is to stop and relax. Give yourself time to descramble your brain by doing something totally different. Have a cup of tea, have a snooze. Then, with your brain rested, tackle the situation from a fresh perspective. You will be amazed what a difference it makes.

Another thing that the extract from *Jock of the Bushveld* reveals is that it is always when we set out on a journey that we fail to notice vital information about our whereabouts. At the start of this tale, Jock and his owner are chasing after a kudu ('koodoo'). In my incident on the night drive, our concentration was directed totally towards a leopard we were following. Whenever you are going out on a walk in a locality that is new to you, the time when you should be most

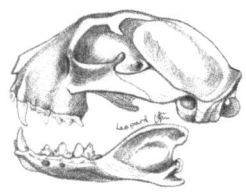

alert to significant landmarks – distinctive trees, unusual rocks, patches of tall grass, dry riverbeds – is right at the beginning of your walk, which is when you have other more engaging thoughts on your mind.

What usually happens is that you have some definite objective on leaving the camp – you might have seen vultures circling in the distance, or you thought there might be lion about because a baboon was making his alarm call. With your eyes fixed on the far horizon, you set out. An hour later, when you discover that the vultures were only catching thermals, you decide to made a wide detour back to camp. Five hours later you are still walking because you have missed the camp. Why? Because when you should have been noting landmarks, you were gazing up at the sky and you did not register them.

As you leave camp, note the time. Note the time again when you have gone as far as you intend to go on that occasion. You can estimate how long it will take to get back to camp. As you change direction, make a mental note. It is like clicking off degrees of change on a chart. The only way you can do this with any certainty is if you have something to relate to – a range of hills, a very tall tree in the distance. You know where the camp is in relation to the hills, so as you change direction away from your original course you can compare your position with it each time.

As I have mentioned earlier, if you have clients with you, it is important to stop every hour for a break. If you feel that you might be lost, these breaks provide a good opportunity for you to shin up a tree so that you can get your bearings without drawing attention to the fact. Getting up above the level is always useful. If you can climb a tall tree, or get on top of a high rock, you can possibly see the smoke from the camp, or catch sight of a road, which can help you get your bearings. This is also when it is very handy having a tracker or a game scout with you who knows the area well.

Familiar features can look quite different from a different angle. I remember coming on a set of lagoons on an afternoon walk in an area that I was extremely familiar with and being amazed that I had never seen them before. Two factors were responsible for this phenomenon: the first was that I normally approached them from a different angle; the second that I normally visited them in the morning, when the light was on the other side. The change of light and the new approach had completely confused me.

On another occasion, after a very long walk I had made to explore new territory, I was returning to camp on a compass bearing and was expecting to meet a river at any moment. Sure enough, the river appeared when I predicted it would, but much to my amazement it was running in the wrong direction. Instead of running from left to right, it was running from right to left. What had actually happened was that my compass bearing was out by a few degrees, and instead of hitting the main river I had hit a tributary of it. This explained the direction of flow. Fortunately I was with porters who knew what had happened, but I was completely confused for some time.

This is the moment that I referred to earlier – the moment when you suddenly realise that your mental picture is askew. Then you must sit down and do something different in order to give your mind time to readjust. If you start walking again with your

mental picture unresolved, you will – without any doubt whatsoever – get lost.

The cardinal rule if you do get lost is to stick together. It is a great temptation for someone, the youngest or the fittest, to go steaming off on his own to find help, leaving the others behind. A classic example of this concerned a group of young school children and their leader climbing in the Chimanimani Mountains to the east of Zimbabwe. When they were climbing down the mountain, the clouds came down. The leader speeded up to get down before all visibility was lost. In doing so, he hadn't realised that the children were not following. They were lost on the mountain for many days without food or shelter, and it was only their tenacity and resourcefulness that saved them.

I took a group out one morning in the Selous game park in Tanzania. My aim was to walk from the largest lake, on which the lodge was situated, Nzerakera, to another, smaller lake, Lake Manze. It was overcast with low cloud. There were no shadows. No indication of where the sun was. We started walking and after about an hour I decided to stop so that we could have a drink and a rest. I laid my rifle against a tree.

When it was time to continue the walk I grabbed the rifle, put the strap over my shoulder and starting walking. Palm trees are an indication of water. An hour later I noticed palm trees ahead and told my group that we were nearing the lake. As we approached, I had a funny feeling. Something was wrong. The palm trees were not as I had expected them to be. The shoreline was too flat. There were

no palm trees out in the water as there should have been. I couldn't make sense of anything.

I spoke to my Tanzanian assistant when I could get him alone. He smiled and shook his head. What had happened was that, after our rest break, I had started walking back the way we had come. Retracing our steps. Why? Because I had not noticed where the sun was in the sky because of the low cloud. The lake that we could see was the lake that we had departed from at the start of the walk. I had back-tracked and made a 180° turn without realising it.

I didn't say anything to the group and found a good spot to rest and have our tea and sandwiches. We saw some lion, so the walk was successful in the end. I was in a state of shock for some time because, even though I knew what had happened, I still found it difficult to make sense of everything. Had I been on my own in this instance, I may well have done something stupid, such as going off on a tangent and getting myself really lost. Having an assistant with you from whom you can get another opinion is always very useful.

Droppings

Identifying all the droppings you are likely to find when walking in the bush is a daunting task. Most antelope have droppings that are very similar in shape – the only factor that changes is size, and this can be very slight. A big animal such as a giraffe has relatively small droppings for its size; they are slightly bigger than an eland's, whose are slightly larger than a kudu's. And so on.

Droppings need to be read along with footprints, then it is much easier to be absolutely sure. Droppings will change dramatically if the grass the animal is eating is fresh and full of moisture – consider cowpats when there is abundant new grass in the paddock and the cows are eating masses of it. Droppings that normally appear as individual pellets – as, for instance, a waterbuck's – will appear like a buffalo's if the waterbuck has been eating fresh, juicy grass. Very fresh droppings will have small insects hovering over them; this is particularly so with elephant droppings. Hunters from days gone by would test the body warmth in elephant droppings by pushing a finger into it to estimate how recently the droppings had been made. This has become a favourite ploy of safari guides when trying to impress gullible clients.

You can tell the difference between the droppings of an animal that is exclusively a browser, such as an eland or giraffe, from the droppings of a grazer, such as wildebeest. A browser's droppings are reddish in colour. Impala droppings are very similar in shape and size to peanuts. This has been used to play a trick on a guide who was very fond of peanuts. Someone pushed a bowl of impala droppings towards him

at the bar as he was launching forth about all the amazing animals he had spotted on a night drive. He filled his palm in the normal manner, tossing the pellets with gusto into his mouth as he gulped down his first beer.

Dung beetles favour dung made by animals that chew the cud – in particular, buffalo dung. Its consistency makes it easy to shape into a ball. These dung balls are rolled along the ground and in the process collect a thin covering of mud which, when it dries, forms a hard protective coating so that when the balls are buried they remain intact. Honey badgers are adept at sniffing these out and eating the larvae.

A midden, or toilet, is a place where an animal will deposit its droppings on a regular basis. Middens convey a very powerful olfactory message for any animal that happens to come along. A lot can be read from them if you have the necessary sense organs and the motivation. Middens, like scent markings, are often used as territory markers. The body chemistry of the animals using the midden can be read easily and quickly. Hyena create middens on the borders of their territory and many animals in the clan will use the same midden.

The droppings of civet contain the greatest variety of items since they are omnivorous. Finding one of their middens will reveal what they are eating, which could be seeds, plugs of grass, shell cases of millipedes, fur, and so on. An old game scout I worked with for many years was convinced that the twisted plug of grass enabled the civet to make it to his next midden. Civet middens are used by a single animal and can cover a large area.

Dik-dik use middens, and the male

secretes a substance from his preorbital gland on to a twig at the site. He then places his droppings on top of the female's as a sign to other males that she is taken. Both black and white rhino make use of middens. All the members of an impala herd will use a midden. They first urinate on the heap of droppings then defecate.

Male hippos scatter their dung with their tails on trees at the point where they leave the water at night to feed, and they repeat the process on bushes on the route they take to their nocturnal feeding lawn. Hippo dung is darker and wetter than elephant dung and never contains bark fibres.

Large birds of prey such as owls and eagles regurgitate pellets containing hair, feathers and bones containing matter that is too large to pass through the opening between the stomach and the gut – the pyloric sphincter – for the same reasons that your domestic dog will bring up pieces of bone that he has swallowed and not chewed thoroughly. This ability to vomit is a very important survival attribute. These pellets are a useful means of telling what the bird is feeding on.

In addition to owls and eagles, herons, gulls, storks and kingfishers also do this. I once found the beak of a kingfisher in an owl pellet, which indicated that owls hunt roosting birds at night. For instance, you can often find where a Pel's Fishing Owl sleeps during the day by locating pellets containing fish scales under a tree. Verreaux's Eagle Owls are the same: their droppings and pellets provide a clear indication of where they roost during the day. Fish Eagles favour a single perch on which to eat their prey, usually barbel. You will find fish heads and fins under the tree, along with their droppings.

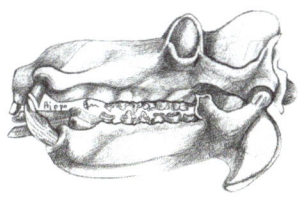

Francolin and Guineafowl droppings have a distinctive while splash that contains uric acid.

Crocodile droppings are yellow when fresh and, as they dry, they turn chalky white because they contain large amounts of calcium derived from the bones of the fish they eat. You can use dried crocodile droppings instead of blackboard chalk. Hyena droppings are similar – they also turn white when they are exposed to sunlight as they contain a high concentration of calcium. Crocodile droppings along a shoreline can often be the only indicator of the presence of a large crocodile in a pool that you thought was safe to swim in.

Otters feed on fish and crabs and their droppings contain the remains of crab legs and fish scales.

A hare's pellets are large in relation to their small size; they are larger than an impala's. As they eat grass, the colour is straw-coloured.

Monkeys, Ground-Hornbills, baboons and mongooses will work through fresh elephant dung to extract undigested fruit kernels and insects. Mongoose droppings contain the shell cases of insects and millipedes, along with feathers and hair from the rodents they feed on.

Baboons are omnivorous, so their droppings will normally contain seeds as well as hair and feathers. They are adept at placing their droppings on the top of termite mounds. They remind me of meringues. You can find where baboons roost at night by the large quantities of droppings under tall trees. It is unwise to pitch your tent underneath a tree that is a roosting tree for baboon because it will be covered in droppings by the morning.

You can sometimes find the hoofs of impala in leopard droppings. Leopard dung usually contains a

lot of antelope hair. Lion droppings produced shortly after a kill are very dark in colour as they are full of blood. Avoid touching lion droppings as they contain harmful bacteria. Lion will roll in buffalo droppings before a hunt. In lion and leopard droppings, one often finds the hoofs of small antelope along with bone fragments and hair. Lion droppings deposited soon after a big feast are very black, consisting of digested blood and muscle. At other times they will contain mainly fur and bone fragments. Leopard dung when old goes white like hyena droppings. Hooded vultures follow lion around in order to eat their droppings.

Elephant dung is full of partially digested fruit. Depending on the season, it could contain marula fruit, *Diospyros mespiliformis* (jackal berry) seeds, *Faidherbia albida* seeds, or even baobab seeds. Squirrels, baboons, monkeys and slender mongooses pull fresh elephant droppings apart in search of seeds and dung-beetle larvae. Elephant droppings are supposed to be very good as compost for roses; with time, they are eaten by termites. Elephant droppings that have been lying around for several months will sprout mushrooms and young trees. Many seeds will only germinate if they have passed through the gut of an animal.

Porcupine droppings remind me of strings of cocktail sausages. They are linked because the porcupine eat roots and these become intertwined.

I was caught out when working in Tanzania alongside the Serengeti National Park when what I thought was buffalo dung was in fact dung from a Maasai cow. Only a Maasai could tell the difference: my Maasai tracker had no doubts about it whatsoever.

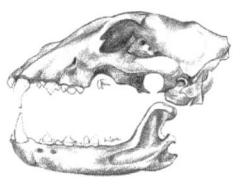

The Kill

Walking around in the bush one is struck by the fact that, on the whole, it is a very clean place to be. Although animals are dying regularly of natural causes, and many others are being killed by large predators, there is no smell of rotting meat, no sign of decaying flesh. The whole business of disposal is handled very efficiently. On occasions when things go wrong, and I will refer to these later, this efficient system ceases to work and the results are very unpleasant.

Once a kill has been made, nature has provided for a series of events that take care of the carcass. This process is an assurance that every little morsel is put to good use with no wastage. What follows here is what I believe could be the course of events after a large animal such as a buffalo has been killed by lion. Let me stress right away that in this case it is imperative that a large predator be involved at the very beginning because if this does not happen the sequence of events will be very different.

Let us say that a young buffalo is efficiently killed by four female lion. As the animal hits the ground, one lion sinks its teeth into the animal's windpipe and the buffalo suffocates to death. Lion have jaws and teeth that have evolved to deal efficiently with a fresh carcass. The shape and composition of the jaw is designed so that the heavy muscles needed for chewing and cutting are attached. The long, curved canines and the incisors are designed for holding on to the prey when it is caught and for delivering the killing bite. The molars at the side and back of the mouth are strong and very sharp, and these are used to cut through hide and tissue. What they have, therefore, is a set of tools that are designed first to

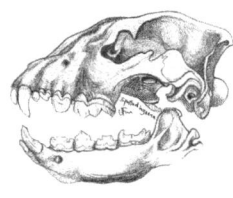

kill the animal, and then to cut up the soft tissue – the muscles, the internal organs, the soft, belly skin – into manageable chunks so that it can be swallowed and digested.

The hide of most animals is tough. In some places it is less tough, and it is for these areas that the lion aim when they start the business of consuming a large mammal. The softest parts are the belly and the anus; the toughest parts are along the back and the sides. When lion attack and immobilise an old male buffalo, it can take several hours before the poor beast actually collapses. All this time the lion are entering the body through the anus and the belly so that the animal is literally being consumed as it stands. This is necessary because the buffalo is so strong and the hide so thick that the lion cannot make any headway anywhere else. At the front, they have to contend with the wicked horns, so there is no choice.

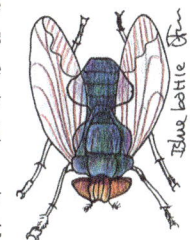

Once the animal is dead, the lion will cut the belly open from tail to chest and set to work on the soft tissue. If the kill has taken place out in the open with no protection from the sun – or, more particularly, from vultures – the females will drag the kill into the shade under a bush or shady tree. At this point, the male lion will make his appearance. He takes little part in the kill unless it proves difficult, whereupon he will lend his greater strength to the operation and, if the kill needs moving, he is often willing to lend his big muscles to that, too. He will feed first while the females, who have done all the work, draw back and wait and watch patiently. Once he is full, he walks away to the shade or to drink, and the females take over. The intestines are drawn from the carcass and eaten first, being pulled through the incisors to remove undigested grass.

While all this has been going on, other players are entering the lists. One of the first birds on the scene is likely to be a Bateleur or a Tawny Eagle – most likely the former. The Bateleur patrols the skies in a very thorough fashion at low altitude and his large eyes never miss a thing. Vultures, which do their patrolling at much greater altitude and are spread out widely, watch the movements of birds such as the Bateleur and often take their cue from them. Once they see a Bateleur going down, the vulture that first spots the movement will lose altitude and investigate. Vultures divide the skies up into aerial territories that are in visual contact with each other and, as soon as a bird occupying the adjoining territory shows signs of having seen something, the message is quickly passed on down the line. In their book, *The Vultures of Africa* (Peter Mundy *et al.*, Randburg: Acorn, 1992), the authors note that vultures as far as thirty-five kilometres away will heed the call to feed.

After the Bateleur, it is the White-headed Vulture that is most likely to make its appearance. These are not gregarious birds and usually appear alone or in pairs. They must seize what they need early because once the mob appears they have little chance of asserting themselves.

Hooded Vultures, which move about in pairs or small groups, often stick with a pride of lion, feeding on their droppings and any 'crumbs that fall from the rich man's table'. Their digestive systems are capable of dealing with the very potent bacteria to be found in the dung. One or more Hooded Vultures may appear early on at a kill simply because they happen to be near and watching events on the ground, as it were. They sneak in and out, snatching small titbits when they can. To show off their dominance to other Hooded Vultures, they may 'blush' – the skin around their faces going a bright red. The Bateleur and Tawny Eagles will also hang around, snatching any morsels. The Tawny is more dominant than the Bateleur and does not tolerate interference gladly. With their small crops, both are soon satisfied and leave the party early.

Once White-backed vultures have started appearing in large numbers, the lion begin to get irritated and chase them off. Until lion have had all they can get from a kill, they will not leave the carcass unguarded because, once they do, the White-backed Vultures take over, and that is the end of it for them. Even if the lion move off to the shade, one will rush back to the carcass as soon as a vulture moves too close.

Lion, as I have noted, will feast on the muscle and the soft organs, crunch up the smaller bones, such as the ends of the ribs, and crack the long bones to reach the marrow, but they do not have the crushing power in their teeth to deal with the hard cartilage of the large joints, the hoofs, the horns or the skull. Nor can they cope effectively with the tough parts of the hide or the thick sinews.

Once the lion move off, either to drink – which they must do after feeding – or to shelter from the sun, the vultures take over. This is also the time when the black-backed jackal makes its move. They may follow the lion at a discreet distance when they know they are hunting and when they are feeding, keeping in the background, moving restlessly back and forth, waiting for their moment – they know that when it comes, they have to be very quick.

By this time, with all the White-backed

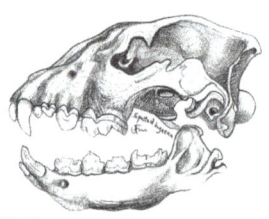

Vultures clustered around the carcass, one or two Lappet-faced Vultures will have appeared and be waiting patiently in the background. When they see an opportunity, they will move in, wings outstretched, and chase off the others to seize chunks of skin and sinew. For this purpose they have a beak that is hooked and toes designed to grip tight for tugging and pulling. Once they have what they desire, they move back discreetly and deal with their prize in an orderly manner without spoiling their feathers with blood and juices.

Hyena, with their good eyesight, will respond to the appearance of vultures even if they haven't picked up the smell. As they fly overhead, a hyena will note the direction and follow. From kills I have observed, the hyena have remained on the outskirts and did not tempt providence by competing with the lion while they were still feeding. This was the case when only one or two hyena were present. If the numbers of hyena allowed, I am sure they could take over a kill and chase the lions off.

As soon as the lion begin to move away from the kill, the hyena will sneak in and drag off a chunk of meat, usually a part with bone attached that the lion have left for later, or it may be the hide, or the skull of the animal with horns still attached. Hyena are extremely strong in the neck and shoulders and I have seen one half-drag, half-lift the skull and horns of a big male buffalo some hundred yards to get it away from the others. Hyena will soak these skulls in water to soften them up; this may also be a way of hiding them from other hyena. The skull of a dried-out male hyaena weighs as much as three kilograms. They are equipped with large canines and incisors that enable them to hold on to their prey and to tear,

but also have huge premolars for crushing bone and carnassial teeth for cutting hides and tendons.

I have seen a large crocodile feeding alongside three lion. The lion killed within eighty metres of the main river. The crocodile smelled the kill and climbed the bank and helped himself. He would have dragged the remains of the kill down to the river later.

Once the White-backed Vultures are allowed to dominate a kill, they will strip it so that all that remains is the spine, the ribs, the hoofs, the long bones of the legs, the pelvis and the skull. According to Mundy *et al.*, it takes fourteen minutes for a Lappet-faced Vulture or a White-headed Vulture to fill its crop and six minutes for a Hooded Vulture. Mundy describes the crop as a 'shopping basket' into which a vulture packs what meat he is unable to swallow.

The hyena will polish off the skull, the leg bones, the pelvis, the hide, any gristle and the hoofs.

I once disturbed three lion feeding on an adult zebra, which permitted free access for the White-backed Vultures. While this was going on we brewed up some tea which we drank while watching them. By the time the tea was finished and the sandwiches eaten, the vultures had eaten the best of the zebra – all in the space of an hour. Vultures can become so gorged with meat that they are incapable of taking off. In his book, *Birds of Prey of Southern Africa* (Cape Town: David Philip, 1982), Peter Steyn recounts fifty White-backed Vultures consuming twenty-three kilograms of meat in three minutes.

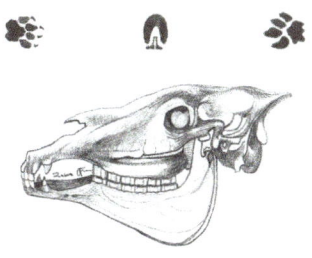

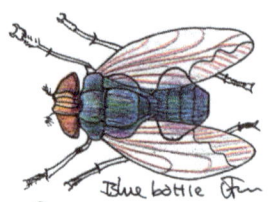

As I mentioned at the beginning of this section, for a carcass to be disposed of efficiently it is essential that one of the large predators is involved at the outset. Their presence is essential to open up the carcass. If an animal dies from disease, particularly if it is an epidemic, or from drought, and lion are unable to attend to the carcass, the vultures are unable to do their duty and the carcass simply rots. This was the case in the Luangwa Valley when there was an outbreak of anthrax. There were so many dead animals about that the lion ignored the great majority and they just rotted away. The stink was indescribable.

Once a kill has been properly dealt with in the right order, all that remains to be seen is a dark stain on the ground with the grass all trampled, a few dark wing feathers, the odd white chest feather, and some white splashes on the ground, attesting to the presence of a large number of vultures. Some distance away will be the half-digested grass removed from the intestines of the animal and trampled down by the feet of vultures and lion, fast losing its green colour and turning brown.

Some distance away in the short grass will be heaps of hyena droppings, lime green at first, but turning white as they dry. Lion droppings will also be present close to the kill site, black and moist, without substance when the kill is new, and fibrous and twisted later, containing hair and chips of bone and small hoofs. At this point, the dung beetles get to work on any dung, which they eat or make into balls to implant their eggs in.

And what of maggots, the larvae of bluebottle flies? There are two species that compete with one another. *Chrysomya albiceps* and *C. marginalis*.

In summer, once the fly has laid its eggs, they take only twelve hours to hatch. This means that vultures have only twelve hours to feed without competition from maggots. These are visible only when the kill has not been dealt with efficiently by large carnivores. In this case, the hide remains intact, and it becomes as tough as armour as it dries out. A few maggots might appear in the nasal cavities of the skull, in places that are out of reach.

After a week, only the horns remain. To dispose of these, a moth, *Ceratophaga vastella*, which has creamy-yellow forewings and greyish hindwings, lays eggs on the horn. The eggs hatch and the larvae begin to dissolve the keratin by exuding special enzymes. While this is going on, it constructs a protective home for itself out of faecal pellets in the form of a slender tube. These tubes will, after some time, cover the horns like white barnacles.

Hyena will return to a kill site and gnaw on any dry bones that remain. And, after dark, porcupines will deal with any that the hyena couldn't chew.

Hyena can crack even the largest bones with their formidable teeth. On a very old elephant carcass, all that remains are strange, round, bony balls that bear little resemblance to anything anatomical. These are the ball joints of the long leg bones. They are, to all intents and purposes, indestructible.

White-headed Vultures can satisfy their food needs by feeding on small animals that have died from misadventure. I have come upon several feeding on the remains of a Nile monitor lizard that had been killed by a Martial Eagle and abandoned. On another occasion I found them feeding on the remains of a stork. They are clean feeders, unlike the White-backed Vultures, which do not mind soiling their feathers.

When vultures have congregated in the skies above a guaranteed source of food – when there is an outbreak of disease or during the wildebeest migrations on the Mara river when many drown – they will respond within three minutes to the presence of a carcass. In the North Luangwa park, which had suffered from a long history of subsistence poaching, one had to sit down for only a few minutes in the shade at midday for a Hooded Vulture to appear in a tree close by to observe developments. They had learned from experience to associate meat with human beings.

Leopard are fastidious eaters and will lick all the hair from the abdomen of a baboon before they start slitting it open; they will also pluck the feathers from a Guineafowl before eating it. With an antelope, they will draw the intestines from the body and bury them before dragging the rest up a tree; this makes it lighter and easier to carry. They need time for this. If a leopard is in the vicinity of the lion kill and smells the meat, it will close in to a safe distance to watch and wait.

Leopard feed on carrion if they can find it, but they will never endanger their own lives to obtain it: they will never approach a kill with lion in attendance, but much later, when the lion have withdrawn, they may sidle up in search of scraps. I once surprised a leopard in a bush on the edge of a large clearing in which lion were feasting on a buffalo. His sense organs were so sated with the smell of buffalo meat that he didn't hear us approach. When he did perceive us, we were only a few metres away from him and he took off in a great fit of temper.

Conservation

His footprint, little master, is small and like no other man's and when you see it you know it at once from those of other men.
Laurens van der Post, *The Lost World of the Kalahari* (London: Hogarth Press, 1958), 63.

As a schoolboy very much concerned with nature and particularly with survival in the bush, when I read *The Lost World of the Kalahari* I became bewitched by the Bushmen, or Khoisan, as they prefer to be called. Their paintings were very much in evidence on the rocks in the caves we visited on Sunday outings from boarding school.

Whenever I could, I searched out articles about them, and tried to find more about these diminutive people who had a complex about their height. So as not to hurt their feelings when meeting them on a path, you had to greet them by saying, 'I saw you from a long way off.' Laurens van der Post describes meeting a Bushman in his book:

'Good-day, I saw you from afar and I am dying of hunger.'

The young man stuck his spear in the sand and with his right hand raised, palm open and fingers up, walked shyly towards us, saying ...
'Good day! I have been dead but now that you have come, I live again.'

I spent some time researching a script for a documentary film about the Bushmen. What particularly interested me was their ability to live in harmony with nature.

I read an interesting article written by an anthropologist living in Botswana who related how a group of Khoisan, having wounded a large antelope, probably an eland, tracked it for days. Coming up to it, they found a group of lion feeding off it. The hunters began talking to the lion saying something to the effect of, 'Come on you guys, we shot it, we did all the work, hand it over now, don't make a fuss.' Talking like this, they walked up to the lion, who slunk away reluctantly but in no doubt as to who was in control.

Years later, the same researcher returned to the area and discovered that, in his absence, herdsmen and their cattle had taken possession of the land. Before, where a good understanding had existed between predators and people, now the lion were causing problems, attacking cattle and often attacking the cattlemen themselves. The subtle balance that had existed between man and beast had gone.

When I stand on top of a kopje that has at some time in the long distant past been home to families of Khoisan hunters and look out over the land, I often wonder what it must have been like to live then, before the arrival of the 'Big People' with their cattle and goats, before the arrival of the wheel and the high-velocity rifle.

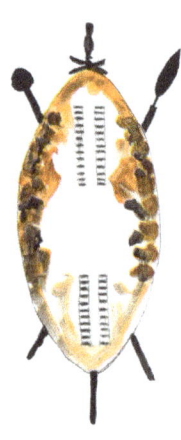

In the middle of the nineteenth century, the period of empire-building, there was an enormous fascination for exploration. Most of the uncharted regions of the earth had largely been explored, leaving Africa and its strange and marvellous creatures still to be discovered. Writers such as Rider Haggard and John Buchan added to the public euphoria about Africa and wrote of lost cities, of individuals such as Prester John and the Queen of Sheba, of gold and ivory, and other valuable commodities waiting to be discovered and exploited.

The motives that drove those early explorers differed considerably. For a few, such as Livingstone and Moffat, it was a desire to stamp out the curse of slavery and produce a more tolerant society where the tribes could live in harmony with one another. For the likes of Samuel Baker, James Grant, John Speke and Richard Burton, it was the challenge of exploration and the fame that went with it. For a great many others, it was sheer lust for the sport of killing. To be fair, along with this lust for killing went a certain amount of scientific study.

Several of these early big-game hunters were artists, and they have produced valuable sketches and paintings of their early impressions of the countryside, its animals and its people. Cornwallis Harris was one of these. Many wrote books about their experiences, and these fired up another generation of men and women for whom the lure of weird and wonderful places, of exotic creatures and savage tribesmen became an irresistible urge. Many of these individuals came from good aristocratic families with considerable wealth to draw on – even in those days, outfitting a safari was an expensive business involving the purchase of a robust ox-wagon, the oxen to pull it, ammunition and powder for several months, trade goods such as beads and calico for barter, as well as essentials such as sugar, salt, tea and coffee – not forgetting quinine – to last the duration of the trip.

A Cape ox-wagon was fifteen feet long, two foot nine inches wide, and the rear wheels were five feet in circumference; the front wheels were slightly smaller. Even in those days a good sturdy wagon cost more than eighty pounds. The whole structure was shaded by a tarpaulin stretched over

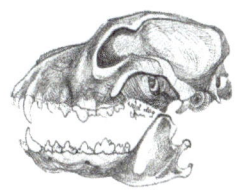

a hooped structure. Then the oxen to pull it had to be procured. A heavily loaded wagon required anything up to fourteen span of oxen to pull it; one span was a pair of oxen. These oxen often succumbed to wild animals or to the dreaded tsetse fly.

David Livingstone did not have huge financial resources at his disposal, and for his journey to Lake Ngami in 1849 in search of a base for a mission station, he had to rely on the generosity of William Cotton Oswell, who, like Frederick Courteney Selous, was a former pupil of Rugby School, whose headmaster was the famous Thomas Arnold.

One of the joys of being in the bush was that you could behave exactly as you wished, free from the constraining influences of Victorian society. Roualeyn George Gordon-Cumming was a wild Scot who galloped about on horseback in pursuit of game with the Gordon tartan of his kilt flapping in the wind and a total disregard for his own safety. William Charles Baldwin was an Englishman who used to gallop after ostrich, bludgeoning them with iron stirrups tied to a length of rope. All good sport. For many of these adventurers, if they could shoot enough elephant and get the ivory back to the Cape, they could offset the cost of the expedition and afford to finance their next safari into the interior.

The game at that time was plentiful. Springbok on their migrations in search of fresh grazing could be numbered in their hundreds of thousands. S.C. Cronwright-Schreiner, *The Migratory Springbucks of South Africa (The Trekbokke)* (London: T.Fisher Unwin, 1925), estimated that migrating springbok covered an area a hundred miles or more long by fifteen miles wide. Thousands and thousands of springbok were shot for their hides. The opening

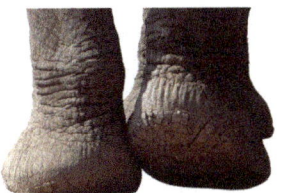

up of South Africa for ranching, and the introduction of rinderpest, very quickly reduced them to a tiny fraction of their earlier numbers. The quagga, a subspecies of the zebra, became extinct at about this time, along with the blue antelope or bloubok.

Before and just after the First World War there was an influx of settlers to East Africa, and this was the prelude to the Big Game Safari. These hunting safaris destroyed thousands of animals.

Before European settlement in Africa, the management of animal species lay with the local chief. In many communities, especially those with plentiful game species, and in particular elephant, the use of the products of these animals – the meat, hides and tusks – were subject to the chief's approval. Often only special hunters were given the right to hunt elephant. The tusks automatically became the property of the chief.

With the arrival of the Europeans came modern, high-velocity weapons and an improvement in the health of the indigenous people following introduction of health care. The population increased dramatically and with it the need for game meat. The British colonial governments of the day decided that it was necessary to introduce strict controls to protect the biodiversity of the region. The privilege of hunting that the indigenous people had accepted as their God-given right was withdrawn. Wild animals became the property of the Crown; certain species became known as 'royal game'. Hunting was permitted only on licences issued by the colonial government. This control even extended to animals on private land but, with a cheap landholder's licence, any number of animals could be shot if this was considered necessary for the livelihood of that farmer.

Among the indigenous populations, only chiefs and headmen had access to firearms, and the snaring of game became illegal on humanitarian grounds. The indigenous people therefore found themselves unable to kill the animals that threatened their crops and their livelihoods.

An old Shangaan poacher caught snaring game in the lowveld of Southern Rhodesia in the 1960s is reported to have said: 'I only use snares because we are not allowed to use guns to shoot game any more. Last week my employer killed 27 zebra in one afternoon. Is that right?' When the District Commissioner, a fervent conservationist, consulted the white farmer about the incident he was indignant. 'That old man can't count. I shot 31 zebra that day.' (Allan Wright, *Grey Ghosts at Buffalo Bend* (Salisbury: Galaxie, 1976.) On his farmer's licence he was entitled to shoot a hundred or more zebra in a day if he so wished.

At the same time, the government's reputation was further tarnished when it embarked on a very misguided campaign to control the spread of tsetse fly through the wholesale slaughter of wild animals along corridors adjoining ranching land. Hundreds of thousands of animals were destroyed in this manner without appreciably limiting the spread of the tsetse fly.

From 1930 onwards, many of the national parks that we know today in southern Africa came into being. This control was originally focused on the game, hence the name 'game parks'; later this was extended to cover all living species. Many rural people living in these areas were moved out, lock, stock and barrel, to adjacent areas outside the park and told to cultivate the land rather than depend

on game meat for food, which was how they had survived before. For many tribes, killing animals for food was traditionally what they knew how to do. They had no skills as farmers. In any case, the land in areas where game is prolific is normally marginal, poor-quality land where agriculture does not prosper; when it does, it is targeted by elephant, hippo and baboon. Hunting for these individuals was their birthright, and they were resentful. Like the American Indians, when they lost their land, they also lost their ancestral burial grounds and contact with their ancestral spirits. Once their old tribal lands had been confiscated, they derived no benefit from the tourism that followed either: all the revenue went straight to the treasury. In addition to losing their land, they received no compensation for its loss.

Zambia in the late 1970s saw the beginning of commercial poaching of rhinoceros on a very large scale. Rhino horn has been used in countries such as China for thousands of years as a general medicine, with apparent powers to cure a multitude of household ailments, even the common cold. Because of the shape of the horn, and the legendary staying power of the male rhinoceros during copulation, it was also perceived to have powers as an aphrodisiac. This is not true. Rhino horn is simply matted hair. Its properties are no different from the horn of any other animal. In some circles, the tail of a baboon is supposed to have similar powers.

When the price of oil rose dramatically between 1973 and 1974 from US$3.5 to US$9.3 a barrel, the oil-producing states experienced a massive surplus of billions of dollars. The wages of oil-workers rose dramatically. Poor Yemenis forced to work as labourers in Saudi Arabia returned home with

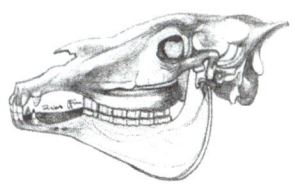

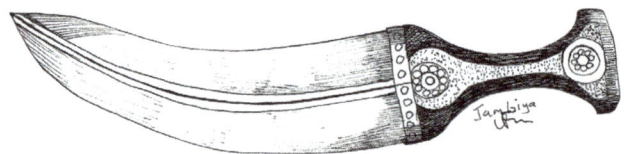

pockets bulging with hard currency. With this they were able to purchase the traditional dagger, the janbiya, with its richly carved rhino-horn handle that bestowed on them considerable esteem, hitherto restricted to the very rich and the nobility. Suddenly the demand for rhino horn went through the roof and the rhino became an animal with a large prize on its head. In the Yemen, the wholesale price of rhino horn went from US$764 for one kilo in 1980 to US$1,159 in 1985.

Within a very few years, the rhino was on the point of extinction in Zambia, where once it had been plentiful. When the poachers ran out of targets they crossed the Zambezi and continued their work in Zimbabwe. Desperate measures were taken there to protect the rhino. One of these was to dart and de-horn all the rhino in the national parks and move them to protected areas, either on private land or in specially protected areas inside national parks. This seems to have worked for the time being.

It is easy to appreciate why traditional hunters who had been deprived of the right to hunt became such willing and skilful poachers. They could not understand why they were not allowed to hunt the elephant that destroyed their crops, yet in the Luangwa Valley in the 1970s an organised cull was necessary to reduce their numbers to manageable levels. There didn't seem to be any logic in any of this.

Game ranching came into being in Zimbabwe in 1959. A certain number of animals were shot at night on private land using spotlights. This realised benefits from venison and hides. Many cattlemen, realising that game had great potential from consumptive as well as non-consumptive tourism, phased out their cattle and began to acquire game species. Many wild animals were sold at auction for these purposes.

As individuals, each one of us has a responsibility to ensure that when we visit the bush we leave it in the same or a better state than it was in when we arrived. Each one of us – irrespective of whether we are engaged professionally or as amateurs in the wildlife industry – has an obligation to protect the wild areas of our land in all its marvellous diversity.

As I have mentioned earlier, there is no such thing as a perfect wilderness area: such a place can exist only in a vacuum because, as soon as someone gets to hear about it, the factors that make it what it is soon disappear. Mankind, uncontrolled, has the capacity to destroy what is special on this earth for its own selfish gain. Therefore, if you know of a special place that you like to visit, make every effort to ensure that it remains special. Our environment is very fragile. Countries that manage their natural resources wisely are countries where their people are happy and contented.

To a lot of people, trophy hunting of wild animals is abhorrent. It is on a par with the killing of seals and whales – inhumane and barbaric. It is an emotive issue and arouses high feelings in many people. In developing countries with small budgets to allocate to conservation, running game parks is an expensive business that is far beyond their means. Their alternative is to deregulate these areas and allow communal farmers right of way for their cattle. This would mean that the wild areas of Africa would soon disappear, and with them the animals that we love to observe and photograph. Zambia, for example,

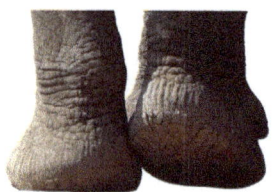

had eighteen national parks at independence in 1964. Nearly twenty-five years later, eleven of these were national parks in name only. Only four of the remainder had enough game, or the facilities and infrastructure, to attract tourists in any number and generate any income.

One way to ensure that sufficient money is available to manage national parks is through trophy hunting. Hunting has always been, and always will be, a popular pastime for some. It is not cheap, and only those with a lot of money can afford it. Tapping into this source of revenue can provide large amounts of money that goes towards protecting the game in national parks. Hunting areas are set up along the boundaries of the parks so that, when populations of certain game species rise, these animals leave the park and enter the hunting areas. Each year, estimates of the number of game species that can be shot would be determined by scientists who monitor the situation very carefully. Licences are then issued for this number only, and hunting companies lease these areas from the government. The hunting clients pay for each animal they shoot – the rarer the animal, the higher the fee. These amounts are charged in foreign currency.

The hunter is only after trophy animals – those with the largest horns. Females are not included. In theory, old males are expendable because there will always be another male waiting to take his place. Hunting companies manage the game in their areas well because it is in their own interests to do so. If they permit their clients to shoot adolescent bulls, rather than those whose breeding prowess is on the wane, then the breeding pool will be diminished and their professions will be put at risk. Hunting for the

big bulls makes the task of hunting a difficult and exacting task. The old males are more wary, more canny, and more difficult to shoot. Days can go by in pursuit of one animal with a particularly large set of horns.

Records will be kept for all species. Strict rules are laid down that govern the methods used in the hunt so that the killing is done humanely. If it is not, penalties are severe. Professional hunters have to pass stringent tests before they are allowed to work in the profession.

Ultimately, although it may seem unethical to allow trophy hunting, it is very necessary. The same argument can be applied to Scottish grouse. If there was not such a demand for grouse-shooting, the heather on the moors that grouse rely on for food would have been ripped out long ago and replaced with pasture for sheep. It is just another form of husbandry, like cattle ranching, and, if done properly, it protects wild animals because it gives animals a value in monetary terms, which contributes towards their protection.

When you are camping or moving through a protected area, be careful that you do not damage trees. If you have to use a tree as an anchor to lever your vehicle out of trouble with a winch, always wrap a tarpaulin round the tree first so that you do not cut into the bark with your cable or strap. Just because a tree obscures your view is not sufficient reason to cut it down.

These days, thankfully, the climate of awareness about the environment is changing, so we rarely find individuals carving their names into tree trunks or

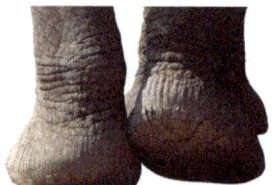

painting their names on rock faces. But the pressure on the general public to behave properly has to be maintained.

Creating your own track through virgin bush may well seem harmless at the time, but it is amazing how quickly a 'once off' track can develop into a permanent fixture: large game find the going easier on a track, so they will choose to use it rather than ploughing through scrub. Once tall grass becomes damaged, it becomes an easy target for grazers. It takes only one good rainy season for your track to become a gutter, and without the long grass to hold the soil together, the fragile surface is easily eroded.

You can see the effect that hippo have on river banks due to their frequent use of one or more exit routes from the river each evening. As they flatten these paths, day in, day out, these become gutters for surplus surface water when the rains come. Very soon they are deep trenches. As they extend further and further inland, they connect with others to form deep channels. After a period of time these in turn become small streams so that at some stage they will be capable of diverting the flow of water away from the main channel of a river, causing the original one to dry up altogether. This sudden loss of water in critical areas can cause riverine vegetation to wither away and die, and beautiful stands of trees that have stood for hundreds of years start to experience stress. Once stressed, they are vulnerable to disease and many die; others that find themselves on the very edge of a new channel have their roots exposed and will eventually topple over. In the space of a few years, what was once a stable area offering sustained growth to mature trees and vegetation, and with them shelter for birds and animals, suddenly disappears.

When I was walking in Malawi, I was surprised to come face-to-face with the remains of an old British anti-slaving fort perched on top of a high saddle overlooking Lake Malawi. I visited the government mapping office and obtained an aerial photo of the whole area. Clear to see was the original mochila path. A mochila was like a hammock, carried on the shoulders of four bearers and used to carry important persons. On a later expedition I found where this path began, and followed it right up to the old fort. It had survived for more than a hundred years and had probably not been used as such for half that period while the rest of the brick structures had disintegrated. It was easy to see how this had happened: the path had become a conduit for rainwater, and this was what had preserved it over all those years. This, I hope, goes to show that what might start off as a minor track can, with the assistance of time, animals and the elements, soon turn into a riverbed that will remain for ever.

Today, with off-roading becoming a serious hobby for many people, areas that were once unknown, except to a tiny minority of local inhabitants, and impossible to reach except with extra-rugged vehicles are now firmly on the beaten track. I shudder when I see off-roaders driving up and down the sand dunes in Namibia. It reminds me of the damage that was done to the ancient ditches depicting animals on the Nazca plain in Peru by 4×4 drivers. These can only be seen in their entirety from the air, and have given rise to the theory that they might have been created by people from outer space.

A friend of mine, like me, had been moved by reading *The Lost World of the Kalahari*, in which Laurens van der Post describes the mystery of the

Tsodilo Hills, a significant refuge and very ancient spiritual home of the Khoisan people in that part of Botswana. In the book, van der Post has as his guide a local spirit healer. So as not to offend the local spirits, who he says are very powerful, nobody in the party must kill an animal because the ancestral spirits of each species reside in the hills. The party become separated and, before van der Post can pass on this information, the advanced party shoots some wild dog. Needless to say, as a result of this the spirits are angry and all their work comes to nothing.

After many years of wanting to make a trip there, my friend at long last had a suitable vehicle and decided to make the journey. On reaching the place, its mystery and uniqueness was shattered because, camped at the site, was a group of noisy overlanders with radios blaring and their washing hanging out to dry on the bushes. Gone was the mystique of the place that van der Post had so skilfully created in his book.

I recently enjoyed a story in *Getaway* magazine of an individual with a new Mitsubishi Pajero who had driven on to a public beach one evening to show off to his girlfriend, only to get stuck in the wet sand. When the tide turned, his precious vehicle was stranded, at the mercy of the waves with the incoming tide that tossed it about like a blow-up toy.

It is very easy when encountering indigenous people in remote areas to go barging into places such as caves and ancient ruins, or even into market places, without really taking into account their traditions and beliefs. One should always be sensible to local feelings and take the necessary steps not to give offence.

Chief Seattle, American Indian, in conversation with the Governor of Washington Territory over the issue of land in 1855 when the intention by the authorities was to send the Indians to reservations so that their lands could be controlled by government.

The sight of your cities pains the eyes of the red man. But perhaps it is because I am a savage and do not understand. There is no quiet place in the white man's cities. No place to hear the unfurling of leaves in spring or the rustle of an insect's wings. But perhaps it is because I am a savage and do not understand. The clatter only seems to insult the ears. And what is there to life if a man cannot hear the lonely cry of the whippoorwill [nightjar] or the arguments of the frogs around a pond at night? I am a red man, and I don't understand.

The air is precious to the red man, for all things share the same breath – the beast, the tree, the man: they all share the same breath. The white man does not seem to notice the air he breathes. Like a man dying for many days he is numb to the stench.

The white man must treat the beasts of this land as his brothers. I am a savage and I do not understand any other way. I have seen a thousand rotting buffaloes on the prairie, left by the white man who shot them from a passing train. I am a savage and do not understand how the smoking iron horse can be more important than the buffalo that we kill only to stay alive.

What is man without the beasts? If all the beasts were gone, man would die from a great loneliness of spirit. For whatever happens to the beasts, soon happens to man. All things are connected.

Whatever befalls the earth befalls the sons of

the earth. If men spit upon the ground, they spit upon themselves. This we know: the earth does not belong to man; man belongs to the earth. This we know. All things are connected like the blood which unites one family. All things are connected. Whatever befalls the earth befalls the sons of the earth. Man did not weave the web of life: he is merely a strand in it. Whatever he does to the web, he does to himself.

That destiny is a mystery to us, for we do not understand when the buffalo are all slaughtered, the wild horses are tamed, the secret corners of the forest heavy with scent of many men, and the view of the ripe hills blotted by talking wires.

Where is the thicket? Gone.

Where is the eagle? Gone.

The end of living, and the beginning of survival.

Lightning Source UK Ltd.
Milton Keynes UK
UKHW051113060223
416527UK00003B/15